Vignettes & Memories

Vignettes & Memories

REFLECTIONS
FROM A CAMBRIDGE
DRAWING-ROOM

LOUIS T. STANLEY

ROBSON BOOKS

*To my wife Jean who shares my
recollections of these happenings
over many decades*

First published in Great Britain in 2001 by
Robson Books
10 Blenheim Court, Brewery Road, London N7 9NY

A member of the Chrysalis Group plc

British Library Cataloguing in Publication Data
A catalogue record for this title is available from the
British Library

ISBN 1 86105 430 0

Designed by
JOHN HERITAGE

Printed in Great Britain by
Creative Print & Design (Wales)
Ebbw Vale

CONTENTS

~

FOREWORD

~

LOUIS STANLEY IS A MOST remarkable man, and it is always good to
greet a new book from him in which he takes the opportunity to
chronicle the lives of selected people of distinction, as he has come
across them; this time as we glide effortlessly, if uncertainly, into
the twenty-first century.

It is comparatively rare that you find someone who is as
knowledgeable and experienced in such a wide range of human
activities as Louis Stanley, and one who has travelled so widely and
met such an astonishing number of people, many with whom he has
established lasting friendships.

Mind you, he does not have to meet a celebrity for very long,
before, with the help of his acute powers of observation, a deep
knowledge of human nature and considerable supplementary
research, is able to produce the most perceptive and penetrating
pen portraits of his subjects. Pen portraits, moreover, which are
often so revealing that, however much or little space he allots them,
the reader is made to feel there is really nothing left to know or say
about them.

The exceptional men and women Louis Stanley writes about
with such insight and often personal knowledge come from a
spectrum of professions and occupations, with a range of skills both
physical and reflective. These portraits are linked together by a
narrative of events, giving the author the opportunity to express his

own strong, down-to-earth and sometimes controversial views and judgements. This makes for highly stimulating reading.

Every reader will have their favourite chapter. Mine, I think, was the one headed 'Saints and Heretics', which I found provided much food for thought as well as being deeply enlightening.

Above all, Louis Stanley writes beautifully in a style which, although economical, flows forward in an utterly compelling and fascinating fashion, making this the ideal book to dip into on holiday, or in bed, as the particular mood or interest of the reader dictates. At the same time, this new offering from the author provides a quite serious *vade mecum* of some aspects of our own times.

I wish the book all possible success.

FIELD MARSHAL LORD BRAMALL

CHAPTER ONE

POWER OF THE PEN

~

THE WRITERS IN *POWER OF THE PEN* created their own world dyed through and through with imagination and delicately observed actualities. Oliver Elton once wrote of Herrick: "A stormy age is incomplete without at least one artist who sits by himself and cares only for his craft." It is a thought which we may reserve for each of these writers.

SOMERSET MAUGHAM

DURING THE MONACO GRAND PRIX WEEK, we were invited by Somerset Maugham to his home on Cap Ferrat between Nice and Monte Carlo. In the past I had tried to persuade the author to watch the race from our suite overlooking Casino Square. Reaction never varied. He declined. He hated motor-racing and abominated the thunderous noise of the engines, but, at the same time, was always generous with praise for our successes in this prestigious race.

There was no hesitation on our part. After the hype, gloss and chatter in the Hôtel de Paris and hectic routine preparations of BRM cars, it offered a complete contrast. Nothing would have changed . . . the Moorish sign against evil engraved on the gate was the welcoming omen (the symbol used by his publishers as a trademark, stamped on the cover of all his books) . . . green shutters of the Villa Mauresque . . . tree-shaded gardens . . . rooms bathed in sunlight . . . roof-top study with panoramic view of the Mediterranean . . . velvet-covered sofas in the drawing-room . . . Ming figures . . . a timeless capsule of a household smoothly run by long-serving staff with Alan Searle, secretary/companion hovering attentively in the background . . . everything presided over by Somerset Maugham like an inscrutable Chinese mandarin . . . lined face the colour of parchment. To the outside world he was an enigma, a role he enjoyed.

To the present generation Maugham is only a name, contemporary with Arnold Bennett, John Galsworthy and H.G. Wells. Plays now dated. Books covered with dust. Yet he was a pivotal figure of the 20th-century literary world. His books sold over 80 million copies, translated into innumerable languages. The phenomenal success only came after years struggling to gain recognition. He used to say it was ten years before he made a decent living.

Maugham's mother died when he was eight; his father, solicitor in the British Embassy in Paris, two years later. The boy was placed in the care of an uncle-guardian, a High Church vicar in Whitstable, who had little empathy with the lad inflicted with a speech impediment and French accent. King's School, Canterbury, was a lonely period, followed by Heidelberg, where he became fluent in German.

Career plans suggested chartered accountancy, then switched to medicine with the prospect of a safe country practice. Somehow it didn't work out. Recalling those days, Maugham admitted he was a mediocre student. Spartan life did not appeal. A couple of rooms in Vincent Square, the landlady providing breakfast and high tea for twelve shillings a week; lunch at St. Thomas's cost four pence for buttered scone and glass of milk. Austere fare for someone who wanted to be a writer. On the other hand, Maugham had cause to be grateful for the medical training. He told me that the wards taught him all he knew about human nature. People in pain and fearful of death did not hide their feelings. Harsh reality affected his outlook on life, encouraged mordant asceticism, and created a personal image of one vast shrug of the shoulders in human shape.

He used to say that his first maternity case and first novel *Liza of Lambeth* arrived about the same time, but it was tough going.

Quitting medicine for writing as a profession meant that for ten years his income only averaged £100 a year.

Writing *Of Human Bondage* would have disillusioned most scribes. The first draft was completed in 1898. No publisher was impressed. It was rejected time and again for being too discursive and over-long. The manuscript was set aside for several years, rewritten, and eventually published in 1915; after a slow start, became one of the most important novels of the century. It is certainly a true expression of the author's personality.

Recollections of Maugham are sprinkled with vignettes . . . fastidiousness in dress and habits . . . very small hands that he kept clasping and unclasping . . . slow speech due to the handicap of a stutter . . . partial deafness, though not nearly as bad as he protested . . . sardonic smiles . . . no illusions, as befitted someone who had seen it all before. He would recall experiences as a secret agent in Russia during the First World War, which he incorporated in *Ashenden*.

His base in London was The Dorchester with sitting-room overlooking Hyde Park. Even in his eighties, the routine was unchanged. Dinner served in the suite: quilted smoking-jacket, dark trousers and monogrammed slippers. He enjoyed pink champagne and light conversation with sardonic asides. I recall him saying with a touch of bravado that the previous day he retired to bed about 3a.m., got up as usual at 9a.m., but was not feeling as fresh as usual. He supposed it was one of the signs of approaching old age.

Sadly this stamina faltered. The closing months of his long life were tinged with sadness. Unable to climb the stairs to his beloved roof-top study, he would sit by the French windows or on the patio just gazing with fading eyesight into space. Ironically the rejuvenation injections administered years before by a Swiss doctor to preserve his body had been too effective. His mind was left in a twilight world in which memories did not exist.

After Maugham's death Alan Searle paid one last visit to London. He joined me for lunch. Parkinson's Disease had taken its toll, but he relived the endless days with mind crystal clear. Details were etched in his brain. Searle recalled how the silence in the Villa became almost tangible. Maugham knew he was dying and longed for the end. Searle's loyalty and comfort were powerless. Cynical agnosticism had left no room for hope. A jaundiced approach to death had to be endured.

So passed from the scene a literary legend.

ROBERT GRAVES

I MET ROBERT GRAVES ON SEVERAL OCCASIONS, always an invigorating experience, but only in the mountain village of Deya, with the Mediterranean as backcloth, did the poet come to normal life. Instead of flamboyant gestures, he was relaxed. The idyllic existence had a calming effect. He pointed out Deya, after so many years, was home. England he considered "abroad".

Objects of furniture in Oxford studies tend to be functional. Graves' desk was no exception, yet on it had been written some of the most beautiful lyric poems in the English language. On the shelves were standard reference books, the Bible, Greek and Latin texts, and a copy of *Josephus*. The room was far from tidy. Sheets of notepaper covered with classic handwriting of rejected thoughts. The waste-paper basket was half-full. Graves admitted to being a compulsive redrafter. Writing poems could be slow and laborious. There could be between ten and thirty versions. *Collected Poems* was revised four times. Accepted routine meant half-a-dozen handwritten drafts with final corrections in typescript.

During our conversation Graves could not resist cynical asides. Likes and dislikes were aired. He brushed aside Hemingway's monotonous boasting about wars he had never fought in as verbal bluster. Of his friendship with Lawrence of Arabia at St John's, Oxford, he refuted any suggestion of a homosexual relationship. He regarded unnatural sex as an abomination and had never had cause to use the services of a prostitute. Periodically he would talk of domestic life on his island-refuge where affairs of the world seemed remote. When invited to be a candidate for the Oxford University Chair of Poetry, he became involved in the academic intrigues. Other candidates were Dr Enid Starkie (Somerville), Miss Helen Gardiner (St Hilda's) and Dr Frank Leavis (Downing, Cambridge), all distinguished in academic life and in the world of letters. W.H. Auden had set such a high standard in the post that his successor had to be a major poet. Starkie concentrated on the scientific block; Gardiner tried to rally support from the clergy; Leavis just hoped. Predictions were accurate. Graves had 163 sponsors; Starkie 62; Gardiner 14; Leavis tailed with 8. Duties were not arduous. 15 lectures over five years for a fee of £1500. Graves was a huge success. Students appreciated the laconic recitations of his own poems.

Graves recalled another experience when, sponsored by T.E. Lawrence, John Buchan and Arnold Bennett, he became the first Professor of English Literature at Cairo University, but resigned after a year. He preferred independence, a trait persisting throughout his life. Robert Graves was his own man.

Background had a moulding influence. Half-Irish, half-German, his father an Irish writer; mother Amalia von Ranke, daughter of the German historian. His name linked with the treatment of Graves Disease. He referred to instances of impetuous behaviour. When the First World War was declared in August, 1914, he was staying in the Welsh mountains near Harlech. Without hesitation, he enlisted at the local depot in the Royal Welsh Fusiliers, and had a charmed life; as a front-line infantry officer survived the nightmare horrors of trench-warfare, until the Somme. Serious lung injuries looked hopeless. Officially listed as died of wounds.

Reaction to the horrendous death-toll was expressed in *Goodbye to All That,* one of the most penetrating autobiographical books about that bloody war. He chronicled the annihilation of friends in cryptic fashion, but reserved censure for inhumanity shown by court-martial courts when half-crazed men, many little more than schoolboys, were charged with cowardice and desertion, put before a firing-squad. It was heartless, cold-blooded murder.

On one visit to St John's College, the study floor was still littered. I helped to scoop a bundle of papers in no particular order into a brown paper parcel. We walked to the Broad Street post office, "made his publisher happy", then proceeded to the market. Graves had a silk scarf knotted round his neck, voluminous cloak, floppy Mexican hat and carried a string bag. What happened next was like an Indian bazaar. Haggles over the price at every stall. Eventually exhausted, we lunched at the Mitre, thankfully without querying the bill.

Graves often spoke of a personal dilemma. Poetry was his passion, but prose had to be his living. Only that way could he provide two families with four children from each marriage with the necessities of life and educational expenses. Without that problem we would have been denied the two books on Claudius that created a market for historical novels; his original approach to Greek mythology in *The Greek Myths;* the imaginative scholarship of *King Jesus;* the enquiry into early Christianity in *The Nazarene Gospel Restored* and *The White Goddess* that analysed the springs of poetry. Every volume reflects originality of approach and established Robert Graves as an outstanding literary figure of the century.

In poetry the scale is miniature. It is the lyric not the epic, Chopin not Wagner. He was the successor to Walter Savage Landor as a romantic classicist. Every poem was marked with fervour.

I have said nothing about Robert Graves' physical appearance. Facially he looked like a pugilist due to a broken nose acquired on the rugby field at Charterhouse, an impression heightened by tall build, muscular strength, hardly the demeanour of a poet. To others he had the face and arrogance of a Roman Emperor with detached poise. It is as such that I remember him. In his 90th year his pilgrimage ended beneath the sun on the island home of Deya. He would have approved the final tributes. Neckerchief round his neck, flat-brimmed hat by folded hands, carried to the grave by three sons and three special friends, pall-bearers for England's last love poet.

NORMAN MAILER

NORMAN MAILER HAS BEEN DESCRIBED as a turbulent egomaniac who sweeps everything aside in the compulsive effluvia of his own personality, reputed to quarrel with anyone reluctant to accept him at his own valuation. I found him at the outset impossible to ignore. His very presence was intimidating. Stocky and heavy, humped-shouldered like a natural stand-off half, the bulk was offset with the enduring grin of a Cheshire Cat. Facially Celtic rather than Jewish, he had deepset blue eyes that must have charmed a way out of many a situation and likewise played havoc with the opposite sex. Biological activities proved costly. Four failed marriages and nine children brought financial headaches. Alimony alone meant that more than £500,000 had to be earned to meet the bill. Mailer had a flair for making money, but admitted he was hopeless at figures. His accountant, Edward Lucci, did not disagree. In money matters, Mailer was like a backward reader struggling with Shakespeare. The writer's rueful postscript was that a man never really knows a woman until confronted in court.

Switching from cynicism to Mailer's status as a writer, *The Naked and the Dead* is a brilliant novel based on personal experiences in the Second World War, won wide acclaim as a naturalistic war novel that sold over 2½ million copies in the English language. He branched out in books based on sexual and scatological material and took a stand against cultural conformity. Such books included *An American Dream*, a menacing thriller of sex and power, then *The Armies of the Night*, both Pulitzer Prize winners. Two lengthy novels, *Ancient Evenings*, dealing with Egyptian life and mythologies, and *Harlot's Ghost*, neither of which I have read. *An American Dream* had an intriguing theme in which the hero challenged the Devil himself, then years later in *The Martrying of Mailer* he took a gamble by writing a novel in the first person. Reviewers were caustic. *The New Republic* was vitriolic, showing him on the cover wearing a crown of thorns with the caption "He is Finished." *The New York Times* and *Washington Post Book World* were equally scathing. Mailer ignored the shafts. No longer an atheist or Marxist, he believed in a Manichaean universe in which God is neither all-good or all-powerful. Man's role is to assist divinity in the fight against an equally powerful Devil. It is an impassioned plea rivalling Tolstoy and Dostoevsky.

It is a typical Mailer montage. He listens to God. Now the Almighty has to listen to the writer. We lesser mortals try to pick up the pieces. He cannot help being controversial. His image is detached from his work. He has brawled with actors, stockbrokers and of course wives. Gore Vidal was one of his victims, belittled the CIA, ran for the Mayor of New York, used television as a platform, published indifferent poetry, tried his hand at movies, and now attempts to revise Matthew, Mark, Luke and John and puts himself in the role of Jesus. How can you sum up such a whirlwind-extrovert who pads about in crumpled shorts flaunting his paunch?

In private the image is quite different. I recall an agreeable lunch at the *Savoy* in London when we agreed to a wager of £100 on a race back to *The Dorchester*. We left at the Embankment Entrance. Mailer accelerated away with tyres squealing. Having local knowledge, I went the opposite direction, down a cul-de-sac into a subterranean garage, down a dark passageway, squeezed between stanchions with an inch to spare, along a short no-entry road, and emerged in the Strand. The Dorchester was reached well ahead. Conscience made me refuse the stake-money. Instead I accepted a copy of *An American Dream* with this inscription: . . .

To Louis Stanley after racing to The Dorchester
Norman Mailer 1965

Almost a year later I received this note . . .

142 Columbia Heights
Brooklyn 1, New York
February 3 1966

Dear Mr. Stanley

Just to say Happy New Year, and agree to have lunch at the Dorchester. But probably you'll be here long before I come to England again. So then you must come to my house. I've got a view, and a model of a city of the future which I think may amuse you.

Norman Mailer

The model in question was remarkable. He had built an architectural layout of a miniature town on several levels with all modern amenities and facilities like schools, hospitals, churches, shops and thoroughfares with no two houses the same, occupying a comparatively small area. I took several photographs. Returning to Cambridge, I showed them to the eminent architect, Sir Leslie Martin. He commented that clearly it was the theory of an imaginative architect that could appeal to town planners.

I think of Normal Mailer, now more grizzled, mature, but still volatile, as a brilliant writer, a relevant part of American culture. He is a refreshing one-off.

JOHN MASEFIELD

MY MEMORIES OF JOHN MASEFIELD are tinged with frustration. On visits to his home in Abingdon, the routine never varied.

Afternoon tea, then, if season and weather permitted, we would sit on a bench in the garden overlooking the river. Masefield sat next to Jean. I kept his wife company. Unfortunately she was very deaf. Conversation consisted of a series of abstruse questions on unlikely subjects. It was like being subjected to tricky posers on University Challenge programmes with supercilious Jeremy Paxman having the answers in front of him. My dilemma was even more embarrassing. There came a point when it was demoralising to have to shout one's ignorance. She was a charming lady but adept at gamesmanship.

Masefield was sympathetic. Like his writing, he was urbane. The death of both parents as a child affected the course of his life. Brought up by relatives, then entered the *Conway* at 13 to learn seamanship, an experience that inspired volumes of poems based on the experiences of hardship and frustration like *Salt Water Ballads*, but without doubt *Reynard the Fox* was his best with its vivid word-pictures of the English countryside. Apart from verse he wrote authoritative naval histories and one epic short account, *The Nine Days Wonder* of the Dunkirk evacuation.

In 1930 he was appointed Poet Laureate and awarded the Order of Merit five years later. To many people, his memory is identified by this quotation:

> I must go down to the seas again, to the lonely sea and the sky,
> And all I ask is a tall ship and a star to steer her by

SIR COMPTON MACKENZIE

THERE WERE SO MANY FACETS to Compton MacKenzie, a romantic throw-back to the aesthetic days before the First World War. The poeticised phase of decadence at Oxford encouraged early ambitions to be a poet. The Muse deserted Compton leaving an urge to write. He used to say he was related to half the theatrical families in England having Edward Compton as father, and American mother Virginia Bateman. As a child of the theatre, he had a strong awareness of himself, raconteur, mimic and born improviser. War experiences heightened belief in himself. Attached to Ian Hamilton's staff, he went to the Dardanelles, became Military Control Officer in Athens and Director of Intelligence elsewhere in Greece. Secret Service work suited his temperament and imagination. When hostilities ended, he returned to writing, bought an island in the Hebrides and became involved in Scottish Nationalism. Literary output was prolific. An early book, *Carnival*, was one of my favourites. It mirrored his vein of humour and wilful fancy. It was all there . . . rollicking sense of farce, raffish Cockney humour and the shabby bohemianism of theatrical lodgings. *Whisky Galore* enshrined the hilarious wreck of a ship loaded with thousands of cases of whisky that became a film classic. Even if Compton had never written a word, he would have been a character, high spirited and droll.

The last time I saw him was in his Edinburgh house. Still immature in outlook, he insisted I should inspect his latest acquisition. In the basement he had established a Hairdressing Salon for ladies, engaging two pretty young women who were clearly anxious to please their employer. Having a captive feminine audience appealed.

In his study he showed with pride another novelty. An old-fashioned dentist's chair occupied the centre of the room. Richly upholstered in red velvet, he demonstrated its usefulness after lunch. He made himself comfortable, a swivel writing-desk could swing into place; on either side adjustable book-rests; another swinging table had writing material; on the other side a mini-bar. Often in the afternoon, he felt drowsy. When that happened, a lever by his side converted the chair into a horizontal couch. He couldn't imagine why he hadn't thought of it before.

With advancing years, Compton's imagination worked overtime. He asked me what were my earliest recollections. A somewhat strained memory-shift relived an incident when I was three. He accused me of not trying. He could recall incidents from 8 months onward, including a word-picture of sitting on the knee of an old soldier who had fought at the Battle of Waterloo. It sounded a tall story, but I suppose it could have been true. The battle was 1815; Compton was born in 1883. I murmured he must have been a precocious infant.

Right to the end Compton exuded a matchless zest for life which he hoped would continue in a future existence, though perhaps on a less earthy note.

T.S. ELIOT

IN WESTMINSTER ABBEY IS A STONE commemorating the memory of Thomas Stearns Eliot, an American born in St. Louis, Missouri, 1888. Laconic reminder to future generations of one of the greatest literary figures of the century. As a writer, his output was prolific, at times controversial, often incomprehensible through skirting the limits of coherency. Honoured by the Order of Merit and Nobel Prizewinner his place in history is assured.

As an individual, Eliot was an intellectual chameleon, unpredictable, austere, elusive. At the outset, loved by the avante garde, a poet influenced and accepted by Ezra Pound, the cynical voice of the thirties, then inexplicably, he changed course. On the form applying for British citizenship, he described himself as "a classicist in literature, a royalist in politics and an Anglo-Catholic in religion". His creed appalled previous supporters. Overnight, Eliot had become the laureate of High Churchmanship with cogent arguments to support his views, as witness a robust attack on the New English Bible.

Eliot's work was not always easy to understand. In his first full length play *Murder in the Cathedral,* he introduced a form of verse-drama, later copied by Auden, MacNeice and Spender. The martyrdom of Thomas à Becket was enacted in the Canterbury Cathedral chapter house, the author anticipating that future productions would be held in churches for ordinary churchgoers. An imaginative idea, but unfortunately the didactic style proved difficult to understand.

On other occasions, his plays puzzled, almost bewildered

audiences who left the theatre conscious they had sat through a cultural experience without any idea what it was all about. Intellectual snobbery prevented an admission of their difficulty in understanding . . . rather like the Emperor's clothes!

Appreciating Eliot's work could be an acquired taste. Scholarly assessment confirms that *The Waste Land,* whilst not his finest poems, nevertheless made an influential contribution to the emergence of modern verse. He was also Editor of the critical quarterly *The Criterion* in the thirties. *Ash Wednesday* in which he flirted with themes of time and redemption. *Burnt Norton,* first volume of the *Four Quartets.*

At the première of *The Cocktail Party* at the Edinburgh Festival, I recall Eliot's quiet satisfaction, almost smugness, that the critics had failed to spot the parallel with Euripides, though in *The Confidential Clerk* the connection was not missed. The search for parentage by three foundlings was the essence of Greek comedy, the search for identity. *The Elder Statesman* shows the title-character accepting the realities of his real self. These works are variations on moral comedies in verse. To fully appreciate the inner significances, audiences had to be on the same wave-length, an assumption misplaced. The sum-total was a formidable life's work. In lighter vein I recall the series of letters to his godchildren published in lively books of comic verse about cats. In them Eliot pin-points the lawless independence and superior instincts of these feline creatures.

Andrew Lloyd Webber saw the potential behind Eliot's *Old Possum's Book of Practical Cats.* I am sure the author would have approved of the stage production of *Cats,* minor revisions and the addition of eight lines to *The Song of the Jellicles.* He would have been delighted in *Macavity the Mystery Cat,* a fiend in feline shape and a monster of depravity. *Old Deuteronomy,* a cat who lived many lives in succession. *Mr Mistoffelees,* the original conjuring cat. *Grizabella the Glamour Cat,* who haunts many a low resort near the grey Tottenham Court Road. It is easy to recognise the naturally lawless behaviour, intellectual superiority and strong instincts of cats . . . incarnations of the human race, identifiable types meticiously penned by Eliot.

In private life, whilst reserved, Eliot had a rare capacity for fun;

enjoyed wry anecdotes told with dead-pan seriousness. Wary of press intrusion, his private life was just that. His 70th birthday party was very much a family affair with his friend Epstein drinking his health. On a more personal note, I recall visits to *Lord's* with Alan White, chairman of Methuen's, and Tom Eliot. In retrospect it was always sunny and leisured, almost somnolent, with the sound of leather on willow, and prospect of Tavern refreshment . . . today it seems like a mirage.

A.L. ROWSE

THERE ARE SO MANY STORIES about this brilliant historian and Fellow of All Souls, Oxford. The historian could be charming, then in a flash testy and abrasive. My recollection occurred during a light-hearted radio contest of literary knowledge between the Dark and Light Blue Universities. I captained the Cambridge side, Oxford was led by Rowse. Everything went smoothly, until the chairman asked Rowse a trick question. The answer was delayed. Rowse then glowered at the unfortunate fellow and said, "How can you expect me to answer the question when you don't know how to pronounce the word!" Bonhomie evaporated. We went on to win.

GILBERT MURRAY

OUTSIDE A LIMITED CIRCLE, few today have heard of Gilbert Murray, Regius Professor of Greek at Oxford University. Yet this frail, quietly spoken academic was a pivotal figure in the pursuit of lasting peace after the First World War. He was President of the International Committee of Intellectual Co-operation, forerunner of UNESCO; instrumental in founding the League of Nations Union; fifteen years as Chairman before becoming Co-President with the statesman Viscount Cecil. Even more significant was his role in drafting the Covenant at the International Disarmament Conference in Geneva. From the outset it was a thankless task. America declined to join the League. Japan, Italy and Germany stayed on the sidelines, uninterested in peace ploys. Hopes that the United States would take the lead were dashed. Neutrality was safer. It was just as depressing at home with a National Government in power. Cynical disenchantment with politics, widespread; grief for the dead; economic hardships; mass unemployment; endless discussions by technical quangoes.

I experienced something of this negative attitude in lively discussions in House of Commons committee rooms and Chatham House, where Murray had endorsed my membership of the Royal Institute of International Affairs, an offshoot of the Foreign Office. It was a frustrating period, yet Murray never lost the pioneering zeal, though, as a practical idealist, he realised it was an impossible dream. It always will be. Smouldering ruins of Grozny in the bloody battle for the Chechen capital and Russia's defiance of United Nations censure have shown we never learn.

Away from the cauldron of nationalistic hatred, Gilbert Murray found peace at Yatscombe, his home at Boar's Hill near Oxford. There he became the Greek scholar, poet, writer of plays and man of letters. Hereditary strains influenced his career. Born in Australia, son of the President of the Legislative Council of New South Wales; mother, cousin of Sir W. C. Gilbert of Gilbert and Sullivan renown; brother Hubert, Governor of Papua; married Lady Mary Howard, daughter of the 9th Earl of Carlisle, beautiful, eccentric and radical, she played a significant role as hostess of a cross-section of society. George Bernard Shaw played a prominent part in Murray's life persuading him to translate Greek playwrights, like Euripedes, Sophocles and Aeschylus, into English verse. Adapting a style based on William Morris and Swinburne, the result was so successful that Greek plays became an integral part of the English theatre. The innovation attracted public interest like Seamus Heaney's translation of *Beowulf* into modrn English poetry in 1999. Murray looked for more practical confirmation. With William Archer's help, he booked the Lyric Theatre for four nights, then presented *Hippolytus* with a private theatrical company, Edith Oliver as Phaedra, Bryden for Theseus and Granville Barker as a Messenger. The experiment was immensely successful. Bernard Shaw also wrote a play, originally called *Murray's Mother-in-law*, later changed to *Major Barbara* in which both Gilbert and Mary are portrayed and caricatured.

Lighter memories. I recall Murray's passion for tennis that lasted well into his eighties. When the Second World War ended, the tennis outlook in Australia was bleak. With men like Jack Bromwich, Adrian Quist and Jack Crawford now veterans, it would be years before Australia could compete on level terms with the world's best. Harry Hopman told Murray he had found a promising youngster at Box Hill High School in Melbourne, recruited him into his Junior Training Squad to see what intensive coaching could do. It did. In his first season Frank Sedgman became Junior Champion of Australia, eventually winning a Wimbledon Singles title by beating Jaroslav Drobny in the final. Unlike peace-keeping setbacks, Murray's optimism proved justified.

Listening to Murray reminiscing was like opening the pages of history with figures like Asquith coming to life; expressing agreement with the foreign policy of Sir Edward Grey, even though it meant falling out with his pacifist friend, Bertrand Russell; more personal were his thoughts of Marie Curie, the discoverer of radium. On one occasion he invited us to listen to a radio programme recorded in the Yatscombe conservatory. It was interesting to watch reactions as he heard himself recalling academic episodes with Professor Verrall, the Euripides scholar; smiling at sceptical comments on Mrs Verrall's experiences in psychical research; and an unlikely incident when Bertha Phillpots, austere Mistress of Girton, showed him how to enter Professor Chadwick's house without a key by climbing through a small window into a boot hole!

Visiting the Old Mill House, Murray made comparisons. Yatscombe was wilder with no hint of manicured lawns, and one similarity. Yatscombe had impenetrable thickets like our Secret Garden. Afterwards he drily remarked that whilst lacking the legend of the elusive boar, at least we could claim the Miller of Trumpington.

Gilbert Murray died at Boar's Hill in his 92nd year, Mary having passed away three years earlier. I think of this scholar, poet, peace-crusader and his beautiful wife with affection. He was a truly civilised man . . . worthily admitted to the Order of Merit.

E. M. FORSTER

E. M. FORSTER WAS THE MOST IMPORTANT NOVELIST of his generation, yet few knew him well. Often accused of being hermitic, one critic complained that he warmed both hands before the fire of life and put it out. Harsh and unfair. I always found him courteous and thoughtful, especially in his high-ceilinged, spacious rooms in King's College, Cambridge. Everything had an air of permanence. Furnishings suggested William Morris, blue-and-white ceramics, Indian shawls draped over armchairs, Victorian knick-knacks, pastel portraits, books galore, and a grand piano. Sunlight always seemed to pour through the long windows with a backcloth of immaculate lawns, fountain with bronze figure of the founder, Henry VI, and King's Chapel in all its Gothic splendour. On all sides beauty of vision . . . leisured tempo that tinged his writing. I was never surprised by the admission that he was influenced by Jane Austen, Samuel Butler and Proust. He used to say that Cambridge, and King's in particular, held everything he desired. "I shall never tire of it." He never did. Routines seldom varied. Glass of sherry before soup and sandwiches in the pale green Combination Room.

His beginnings were character-moulding. Unhappy at never knowing his father who died when he was an infant, reared by his mother and spoilt by maiden aunts, Forster relived childhood memories of *Rooknest* at Stevenage in his novel *Howards Way*. In 1933 uprooted so he could attend Tunbridge School as a day boy. It was an unhappy period. He hated the conceited venality of the public-school system. Purgatory ended when he came to King's as a Classical Exhibitioner. Freudian and Jungian undertones were swept away by the freedom of Cambridge.

There was a darker side. The impressionable young man came under the influence of Lowes Dickinson, his mentor, Fellow of King's and recruiter for the secret intellectual club known as the *Apostles*. Flattered by the advances, Forster became initiated into an elitist atmosphere in which homosexuality was accepted as the Higher Sodomy. In this hothouse atmosphere Forster accepted homosexuality as a way of life. On the positive side it led to involvement in the Bloomsbury set that included Leonard Woolf, Vanessa Bell, Roger Fry, Lytton Strachey, Virginia Woolf and Maynard Keynes . . . friendships that lasted a lifetime, several survivors attending the lunch party to mark Forster's 80th birthday.

As a novelist, Forster used to say that his college supervisor was the first to encourage him to write. At the outset he was conscious of specific weaknesses that had an adverse effect. He pinpointed three types of people: the person he thought he was; those who irritated him; and people he wanted to be. Experience soon changed such Walter Mitty ideas.

Isolating one work, I think of *A Passage to India*, Forster's last and greatest novel, certainly his most philosophical. Such was its success that it gained the *Femina Vie-Heuresse* and *James Tait Black* prizes and was translated into 21 languages. He began it in 1912, interrupted by the war years, later becoming Private Secretary to the Maharajah of Dewar State, an experience that convinced him of the inaccuracies in his book about India. The manuscript was drastically revised, the abridged version giving a truer reflection of the oriental mind. The thorny question of Anglo-Indian relations was handled with a sympathetic understanding that gained approval from both Hindus and Muslims.

It is brilliantly written, with traumatic scenes, and an intriguing episode that is never explained. It begs the question whether on a visit to the Marabar Caves the young woman was raped by the Muslim doctor or whether it was an hallucination, an offence that would have ruined the medic's career. The woman retracted the charge in the witness-box, but the truth was never revealed. Forster refused to comment. Sir David Lean unsuccessfully tried to find the answer in his epic film that had eleven Oscar nominations.

Be that as it may. After this novel, Forster's flow of writing ceased. Asked why, he said that inspiration died, adding that his reputation seemed to grow with every book he didn't write.

His 90th birthday was marked by a concert in King's Chapel. Forster took immense care in selecting the music. In his rooms the grand piano was not just for effect. He played a limited repertoire of Beethoven and Verdi. Results were not always pleasing to those with a susceptible ear, but it gave him immense pleasure on a par with recollections of assisting Eric Crozier in writing the libretto for Benjamin Britten's opera *Billy Budd*. The 90th concert also coincided with the announcement that he had been admitted to the Order of Merit, an honour that had real significance after earlier refusing a knighthood offered by Clement Attlee.

As often happens, old age brought hardships. With frail, failing eyesight, shuffling about in grimy raincoat and worn cloth cap, Forster looked for a touch of loving care denied in impersonal college surroundings. He turned to the homosexual relationship formed years before with a young policeman, who later married. Even so, the relationship had continued. With characteristic courtesy, Forster had become fond of the wife, an emotion reciprocated. In their semi-detached house in a Coventry suburb, Forster at last found affection and solace. On 7th June, 1970 the curtain fell. I find it impossible not to speculate what Forster's life might have been had he not been ensnared into the elitist web of the *Apostles*.

He was enigmatic, but his faith was simple. "The people I respect must behave as if they were immortal and as if society were eternal. Both assumptions are false; both of them must be accepted as true if we are to go on working and eating and loving, and we are to keep open a few breathing holes for the human spirit."

STEPHEN POTTER

APART FROM WRITING SEVERAL erudite books of scholarly nature, Stephen Potter had the distinction of introducing a new word to the English language following a series of books on Gamesmanship. One in particular, *The Complete Golf Gamesmanship*, had personal consequences, mainly on the greens. Sinking a simple putt was nerve-racking against a background of sly comments and fidgety movements. Psychologically it added strokes to a round. Another irritating habit was typing a personal letter without spacing. Deciphering was tiresome. In spite of such tactics, Stephen was excellent company and radiated charm, but had to endure the backlash that shadows every humorist. Such was his reputation for gamesmanship that innocent actions became suspect. He was a prisoner of his own ploy but adept at turning an instant apology into a defence possibility. Refusing to conform, he created an ambience in which ludicrous anomalies became believable, suggesting he was a simpleton instead of being as sharp as a tack.

His marriage to the distinguished painter Marian Anderson in 1927 ended in divorce twenty-eight years later, then immediately he became tied up with Heather Jenner, founder of the successful

Marriage Bureau in Bond Street, London. Although opposites in temperament, it brought a form of mutual happiness. Heather, handsome, incisive and a strong personality, swept Stephen off his feet, held control. In the early days he acted like a love-stricken male but became resigned to submission with occasional lapses. One such occasion was a week-end visit to the Old Mill House with the understanding that departure would be immediately after breakfast on the Monday morning, as I had a luncheon appointment in London. The weekend went blissfully. Monday breakfast. Stephen came down with apologetic news as Heather had decided to stay in bed. Eleven o'clock: she was still between the sheets and refusing to get up. Ruefully Stephen said that in her mood, nothing could be done. I suggested gamesmanship might help. We had to leave for London. Heather emerged, ruffled, hastily made-up and surly. Stephen, mindful of honeymoon days, acted as porter.

When Stephen died, the mould was broken. It is difficult to believe that he was born a hundred years ago.

DR. FRANK LEAVIS VERSUS SIR CHARLES SNOW

FRANK LEAVIS WAS A FORMIDABLE OPPONENT, an acerbic academic who resented the accusations in the *Two Cultures* that universities had found new scientific cultures with irrelevant comparisons between scientific and literary values. In the *Rede Lecture*, Snow further developed the theme by adding inflammatory arguments. Leavis said Snow had insulted literary traditions with doses of High Table snobbery. His counter-attack was carefully planned. He chose as a platform the *Richmond Lectures* created during the Second World War by Sir Herbert Richmond, then Master of Downing, as a platform. The Lecture, held in the College Hall, was not open to the public, but such was the bitterness of the Leavis/Snow feud, it attracted media and national press interest.

They were not disappointed. Opening remarks set the tone. "If confidence in oneself as a master-mind, qualified by capacity, insight and knowledge to pronounce authoritatively on the frightening problems of our civilisation, is genius, then there can be no doubt about Sir Charles Snow's." Referring to the *Two Cultures*, Leavis scathingly commented on its "utter lack of intellectual distinction and embarrassing vulgarity of style . . . a document for the study of clichés". Snow's reputation as a writer was flawed . . . with scant knowledge of what constituted creative literature . . . reflected shallow materialistic philosophies worthy of Sunday newspaper reviews and *New Stateman* pontifications.

The aftermath upset the world of literary criticism, split the English Faculty at Cambridge University into rival camps, and destroyed Snow's reputation as being intellectually negligible. Leavis had reason to be satisfied.

In private Leavis was quite different, an agreeable eccentric who was always good value if you had the patience to listen. I knew when he parked his obsolete bicycle in the Old Mill House courtyard that I was about to listen to an up-to-date, blow-by-blow resumé of literary in-fighting. He hated conventional dress, open-necked shirts in preference to ties, old-fashioned khaki shorts, knapsack as brief-case. Once inside, he would sink into an armchair, sitting sideways with legs across the arm. Invariably provocative, but courteous in argument.

As a guest he was hopeless. Set views on diet with no main meal after lunch, meant that guests felt embarrassed at enjoying dinner with Frank staring at an empty plate. Still, that idiosyncrasy was preferable to Snow's habits. He was such a tactile person that care had to be excised about the female guests on both sides. To maintain a balance, one was straight-laced, the other had Germaine Greer's foibles. At least other diners enjoyed their reactions.

One thing Snow and Leavis shared. Both had reactions to disappointments. The former was embittered that Leavis' devastating attack had killed any hope of Nobel Prize recognition. Leavis regretted that the Chair of Poetry at Oxford University had gone to Robert Graves. Had both ambitions been realised, Snow would have become even more overbearing; Leavis might have donned the gown of conformity.

SIR JOHN BETJEMAN

WE MET ONE AFTERNOON in the Cotswold village of Burford, the *Bay Tree* making an ideal backcloth for Sir John Betjeman, by popular acclaim the people's Poet Laureate. The experience became escapism from living in the present, a world in which to appreciate tea parties, Joan Hunter-Dunn playing tennis at dusk, memories of gas-lit Victorian churches, mischievous microscopic observations about suburbia. In retrospect we talked of Irish music-halls, plastic macs, haemorrhoids, choice of tea or whisky. He had just visited an industrial dormitory with skyscraper housing-blocks, where people lived in a silent vertical life cut off in airy silence. Occasional wry remarks on doleful suburbia that inspired the lines "Come friendly bombs, and fall on Slough."

On personal matters, Betjeman was like his verse, neither heated or dishevelled. He had a fear of old age and death, the mystery of being brought apprehension. In 1933 he married Penelope Valentine Hester, only daughter of Field-Marshal Sir Philip Chetwode, then Commander-in-Chief in India; amicably separated; then cared for by his friend, Lady Elizabeth Cavendish, sister of the Duke of Devonshire.

John Betjeman died in 1984 at his home in Trebetherick, Cornwall, and is buried in the churchyard at St. Enodoc. The setting was in keeping. Nestling in the middle of sandhills is a 13th-century church spire. For many years it was buried in the sands. An annual Service used to be held when a path had to be cut. It was finally dug out and restored in 1863. That May day the dunes were wreathed in mists as Betjeman's coffin was carried by mourners in slow procession along a winding path in falling rain, a poignant requiem to this much loved poet.

JOHN GALSWORTHY

IT IS TRUE TO SAY THAT WHILE NOVELISTS belong to their own day, great novelists are not confined to this time-scale because men and women have changed so little. John Galsworthy is an example. It is unfair to base an opinion on the strength of two meetings, but Galsworthy left a lasting impression, so outwardly composed with total absence of emotion. He was a true-to-life image of the Upper Middle Class of his time, but critical of the class. In a privileged way, he attacked privilege. In short, almost play-acted the role of Soames in *The Forsyte Saga*, Galsworthy wrote into the plot many of his likes and dislikes. Whilst upholding Victorian values, the author reveals his taste for property, the acting of "owning" that included Soames's wife, Irene. Galsworthy further explained that Irene was modelled on the life of his own wife, Ada. Sexist undercurrents were rife.

Joseph Conrad described Galsworthy as a "humanitarian moralist". It was an accurate description. My comparison was the English Ibsen. Galsworthy felt Turgenev would be nearer the mark. They shared similar views on society. As a playwright, Galsworthy used the stage as platforms for introducing social reforms. *The Silver Box, Justice*, and *The Skin Game* were well received in London's West End Theatres.

Surprisingly he refused a knighthood in 1918, but was appointed Order of Merit in 1929 and awarded the Nobel Prize for literature three years later. His writing has stood the test of time.

CECIL DAY-LEWIS

WHEN IT COMES TO CECIL DAY-LEWIS, it is difficult to decide which comes first – personal life or work. The former was more than colourful. Hot blood flowed in his veins. He married Constance, daughter of a Sherborne housemaster; then had a passionate affair with Billie Currall, feisty wife of a neighbour in Devon, that produced a son; began a relationship with Rosamond Lehmann, the novelist, the infatuation lasting until 1949; then fell in love with actress Jill, daughter of the film producer, Sir Michael Balcon.

The role of Lothario improved his charismatic techniques. The gloss never wore off. He was an agreeable companion, but I could never understand why Jill, so fastidious, did not insist on Cecil taking advice from a cosmetic dentist to improve the sight of an unpleasant row of mis-shapen teeth. I could only assume that his conquests shut their eyes and thought of England.

As a poet he was outstanding. At Wadham College he met Wystan Auden and collaborated in *Oxford Poetry*, becoming with Spender the left-wing poets of the thirties. Of his work, he was the least complex, one of the most scholarly, yet the symbols he used were simple and unsophisticated, dealing with youth and age. He belonged to the traditional minor Romantics. In 1951 he was elected Professor of Poetry at Oxford; that same year the BBC broadcast his translation of Virgil's *Aeneid*; became involved in publishing joining Chatto and Windus as director under the chairmanship of Norah Smallwood. In 1968 he succeeded John Masefield as Poet Laureate. Four years later whilst staying with his wife Jill at the Hadley Wood home of Elizabeth Jane Howard and Kingsley Amis, he was taken ill and died.

Cecil Day-Lewis was a poet who never grew out of childhood.

> I practised
> Words like a secret vice; words perpetually
> Flung up, encroached on, crumbling, superseded,
> Real to me as wet sand to a child's fingers,
> More real than the quaking asphalt of the sea front
> Or the rook-babble of bathers . . .

JAMES BRIDIE

FEW PEOPLE OUTSIDE THE MEDICAL PROFESSION have heard of Osborne Henry Mayor. He was Consulting Physician of the Victoria Infirmary and Professor of Medicine in Anderson College, Glasgow. His status was high and respected, but it was as a playwright under the name of James Bridie that he was best known. Forty plays appeared under the pseudonym. The list included *The Switchback,* presented by Sir Barry Jackson in Birmingham; Henry Ainley in the leading part of the London production of *The Anatomist*; Alastair Sim starring in *Mr. Bolfrey*; Dame Edith Evans led in *Daphne Laureola*, whilst memorable biblical plays were *Tobias and the Angel*; *Jonah and the Whale, Susannah and the Elders*. No mean record for the secondary career of a Scottish medic. In private he would talk about almost anything except his medical activities as a doctor, but admitted, like Somerset Maugham, that his work had taught him pretty well all he knew about human nature. Only once did his formal professional approach falter. I shared a public debate in the University on the subject of euthanasia. He took a compassionate line, arguing that a terminal illness involving great pain required a humane approach. Provided it was established without reasonable doubt that the case was medically hopeless, it was right to end such fruitless suffering. On four occasions he had made that decision. The following morning the Scottish *Daily Express* carried the headline "James Bridie Commits Four Murders." It required the tact of Bridie to get Mayor out of an embarrassing situation.

ROBERT FROST

OCTOGENARIANS ARE USUALLY FRAIL. Robert Frost was an exception. This rough-hewn man with a slab granite face and abundant white hair displayed amazing energy that belied his eighty-three years when he came into the Old Mill House courtyard accompanied by S.C. Roberts, Master of Pembroke College. Links with Rupert Brooke were recalled through our house being so close to the Old Vicarage at Granchester and the fact there was still honey for tea at the *Orchard,* memories unaffected by the likes of Lord Archer. During his stay the University of London invited him to give a series of lectures that proved immensely popular. This American poet not only influenced a generation of budding American poets, he was also an acknowledged American institution. The reputation surprised him. In a rich baritone voice and a touch of ironic humour, he confessed to despising fashion as a poet, yet he was fashionable. His accessible colloquial blank verse, spiced with New England speech-patterns, is written with an individual voice and penetrating insight. He wrote poems in the plainest terms, yet critics analysed his work in terms of the greatest complexity. The output earned four Pulitzer Prizes. The United States Senate issued a citation in honour of his poetry. He was the only American poet to receive honorary degrees from both Oxford and Cambridge. The Master of Pembroke drily remarked that whilst Lowell had been similarly honoured in 1873, it was in part recognition of diplomatic service, whilst Longfellow five years earlier received similar degrees but not at the same time. On balance Frost took the points.

Frost's writing was colloquial yet simple. He enjoyed both sardines and caviare, and did not refer to heaven as a bed-sitting-room. He confessed that in self-evaluation, he felt his life had been half-achievement, not much of a farmer, question-mark on poetic prowess with an output of some ten pages a year over a span of sixty years, indulgent self-pessimism that did not match universal acclaim. . . . Quizzically he requested that the epitaph on his gravestone should read . . . "I had a lover's quarrel with the world." Robert Frost was a gentle genius in big black boots.

BERTRAND RUSSELL

LYTTON STRACHEY USED TO SAY that Bertrand Russell belonged to the dangerous class of great gnomes. It was an apt description of a man whose life-span lasted ninety years, the survivor of a dead era. Grandson of Prime Minister John Russell, he told how he visited Napoleon in Elba, whilst his maternal grandmother was a friend of the Young Pretender's widow. In a reminiscent mood he would recall how in 1889 he dined with Gladstone, who asked him why he was given excellent port in a claret glass. For once he didn't know the answer.

The 3rd Earl Russell, to give his real title, was the younger son of Viscount Amberley; mother died when he was two; father, a year later; taught at home by tutors until he was 18, then entered Trinity College, Cambridge – the outset of a brilliant career . . . that produced *Principia Mathematica*, one of the most significant contributions of the century. He would recall how the book very nearly was rejected as the publisher calculated it would show a loss of £6500. Russell and the co-author, Alfred Whitehead, agreed to bear half the cost, plus £200 guarantee by the Royal Society. Between the ten years work was rewarded by minus £59. Russell remembered the manuscript being delivered to the publisher in a horse-drawn cab. His own description of its contents summarised the theme. "Mathematics may be defined as the subject in which we never know what we are talking about, nor whether what we are saying is true." Laymen unable to understand the theories could take heart. The dilemma was shared. Russell's own views were expressed years later . . . "when I was young I liked mathematics, when this became too difficult to me, I took to philosophy, when philosophy became too difficult, I turned to politics."

Self-deprecatory reflections were hardly justified. His long life was marked by innumerable honours; pacifist protestations cost him Trinity lectureship; disqualified from an academic post at City College in New York because of over-liberal views on morality;

commented that his book *Introduction to Mathematical Philosophy* was written in prison; in spite of the sentence, he was awarded the Order of Merit; then in his nineties he and his wife took part in a mass-sitdown in Whitehall and demonstrated, which resulted in two months prison sentence, reduced to a week because of their age. He never changed from being a rebel advocate of free thought and free speech. Some utterances have a familiar note today . . . "Since the Labour Party turned Tory, I have no political party!"

Away from controversy Russell was a compulsive womanizer. Marital fidelity meant nothing. Four official wives, he added Lady Ottoline Morrell as his mistress; tried unsuccessfully to seduce Evelyn Whitehead, wife of his teacher; and a sequence of females who took his fancy. Nora was the wife I knew, dogmatic, reformer, with a roving eye. Over many years, it was a repetitive saga. The remarkable feat is that in appearance Russell was not attractive, yet at social occasions he was invariably encircled by pretty young women who overlooked his incessant pipe-smoking, short stature, clipped donnish voice, white hair and irritating, high-pitched laugh.

Reputations compensate for physical drawbacks. I took part in a broadcast discussion on the subject of belief in God. Russell's formative years as a child were influenced by the Amberleys, atheist guardians with unconventional views on morals and religion. John Stuart Mill became a secular godfather. Traditional arguments failed against the conviction that all forms of religion were not only false but harmful.

J.B. PRIESTLEY

RECOLLECTIONS OF J.B. PRIESTLEY are linked with reassuring wartime broadcasts to counter the sneering voice of Lord Haw Haw's Nazi propaganda. Priestley's regional accent was as compelling as *The Good Companions*, just as the pages of *Angel Pavement* captured the flavour of London life. In his Albany apartments, lack of space meant that everything was carefully chosen, particularly the paintings. He talked about his preoccupation with theories of time, but was cut short by his wife, Jacquetta Hawkes, distinguished author in her own right, and daughter of Sir Gowland Hopkins, discoverer of vitamins.

That afternoon Priestley gave me a copy of his latest book, *Margin Released*. I was puzzled by the significance of the title. He explained that anyone who used typewriters would know that the machines have a key labelled *Margin Release* for the benefit of careless typists. He intended it to suggest more than its practical purpose . . . something that had a conceited reticence at one end and a diffident humility at the other. The inference seemed strained, but at least we were spared an anagram.

The list of his plays, novels and essays is remarkable proof of literary endeavour. Priestley was a born story-teller of imagination, and craftsmanship.

W.H. AUDEN

W.H. AUDEN WAS SUCH A CONTRADICTION I found it difficult to discover the real man behind the ellipsis of personality and literary output. To some he is the foremost English poet of the century, yet there is a dilemma which he recognised when he said, "Life, as I experience it, is primarily a continuous succession of choices between alternatives." Referring to himself as a voyageur, he wrote, "The journey of life is infinitely long and its possible destinations infinitely distant from one another, but the time spent in actual travel is infinitesimally small, the hours the traveller measures are those in which he is at rest between the three or four decisive instants of transportation which are all he needs and all he gets to carry him the whole way."

There are many turning-points in the pilgrimage of this poet, essayist and librettist. He was born 1907 in York, educated at St. Edmunds, Hindhead, where he met Isherwood, who was to figure so prominently in his life. At Christ Church, Oxford, he began to write poetry and was influenced by T.S. Eliot's *The Waste Land* that had just been published. About this time Auden became homosexual.

Academically he was not brilliant at Oxford, leaving with a Third Class in English Literature. Had his first book published, *Poems,* forty-five copies being printed privately by Stephen Spender. Left for Berlin where he became interested in Homer Lane's movement. Uninhibited love was a liberating force; but it lost its appeal, so from Freudian psychoanalysis he turned to Marxism. It was a period of experiment that was unsettling. One incident puzzled me. On a visit to the Old Mill House, I asked Auden what possessed him to marry Erika Mann. It began when the girl, daughter of Thomas Mann, realised she was on the Nazi hit-list. The solution was to acquire a British passport. She asked Isherwood if he would marry her. He declined but suggested Auden. The first meeting was at a railway station, details discussed and the wedding followed. Auden's answer was practical. He had no interest in women from a sex point of view. The girl needed help. He obliged. The union was never consummated. I remarked that chivalry could be taken too far.

In 1937 Auden was in Spain and volunteered to drive an ambulance for the Republicans. The experience led to the political poem, *Spain*. Travelled to China, collaborating with Spencer to write *Journey to a War*, went to America where he met Chester Kallman in New York, began a passionate relationship with the young poet, an affair that went through stormy moments through Kallman's flirtatious approaches to other men. They later collaborated in writing the libretto of *The Rake's Progress* with music by Igor Stravinsky. When the war ended, Auden rented a flat in Ischia, later buying a house in the village of Kirchstetten, near Vienna. In 1956 he was elected Professor of Poetry at Oxford University, thoroughly enjoyed the experience, making regular contacts with students by holding open house sessions sat in the *Cadena* cafe in the Cornmarket. Envious of E.M. Forster's luxury of enjoying life-tenure rooms at King's College in Cambridge, he requested similar facilities at Christ Church, eventually being given a grace-and-favour cottage in the college grounds. It should have been a happy arrangement, but sadly it proved impossible to recapture the pleasures of yesterday. Oxford had changed. Industry and tourists ruined the former tranquillity. The new generation of undergraduates had little in common with the poet, who at times imbibed too much wine at High Table.

Auden's closing years were far from happy. Nothing went right. He quarrelled with Benjamin Britten, a rift never resolved. He was not only lonely, but apprehensive. He had no peace in New York, obsessed with the fear that he could die in his apartment without anyone knowing. His friend, Reinhold Niebuhr, the theologian, offered comfort to no avail. Auden had hoped that when Day-Lewis died, he might succeed him as Poet Laureate. It was not to be. In 1973 he gave a reading in Vienna and died suddenly that night. He was buried at Kirchstetten. The following year, a memorial stone was laid in Westminster Abbey.

ROBERT LOWELL AND EZRA POUND

I RECALL TWO HIGHLY CONTROVERSIAL MEN OF LETTERS . . . Robert Lowell and Ezra Pound. The former was hailed as the most significant American poet since T. S. Eliot, but not to everybody's taste; the latter regarded by many critics as aesthetically and culturally an outstanding literary figure of the century . . . again an acquired taste. Robert Graves dismissed him as a charlatan. In Lowell's case I had difficulties. He was a new talent and had established a fresh approach to verse, often breaking fresh ground by dealing with subjects usually taboo, like spasms of a nervous breakdown. Elitist critics called such lines confessional verse, a distinction that meant little to me. The same applied to Lowell's attempt to turn modern verse into drama, like W. H. Auden and Dylan Thomas, but well short of T. S. Eliot's *Murder in the Cathedral*. He launched three plays, two directed by Jonathan Miller in New York. I found them dreary, stark, with miserable endings. They were collector's items.

Lowell was always prepared to defend his corner when we met in his New York apartment, which had been converted from an old Mission. The studio had a complete wall of glass, an austere backcloth for the poet's individualistic tastes. In discussions about the exploitation of modern views, I said that the description of how his mother's body was returned from Italy for burial in the United States was distasteful:

> Mother travelled first-class in the hold;/
> her *risorgimento* black and gold casket/
> . . . in the grandiloquent lettering on mother's
> coffin/ Lowell had been mis-spelled *Lowel*./
> The corpse was wrapped like *panetone* in Italian tinfoil.

Lowell thought I was too thin-skinned. After all, it was an accurate description, maybe dramatised, but it was what happened! He used similar stark observations about life in a lunatic asylum . . . "These victorious figures of bravado ossified young." It is a matter of taste. Mine was unsympathetic. It had wide appeal. The style earned innumerable prizes, including a Pulitzer.

I have always regretted never having met Ezra Pound. Lowell's comments on the troubled life of this tormented man were reinforced by the framed portrait that surveyed the room like a disdainful Old Testament prophet. When I asked if he thought Pound was really mad, he replied that any mental instability must have been aggravated by the barbaric treatment meted out by American soldiers. He thought that naivety caused many problems, insensitivity to reactions. During the years in London living in a small flat near Kensington High Street, he became a mobile landmark with uncombed hair and red beard plus Mid-West accent. He was not over-popular with the more conservative residents of that locality.

In sympathy with Mussolini's policies, he was in a dilemma at the outbreak of war; tried to join the diplomatic train taking Americans from Italy to Lisbon, but permission was refused, largely because of his broadcasts from Rome Radio. They were legal but foolish. When the United States entered the war, Pound asked the Italian Minister of Popular Culture for continuation of the talks provided there would be no directives or censorship. In spite of such assurances in 1945 these broadcasts led to Pound being indicted on 13 grounds in his absence by the Grand Jury of the District Court of Columbia. He was interrogated by the United States Army in Genoa and taken by road to Pisa. What happened next was condemned by Lowell in no uncertain terms. Pound was put in solitary confinement in a barbed wire cage. No roof or protection, he was given three blankets. Guards were ordered not to speak to him. Throughout the night searchlights prevented him sleeping. This continued for six weeks. He had a nervous breakdown and transferred to a tent; had two books with him – a Confucius in Chinese and a Bible, table and writing materials. Whilst there, he composed the first draft of the *Pisan Cantos* in which he embodied the landscape details around the camp and also translated two

Confucian texts. A month later he was flown to Washington to be tried for treason. Medically examined he was declared unfit to plead. Sent to a public mental hospital in Washington suburbs; imprisoned for 15 months in a concrete dormitory without furniture or windows and most of the patients in straitjackets; after 18 months transferred to a small room, with table, typewriter, allowed to write and have visitors. During that period he translated the whole of the canonical Chinese *Book of Odes*, continued working on the *Cantos*, and translated a play of Sophocles.

In 1949 the mood improved. Pound received the Bollingen Award, plus a prize of 1,000 dollars for the *Pisan Cantos*. Controversy followed. Lowell said the decision was right. He served on the panel of judges along with T. S. Eliot, W. H. Auden and Conrad Aitken. Nine years later Pound was released from St. Elizabeth's Mental Hospital. He went to Italy and joined his daughter in her husband's castle in the Tyrol. So ended a callous chapter of vicious punishment.

What verdict can we pass on this man-of-letters? T. S. Eliot once said that the poet always seemed a temporary squatter. In that New York apartment of Richard Lowell's, his spirit seemed at home, at least he found sympathy.

WALTER DE LA MARE

WHEN IT WAS ANNOUNCED that Walter de la Mare had died, the news, although expected, came as a shock. Memories surfaced, heightened by insignificant details that suddenly became important, recollections of my last visit to the secluded house in a Georgian terrace, dominated by a plane tree that vied with the tall windows. I was shown into the small study. Windows looked on to a garden. The centre pane had these words engraved on it by Laurence Whistler:

> Look thy last on all things lovely,
> Every hour. Let no night
> Seal thy sense in deathly slumber
> Till to delight
> Thou have paid thy utmost blessing;

> Since that all things thou wouldst praise
> Beauty took from those who loved them
> In other days.

The housekeeper took me into the bedroom. The poet, leaning back on the pillows, was resting after completing a manuscript on Thomas Hardy. On the folds of the counterpane were an orange, a red-cheeked apple and a threepenny bit. He talked about *The Traveller*, a long metaphysical autobiographical poem of some 700 lines broken into 4-line stanzas. It is haunting, describing how a Traveller and his horse journeyed across a strange land towards death and came to death at last. Walter said it was intended to be both a spiritual and physical journey. He felt he was already nearing that journey's end. In such a frame of mind he was melancholy with a brooding sense of pending tragedy.

To judge him by this poem would be misleading. As a poet he ranks with Blake, Shelley and Bridges, but his lyrical gift ranks him far in excess of any other English poet with command of pure inspiration. He lived in two worlds, one real, the other spun of dreams. Born with a love of words, he captured the wonder of a child with the intensity of enchanted loveliness, isolating things minute, almost magical. Maybe a bubble world, but not once in thirty volumes of poetry and prose did he lose the will-o'-the-wisp touch that created a mosaic of dreams. After that visit he wrote me a letter ending with a regretful note: ". . . If you were on the Bench and I in the dock what must be my Sentence for being in bed on such a morning! I begrudge every green leaf that appears, because it will be gone in October! Could there be anything more infantile."

Walter de la Mare is no more, but his spirit lives on in his imaginative dreams. Old age came to him with vision unimpaired.

LEGENDS OF STAGE AND SCREEN

~

THE PERSONALITIES OF CINEMA and theatre are created by the public. Everyone knows the characters are fantasy, but there is reluctance to surrender disbelief at the box-office. The charade is acceptable because many in the audience see themselves as mirror personalities by identifying with performers who become art objects dealing in illusions rather than artists. One thing is certain. The cult of the personality has become imbedded in our attitude. Some of these performers have no identity other than as actors or actresses. As professionals they have to guard their images. Many remain enigmatic. They play over and over again roles similar to one another and create strong images of themselves. The careers of several well-known stars are masterpieces of such understatement and timing. They sense it is essential for an audience to be comfortable in their presence. By understatement they imply strength rather than insisting upon it, and, as a result, become deliberately out of touch. They play themselves, but today that is not enough. Everyone is curious what these illusory figures are really like. In attempts to please, they become infected with the disease of terminal trendiness and submit themselves to probing by television interviewers.

Maybe in our cynical times it has become the accepted build-up for an embryo star, but it is questionable in the case of an established larger-than-life figure. It can be counter-productive and tends to destroy illusions. Television chat-shows have become the modern equivalent to the old B-type film. The farm-system for new talent seldom adds to the stature of those who have attained the height of a celebrity, gilt-edged drawing-cards in the business.

It is not easy to make a selective choice of those who might be considered eligible for the narrow category of genius. So many factors influence a career . . . The well-trodden routes to the silver screen is for many hopeful starlets by way of the casting couch, but the whim of a producer is not the deciding factor. The camera has the last word. If the lens is unimpressed, the film tests become meaningless. On the other hand, there have been surprises. The camera has singled out a girl in a supporting role who reflects the imagination of that period. One of these was Brigitte Bardot, the teenage sex-symbol who became a tonic for a war-weary generation. Roger Vadim, her first lover and first husband, recognised her unique quality that was confirmed in the film *And God Created Woman.* She became a "natural" for the *paparazzi.* Youngsters copied the piled-up hair, tumbling pony-tail, gingham and jeans. Capricious and petulant, Bardot collected pretty young men, several husbands, quickly became bored and dropped them. She made more than forty films, but only a few are memorable. There was no doubt about her star quality, but the talent in no way reflected genius. Our meeting was something of an anti-climax. Half-expecting a rebellious blonde, I found instead a brunette with eyes heavily coated in mascara, more concerned about her campaign in the defence of animals than recollections of liberated sun-soaked sex. Maybe her priorities were right.

Others in the same category include Jean Harlow, the gold-prospecting tramp of the Thirties and Rita Hayworth, the seductive post-war dream whose rota of husbands included Edward C. Robinson, Orson Welles, Aly Khan, Dick Haynes and James Hill, but the classic example of a camera spotting a potential star was Marilyn Monroe. She had worked hard to gain recognition with endless publicity photographs, including the nude pose of a calendar, but success, when it came, proved overwhelming. The golden girl, who had become a bill-board super-star, turned to drugs. *Some Like It Hot,* filmed under this induced animation, and *Let's Make Love,* proved disastrous. During the shooting she fell in love with Yves Montand. The French actor did not allow the dalliance to upset his marriage to the actress Simone Signoret, but the affair virtually destroyed Monroe's relationship with Arthur Miller. Her last film, *The Misfits,* was equally unfortunate. Filming was difficult, the weather unbearably hot, her co-star, Clark Gable, crumbled under the strain and died of a heart attack a few days after it was finished. Monroe's personal trauma continued. Her marriage ended, the drug problem persisted. Though suspended, she received awards as the best actress and sang at Kennedy's birthday party, then under circumstances that still raise speculation came that fatal overdose. Marilyn Monroe was a tragic figure. She reached the top, accepted success, but knew that the plaudits were dependent on her beauty. Although only 36, she became obsessed with the thought that the passage of time would see her only asset decline. Ambitions were realised too early. Like Bardot, she had vital talent, but fell short of genius.

Even more natural in front of the camera is Sophia Loren. She comes across as a supreme symbol of genuine sexuality. Victoria De Sica tried to described the effect in words . . . "In spite of having the usual womanly defects, she is the only really spiritually honest woman I have ever known." Others have said that Sophia changed into sensual what was spiritual in Greta Garbo. The overall image became a super-star, but again sensuality rarely becomes genius. Many have tried to no avail. Ursula Andress, conscious where her assets lay, emphasised this angle. Unlike Raquel Welsh and Sophia Loren, who declined to appear nude, Ursula had no inhibitions about shedding garments, but the effect, though total, did nothing for her image. Reputations are often enhanced by idiosyncratic touches like the wraith-like quality of Joan Greenwood, the diminutive blonde with an intriguing voice likened to a champagne gargle.

If genius was influenced by looks, I would champion Merle Oberon, whose transcendent beauty with ever-widening eyes seemed to absorb everything. Her acting was outstanding, but somehow the roles were inadequate and the edge of ambition faded. The same might be said of Claire Bloom. When this lovely actress made her name in *Limelight,* she was only a girl of 18, but her potential had been recognised by Charles Chaplin. International stardom became reality after her memorable Juliet at the Old Vic and a brilliant role in *Streetcar*. Her career faltered. Possibly success came too early. Not so for Gertrude Lawrence. Noel Coward, like Chaplin, was quick to spot potential talent, even when Gertrude was a child performer in 1913. His hunch was right. Eventually she became the foremost of Coward's leading ladies. *Private Lives*, *Present Indicative* and *Future Indefinite* were landmarks in a career that highlighted her vitality, humour and glamour, qualities caught in the film of her life entitled *Star*, that featured Julie Andrews in the leading role. Gertrude Lawrence was a rare artist who "lived" the parts, but refused to take herself too seriously. Her sense of humour would have shot down any attempt to equate her with genius.

The same could be said of Ingrid Bergman, whom David Selznick, who built up her career, described as a genius without ostentation.

Assessing "greats" is not easy. Publicity values in the entertainment world are exaggerated. Informed criticism is rare. For that reason I turned to Gloria Swanson, a friend of many years, and asked for honest comments about her contemporaries, many being co-stars. The result was enlightening. Gloria could be tough and had the stamina of a survivor. For three generations she personified romantic fantasy. She was everything to every man. When sound came to movies, her style was adapted to cope with the changed conditions. Publicity gimmicks like the solid gold bathtub in a black marble bathroom were forgotten. She concentrated on the emotional side of her private life, which was anything but private. Torrid would be a more accurate description. Turbulent marriages and a sensational love affair with Joe Kennedy, patriarch of the Kennedy dynasty, an involvement broken through the intervention of Cardinal O'Connell of Boston and the guile of Rose Kennedy . . .

Gloria's caustic tongue had a picnic in reminiscences, recalling clashes of temperament . . . Cary Grant had a limited range as an actor. *North by Northwest* was his best film, not forgetting *To Catch a Thief* that established Grace Kelly. *The Philadelphia Story* earned an Oscar for James Stewart but he was almost word-bound after talkies arrived. She found Rudolph Valentino tiresome with flailing antics almost out of control, at times comic. His love scenes in *Beyond the Reach* were overseered by Elinor Glyn, which Gloria found inhibiting. The nearest I had been to meeting this legend was in a cemetery in Hollywood. A taciturn assistant shifted the moveable ladder, climbed to the top, opened a small elaborate hatch, and came down with the urn containing Valentino's ashes, then solemnly returned it to its niche. So much for the longevity of fame.

Other comments included Harold Lloyd, in a class of his own. In London he told me that his films grossed over 30 million dollars. She found Chaplin indecisive. Lonely and wealthy, he had clung to silence like *City Lights* with sound tracks and no spoken dialogue.

She found Marlon Brando brilliant, but sullen and mumbled. Orson Welles was hardly a charmer, but nothing could detract from his performance in *Citizen Kane*. Over lunch in London I found Welles' physical presence overwhelming with brows contracted above his jowls and eyes bulging reproachfully, like a ghost of Kingsley Amis, but the effect was softened by a voice of superb quality. Orson's career, marred by frustration, was not dissimilar to Gordon Craig. Both were viewed with suspicion because of their many skills. Critics welcome a genius who excels in one thing. Orson's talents were too spread and innovative . . . a huge potential was wasted. Aided by wine, this Hollywood *éminence grise* unburdened the woes that happened after *Citizen Kane*. It began when RKO gave him a carte blanche contract as producer, director, writer and actor to do his own thing. *Citizen Kane* was the result, according to many critics the best film ever made, and Orson was only twenty-six. Such freedom was never repeated. Afterwards everything seemed anti-climax, apart from isolated successes sandwiched between cameo parts in indifferent films and voice-overs. Orson never hid the disappointment, though as raconteur, bitterness was sweetened with anecdote. That afternoon this introspective catalogue of gloom was interrupted by Alexander Korda's wife asking him how he would like to be remembered. Unexpectedly he named the *Citizen Kane* role. My choice was the chilling Harry Lime in *The Third Man*. If only such successes had been repeated, but obesity changed his appearance into a grotesque shape.

Gloria regarded Katherine Hepburn as an oddity, a contradictory creature, over-conscious of her intelligence and lack of it in others, though superb in *The African Queen*. John Ford made a dull man seem interesting. Gary Cooper, the archetypal American, merited a second Academy Award for *High Noon*. Tom Mix she never knew. At the time when Neville Chamberlain thought he had checked Nazi aggression, I had occasion to show the veteran something of the sights of Edinburgh. Back in the Caledonian Hotel we were joined by Professor Brasnett, one of Scotland's leading theologians. Although not socially conscious, Brasnett found that the name of Tom Mix recalled childhood memories. We were invited to lunch the next day at Coates Hall. A cloistered life dictated by moral and spiritual disciplines did not stifle Brasnett's curiosity about life outside the seminary. They were worlds apart. Mix, twice a real-life sheriff, Texas Ranger for three years, soldier of fortune in the Boer War, had fought in the American Army in the Spanish-American War and Boxer Rebellion.

He described how he made his first movie in Oklahoma in 1910, when the Selig Company, out of Chicago, hired him as an extra, but the big chance came when William S. Hart, who preferred realism to the contrived, announced his retirement. Tom Mix took over in more romanticised versions of the simple dramas of heroism in which he was cast as the puritan of the plains, distracted neither by scheming women nor good whisky. He was at pains to point out that he never used doubles for stunts, galloped his own horse, and handled cattle stampedes. Dicey at times, but the risk became an end in itself. Those days had gone for ever. Had no regrets. At times felt they had never been.

He felt life in an academic setting would be austere. His own home was more suited for a cattle baron than a cowboy. Originally his ambition was to outdo the "Falcon's Lair" of Randolph Valentino and 'Pickfair" of Douglas and Mary Pickford, but they belonged to the past like the Keystone Kops and Blanche Sweet. So ended a lunch I have never forgotten.

Noel Coward was only a slight acquaintance, but remembered as a talented, vain homosexual. In contrast Clark Gable seemed uncomplicated, all man with equal appeal to both sexes. Equally outstanding was Humphrey Bogart in *The Maltese Falcon*, due in part to inspired directing by John Huston. Bogart was an acquired taste. His air of sardonic loneliness was unattractive, though obviously not to Lauren Bacall. Nothing can blur for me the memory of Marlene Dietrich in *The Blue Angel*. She had the best of two worlds. Her sexuality appealed to men, her masculinity to women. Greta Garbo was said to have a timeless mystique that men found suggestive of erotic promise, though the indolent movements were probably due to anaemia. She wanted solitude. In late life she had it. I could never take Mary Pickford seriously. In real life the so-called America's sweetheart was a tough mogul in curls. Maurice Chevalier was a delicious rogue with a wicked smile, pink cheeks and great knowingness. He had the charm one would expect from the partner of Mistinguett in the Folies Bergère. I think of Fred Astaire, who danced his way into the hearts of three decades of filmgoers. His contribution to musical films being rightly recognised by an Oscar. Then the great lady of the screen, Bette Davis, who ignored the lines of age. She was always just herself with remarkable resilience. The resentment, bitchiness and vicissitudes she experienced would have broken the spirit of any other actress. In many ways Bette was ahead of her time. Then possibly the finest screen actor of all . . . Spencer Tracy. I can offer no reason. It was just a fact.

VIGNETTES OF MEMORY. I think of Ralph Richardson, the avuncular, pie-loving eccentric whose acting career spanned six decades. So many outstanding roles . . . Peer Gynt, Cyrano de Bergerac, and possibly his greatest as Falstaff, and films like *Spartacus, Gordon of Khartoum* and *Dr. Zhivago*. Off stage in his Regency house on a Nash terrace, he took immense pleasure talking about early firearms, based on his unique collection of antique pistols of every type. One in particular had belonged to the Reverend Alexander Forsyth, called by Richardson the "Church Militant in Action", having taken out the first patent for percussion lock in 1807, but pride of possession was the 750 c.c. BMW cycle. In his seventies, he would don crash helmet and touch the ton-mark with pipe in mouth. It reminded me of the day when Paul Getty, Senior, asked me if he could drive a BRM on a slow lap round Silverstone with no other car on the circuit. It was a gamble to satisfy the whim. Sitting in the cockpit wearing a crash helmet, he resembled an ancient mummy strapped in a mobile coffin. Thankfully all went well.

Unfortunately Richardson's career, like Michael Redgrave's, coincided with the golden era of Laurence Olivier and John Gielgud, both of whom take their place among the élite. Gielgud excelled in cerebral roles. This grand nephew of Ellen Terry made his acting debut at the Old Vic in 1921. No one could forget his Richard of Bordeaux and Hamlet. He used to say he strayed into films, as an afterthought. Among many outstanding portrayals on screen I remember Disraeli in *The Prime Minister;* Louis VII in *Becket;* the sensitive performance as the dying writer in Resnais's *Providence;* and his own favourite of playing Prospero, voicing all the characters in *The Tempest.*

His distinctive voice was as unmistakable as the profile with its aquiline Terry nose. No one could describe Gielgud as an extrovert. He adopted a somewhat lofty approach to his colleagues, which perhaps was understandable. Accumulated a wealth of absent-minded gaffes. One habit I adopted. Choosing a shirt in the Jermyn Street establishment of Turnbull and Asser, he advised me always to have extra cuffs and collars – it added additional life to the garment, later confirmed by Paul Kass, who with Williams, launched this excellent shop.

Laurence Olivier was the colossus of the profession. His record spans the years . . . to isolate a few, I recall the starring role with his future wife Vivien Leigh in *Fire Over England;* acting and directing in the Oscar winning *Henry V; The Prince and the Showgirl* with Marilyn Monroe; and the definitive performance of Archie Rice in *The Entertainer.*

The chameleon-like actor, Alex Guinness; Michael Caine with cockney background; John Mills, with more than 80 films to his credit; Sean Connery with charismatic insouciance that defies Scottish brogue – all these and many others have been rightly named in the Birthday Honours. In some cases it must have been difficult to decide if the recipient should be Knight or Dame. What matters, all were brilliant in their own way.

Dame Peggy Ashcroft was a truly great actress. Intellectually and emotionally, this petite, almost frail figure dominated the scene for over forty years. She was the genius of sensitivity. Glenda Jackson is a contradiction, an actress with a puritanical streak who takes nudity in her stride, a thinking man's Marilyn Monroe without the latter's looks, shape, make-up or social graces. Given the right part, Glenda is still in a class of her own though not in the Lord Mayor's or Tony Blair's harem.

Vivien Leigh was the first lady of the London theatre and behaved accordingly. Her delicate beauty was unforgettable with movements as graceful as a ballet dancer, but appearances were deceptive. She had what the Lunts described as "a whim of iron" with darker sides of depression and manic outbursts. Her rise to stardom began almost by chance. David Selznick searched for two years to find an actress to play Scarlett O'Hara in Margaret Mitchell's *Gone With the Wind*. The quest ended when he saw Vivien Leigh. The subsequent film electrified audiences, won an Oscar and international recognition. Then came the role of Blanche in *A Streetcar Named Desire* and another Oscar. She died of tuberculosis in London, 1967. I remember the exterior lights of the West End theatres darkened for an hour as a gesture of respect. There was a feeling that a genius had slipped away. The eclipse of reputation that befalls the great as soon as they die did not happen to Vivien. The praise was on a lower key because a fresh generation of theatregoers arrived, but her reign was outstanding.

Now for the men who discover, mould and create the stars, directors who set fashions with flair and inspiration. The list is lengthy. I content myself with five. I recall Alfred Hitchcock after lunching with him in The Dorchester, maturely rotund with a body shaped like an inflated embryo. He looked out of the sitting-room window and remarked that a film featuring the hotel would be ideal with so much turf available in Hyde Park to bury the bodies. It had to be that way. His public insisted on gory incidents. Even if he made a film about Cinderella, there would have to be a corpse. Everything was clinical about him. He knew exactly what he wanted. Details were exact, a method of matching the filming of an incident with the mental picture in his head. Action sequences were his pride. He said the secret was to work closely with script writers, preparing the bulk of the work before shooting began. In complete command, Hitchcock's imagination was dictatorial; he had the knack of involving the audience. He argued that every shot should have the meaning of a painting, every movement told us something.

Hitchcock had a grave, throwaway style of sharp, contentious remarks. The seams of his work never showed, nor the intensity of the man who created it; instead casualness and coolness, a taste of relaxed eloquence. He referred to the Lee Harvey Oswald shooting as bringing murder into the living-room where it belonged. He denied thinking that all actors were cattle. He merely treated them like it. When I asked for his views on the new breed of continental directors, he sidestepped by saying, "I am not a moviegoer."

John Huston, legendary figure in movie history, director of such classics as *The Maltese Falcon* and *The African Queen* was a tall figure who dominated everybody. As a director he had the touch of genius; as a private individual he enjoyed the married state with a tally of six wives. A glutton for punishment, at a party a pretty young girl sat on his lap. A female came across and introduced herself . . . "I'm his wife and that woman over there is his mistress. I don't think there's any room for you, honey." I was not surprised he suffered from emphysema that required frequent use of a canister of pure oxygen which he inhaled through a mouthpiece linked by a plastic tube.

The name of John Sturgess is a reminder of such films as *The Magnificent Seven* and *The Great Escape,* each having the unmistakable Sturgess touch, gritty and abrasive. Had a knack of by-passing trouble, but on one occasion the ploys failed. It began when *Grand Prix* was being evaluated as a possible film. John Frankheimer was appointed director. MGM backed the project. Suggested stars were Steve McQueen and Yves Montand. Trouble began over financial terms. McQueen stormed off in a huff, went to Warner Bros, persuaded them to do a similar film and signed a contract. Both companies were now committed to making almost identical films. MGM were shrewd. Exclusive rights were secured for filming on all the World Championship circuits, with the exception of Germany. Warners were left with Nürburgring. Sequences were shot starring Yves Montand and James Garner who substituted McQueen. Several months went by then Sturgess met me in London and asked how the time-schedule was shaping, I could report that MGM were ahead of the dead-line. Sturgess admitted that whilst progress was steady, they would be late. The news caused a crisis. Although having spent millions of dollars on the project, Warners cut their losses and abandoned the film. I was sorry because both films would have reflected the tensions built up by two dynamic directors.

One further director. I recall Cecil de Mille telling me he had invented the screen bathroom. It was true. In his fertile imagination people loved, dined and died in baths and showers. He offered Claudette Colbert the role of Cleopatra with the bait of portraying this scheming woman in scenes of decadence including unusual baths. Gloria Swanson recalled *Male and Female* in which her charms were discreetly shown in a bath without upsetting the censor. The gimmick peaked in *The Sign of the Cross* when Poppaea in the shape of Claudette Colbert, surrounded by flimsily-clad handmaidens, was shown in a sunken bath filled with asses' milk. Unfortunately the heat of arc lamps caused a cheesy crust to settle on the surface. An unsuspecting visitor, mistaking it for a marble floor, stepped on it and disappeared into the unpleasant liquid. Whilst staying in *The Dorchester*, de Mille commented on the Oliver Messel Suite. He liked the amenities but particularly approved the bathroom. He thought the titillating delights of soaks, suds and semi-submerged sex were more than possible in the Messel tub. I suggested it might be an optional extra on the bill.

Other personal recollections include memories of Dame Edith Evans, tireless chatterer, disarmingly outspoken, at times quiveringly indignant. She took sophistication out of the ice-box and set it bubbling on the hob. Her stock-in-trade was nonchalance. On one occasion I sat opposite her at a *Savoy* luncheon when awards were made for outstanding performances during the year in various professions. Next to her was Freddie Mills, the boxer nominated Sportsman of the Year for beating Gus Lesnevich to win the world light-heavyweight title. Full of enthusiasm Mills described how he started boxing at the age of 14; of early days in a travelling fairground-booth; Gipsy Daniels advice; gory details of the Lesnevich fight. Edith Evans listened attentively until the flow stopped, then, looking at the pugilist with quizzical eye, "What did you say your name was?" Mills obliged. "I think you're simply sweet." The compliment given with a coy smile, silenced Mills as effectively as a Lesnevich chop. Talking about the incident afterwards the actress said that in no way had she meant to put Mills down. He was just different to anyone she had met before, totally natural and unaffected.

Embarrassing moments and Edith Evans were no strangers. At Cambridge she muffed her entrance at a Degree Ceremony. In her anxiety not to get out of step during the traditional ceremony, she wrongly anticipated the moment to step forward to shake hands with the Chancellor and was halted when Lord Tedder muttered, "Wait for it, wait for it." The warning had such effect, she became rooted to the ground and had to be nudged forward when the critical moment arrived. There was never such hesitation in her stage role as Lady Bracknell in *The Importance of Being Earnest*. The quivering outraged voice never faltered.

I think of James Mason, that brooding actor with unmistakable voice, who reached his peak in the forties. Among his countless films, I remember in particular *A Star is Born*. After he settled in England following a lengthy stay in America, we saw quite a lot of him and his wife, Clarissa. Although in his eighties, it came as a shock when he died. Shortly afterwards we went with Clarissa to the Garden of the Rose, the Royal Horticultural centre at St. Albans, for the formal naming of the James Mason rose. Sadly Clarissa became embroiled with legal arguments about the Will brought by children of his previous marriage. Unresolved and bitter, Clarissa settled in Australia. It was a sad postscript to an illustrious career.

When money is involved, relationships suffer. This was never the case with Dame Sybil Thorndike and Sir Lewis Casson. In October, 1961, these two active troupers of the old school came to the West End for a six-week run. It was a very special event. Dame Sybil at 79 was about to play the largest part she had ever played, the role of *Saint Teresa of Avila;* her husband, Sir Lewis at 85, also had a larger part than he had played for years.

There was nothing modish about either of these much loved veterans. All their married lives they avoided the gossip columns. She used to say that her career peaked in 1924 when George Bernard Shaw wrote *St. Joan* for her, the play having a run of 244 performances. Neither of them led an interior life. They were great protesters. Sybil, a staunch High Church Anglican and left-wing

Socialist, preached and spoke all her life. Lewis drove a car to help in the 1926 General Strike; both fought hard for Equity.

Unselfconsciously, out of preference, they lived a simple life. On tour it was the old lodgings and landladies, no five-star hotels. Buses not taxis to the theatre. At home in their two-bedroom flat off the King's Road, their hospitality was heart-warming. After one such meal, Sybil talked of an ambition never realised. This grand old lady of the stage wanted to be a composer . . . to have written a work on a par with the *D Minor Concerto* of Bach or even one of the preludes or fugues. It was a throwback to 1899 when, after studying the piano at the Guildhall in London, she gave a recital in Rochester. That career was interrupted by illness. The stage benefited.

I recall Peter Sellers, an anarchic member of the Goon Show, Union leader in *I'm All Right Jack,* the young thug in *The Ladykillers,* and international fame with *Dr. Strangelove* and *The Pink Panther*. As a clown he was exceptional, but suffocated his talents as an actor. His private life was too strenuous for a suspect heart patient. Whilst staying in London, he came across Britt Ekland. An introduction was arranged, an invitation to see *The Pink Panther,* followed by champagne supper. It did the trick. Shortly afterwards they married. Five years later it was dissolved. Next marriage to Miranda Quarry, daughter of Lady Mancroft, who worked in a florist's shop, becoming a publicity assistant on his film *The Magic Christian.* The union lasted four years. Three years later, Lynne Frederick joined the queue.

Fascinated by motor-racing and the thrill of speed under control, he asked if he could drive a BRM during our test session at Silverstone. I dissuaded him because of a suspect heart. Caution was justified. In July 1980 he made an unscheduled trip to London for an engagement with Spike Milligan and Harry Secombe. Had a violent heart attack, given the kiss of life, taken to Middlesex Hospital, but never regained consciousness.

Still on the subject of motor-racing, I think of Princess Grace who conducted herself on official engagements in a manner that conformed with Monegasque protocol. Her special interests in Monaco were the Red Cross, the Garden Club which she founded and the Princess Grace Memorial Hospital. One feature was noticeable. On formal duties, her voice became incisive, didactic, almost hard. This icy manner was explained by some as a sign of repression rather than good breeding. Nothing could have been further from the truth. When the chore was over, she became relaxed and effervescent. As we won the Monaco Grand Prix five times, there were several occasions when she became very much an American in Monte Carlo. She maintained the perfect balance between responsibilities as a mother, wife and woman, and obligations as Princess, and had learned French quickly. She inspired the glamour that appealed to the jet set who flocked to Monaco for its cosmopolitan lifestyle. It all began when Pierre Galante, editor of *Paris Match*, introduced her to Prince Rainier, who fell for her charm and loveliness. Alfred Hitchcock must also take part of the credit by adding the dimensions of worldliness and humour to her role in *Rear Window*. In all, she made eleven films; cast as Gary Cooper's bride in *High Noon;* nominated for a supporting Oscar for *Mogambo* opposite Clark Gable and Ava Gardner; won an Oscar as Bing Crosby's bitter wife in *The Country Girl;* then Hitchcock's *Dial M for Murder* and *To Catch a Thief.* After *High Society* she married Prince Rainier. There was talk of a film comeback, but sensibly she turned it down. She had made her mark. There was little left to prove, except as an older actress, not a better one. Her tragic death in a car crash left Prince Rainier shattered. He has never really recovered.

I think now of two sisters . . . Joan and Jackie Collins, who have made significant impact on the film and literary scenes. The younger, Jackie, has pandered to the taste of her readers; like Lord Archer's prolific pen, this is maybe not literature at its best, but nevertheless she has produced best-sellers. Jackie's novels have brought immense financial returns, well beyond wildest expectations, but she has also known disappointments and personal sadness when her devoted husband, Oscar, died of cancer. Innovative in his enthusiasm, he asked if I would give an assessment of a venture he had launched in Poland Street. It was a state-of-the-art museum chronicling the history of football. Everything was there. Videos recording classic matches, coaching tips by experts, films from archives, photographic gallery of the "greats", comprehensive library, endorsement by Football League officials. Very impressive, quite unique, but I could not see it succeeding.

The average football fan does not read about the game, certainly not in this country. All he wants is to cheer, sing, and shout abuse, behaviour that makes him feel masculine. The prediction was correct. The premises shut.

Jackie's novels provided her sister with stepping-stones to international recognition. *The Stud* with its lead-role of an amoral, libidinous female was portrayed in detail. Critics suggested that it suited Joan and did not require rehearsals, followed by *The Bitch*, both made into films, led to a seven-year stint as Alexis in *Dynasty*.

Joan's private life has been continual trauma; accumulated four husbands, outliving two; many relationships; three children, Sacha and Tara fathered by Anthony Newley, and Katie by Ron Cass. Restless by nature, she has a flat in London, house in Beverly Hills and a pad in St. Tropez . . . no obvious base to settle and regard as a permanent home.

Joan has become as ageless as Marlene Dietrich. Approaching the 70-mark, her heart-shaped face is still exquisite, no lines, no wrinkles, just expressive dark eyes, high lip-gloss and scarlet claws. When married to Ron Kass, their London house was in South Street, epitomising her tastes and outlook at that time. It was comfortable, had an atmosphere of being lived-in, with personal touches and memorabilia; links with John and Robert Kennedy; Art Nouveau pieces from Christie's and Sotheby's. The bedroom might have come from a *Dynasty* set with silk wallpaper, circular ceiling with pleated silk, ornate mirrors, giant-sized waterbed with extravagant covering and a sauna next room. Her hair styles were always noticeable. Had she wanted to become blonde, the odds are it would be electroplated. In relaxed mood, these trimmings were swapped for casual dress, possibly tracksuit or leotard, little make-up, hair screwed-up on top. Preference for wigs was possibly due to hair's thin texture. I recall her coming downstairs with a different style, asked for an opinion, honesty compelling the answer that she looked like a cocker spaniel.

About her husbands, I prefer to talk of only two. Anthony Newley, an all-round entertainer, remembered by his role as the Artful Dodger in David Lean's film *Oliver Twist*. Born in Hackney, his career was indeed colourful. It included affairs with Diana Dors and Barbra Streisand; married to Ann Lynn, a Tiller Girl; made dozens of films, notably *Stop the World – I Want To Get Off.* Asked how he would like to be remembered, he replied with characteristic modesty . . . actor, playwright, author, composer, lyricist and singer. You could take your choice.

Joan's split with Ron Kass was very sad. When they married her film career was at a low level. To counter the blip, Ron went to tremendous lengths to promote her talents. I remember when they were our guests in Monte Carlo for the Monaco Grand Prix. In public they looked an ideal couple, but one evening Ron told how enforced absences through their parallel careers were putting a strain on their marriage. He was considerate to the children and brought Sacha and Tara into our pit at Silverstone, buying a miniature BRM which was "garaged" in the South Street basement, lovingly polished and spruced. The arrival of Katie brought excitement, later overshadowed when the child was nearly killed in a car crash, hospitalized for seven weeks, watched over by both parents until miraculously she came out of the coma. Such joint devotion spoke for itself. They deserved better than divorce.

There were more set-backs. Ron went to Los Angeles and began a successful commercial career. An early-morning distress call from California told its own story. Undergoing a routine medical check-up, the doctor, diagnosing terminal cancer of the liver, said he had only weeks to live. Uncertain what to do, Ron asked for advice. At that time the first liver transplant had been successfully carried out in Addenbroke's Hospital, Cambridge. I contacted the specialist, arranged an appointment, and within 48 hours Ron was in the Old Mill House with medical reports and X-Rays. The result showed the disease was too advanced for surgery, but recommended treatment that should give a year's remission. During the last few weeks, Joan gave immense support and took responsibility for the high cost medical care.

It was a gesture of real affection from a star greatly loved by her public.

ELIZABETH TAYLOR AND RICHARD BURTON

ELIZABETH TAYLOR HAS BEEN the most volatile actress of the century. Everything about her has been tempestuous, no half-measures, conventions ignored, health-wise a survivor when ordinary folk would have died. It began with a riding accident as a teenager that injured her back. She has had two hip replacements; mild stroke; near fatal case of pneumonia; she described what happened, her breathing stopped, clinically dead, she went through a long tunnel, saw a light at the end where her ex-husband Mike Todd was standing. He told her to go back; she did and woke up. Among other health problems a brain tumour was removed; broke a vertebra falling at her 66th birthday party; rumours of heart attacks; when she came to London after the Queen's Honours List to become a Dame, she looked frail but still beautiful. There was a period when, overweight, she entered the Betty Ford Clinic to cure her many addictions.

Contributory causes have included a troubled private life. Her marriages made headline news, and influenced her film career. Nicky Hilton, the first of eight husbands, when she was 18; Michael Wilding, the actor; Mike Todd, killed in an air crash; Eddie Fisher after a scandalous affair; Richard Burton, during the filming of *Cleopatra;* Senator John Warner; and the unfortunate Larry Fortensky . . . clearly a glutton for punishment and the material advantages they brought.

On a personal note, I have many memories. I think of the surprise party given by Elizabeth to celebrate, not only Richard's fiftieth birthday, but the fact they had just remarried in Botswana. She telephoned The Dorchester from Johannesburg and asked that doyen of public relations, Marjorie Lee, to make the necessary arrangements, send invitations and make menu suggestions. With characteristic efficiency, Marjorie asked Oliver Ford, the consultant designer, to prepare the Orchid Room. It was transformed with gold as the dominant motif. The buffet had Burton's favourite dishes. On costermongers' barrows were bangers and mash, fish and chips, tripe and onions, York ham and roast pork. It was a homely night remembered by 150 guests. Unfortunately marital bliss did not last. After the Royal Command World Première of Franco Zeffirelli's *The Taming of the Shrew* starring Elizabeth and Richard, they gave a Supper Dance in the Terrace on the eve of Elizabeth's birthday. Guests included Richard's brothers and sisters with respective families and friends. The birthday cake was wheeled in at midnight;

singing of Happy Birthday was in Welsh.

When I gave a dinner party in London we were in a suite whose kitchen was shared with Elizabeth: guests were from a cross-section of industry, sport and the arts. About six o'clock, the floor manager came to the suite and warned that the table-plan might have to be altered. The Burtons, next door, were having a furious row. I suggested a progress report would be helpful. Half-an-hour later it was no better. He came back. The situation had further deteriorated. Elizabeth had locked herself in the bathroom where her dinner would be served. The plan was altered. Duke Ellington was substituted.

Atmospheric tension between these two explosive creatures would quiver in the air like exposed live wires. Such human electronics requires deft control. It was a compound of legend and unreality in keeping with the fantasy world of movie stars, except that in Elizabeth's case, most of it was true. Her way of life has meant never being off stage. She neither refused nor insisted on showing off. She has no private personality. Thoroughly spoilt, she has collected husbands, diamonds and success as a matter of course. Only illness and death have denied her whims. There were flamboyant gestures like Richard's present of a twin-jet Hawker Siddeley executive aircraft christened *The Elizabeth* at a cost of one million dollars, and fabulous diamonds including the 33.19-carat Krupp diamond as a birthday present. Not to be outdone, Elizabeth reciprocated with a present of a helicopter valued at more than £200,000.

My friendship with Richard spanned many years. He had accepted my invitation to act as patron of the Jim Clark Foundation. Whenever in this country he always wanted to know of the Foundation research projects. He was man of dominating power that became over-flamboyant when he was drunk. Married five times. The brides always looked lovely. Suzy, former wife of James Hunt, I knew from motor-racing days. She had a tough task, but succeeded in breaking his drink problem, though with many lapses. There could never be a replacement for Elizabeth, the Cleopatra to his Antony. They had differences and violent rows, a volatile almost volcanic relationship when anything could happen and often did. Richard would tease by saying she had put on too much weight, inviting a cutting retort that he was enslaved by what Ben Jonson called "the fury of the gullet and groin".

At times Richard's repartee was lusty, particularly on the size of Elizabeth's "rump". Once over drinks with a group that included Alistair Maclean. Someone recalled how the artist who painted Helen of Troy used five young women as models to produce a synthetic ideal of beauty by taking the arms of one model, the shoulders of another, the breasts of a third, and so on. Richard applied a similar synthetic model of his wife with relevant parts recalled from memory, but ended by saying he preferred the statue of Venus Callipyge, better known as the Venus of Beautiful Buttocks.

Richard's last wife, Sally Hay was twenty-two years younger, but the age-gap seemed not to matter. They met on the set of Wagner in Austria and married in Las Vegas. Sally was unlike his usual type. Clearly they were happy. She was good for him. We met a week before he died. He looked leaner, fitter and alert. His sudden death came as a terrible shock, but Sally responded to his whimsical humour. He had made a bet with old friends, Peter O'Toole and Stanley Baker (who predeceased him) that no one would see him without at least one item of clothing that was red. Sally chose a jacket, polo-necked sweater and trousers all red, so in death Richard had the last laugh.

One final memory of Elizabeth. We were invited to a luncheon party in the South of France. Among the guests were Cristina, then wife of Henry Ford. Next to me sat Elizabeth. Trivialities were discussed, feline insincerity mixed with sophisticated bitchiness. It became a contest of verbal gamesmanship. Elizabeth won hands down with the assurance of someone dealing herself a fifth ace in a card game with a child.

In spite of being frail, Elizabeth's recuperative powers are incredible as her medical history testifies . . . thirty major operations, forty hospitalisations, two skirmishes with death, and two spells in Hollywood's Betty Ford Centre. Elizabeth is a survivor. Unexpectedly she decided after an absence of several years to face the cameras once again. The script was too tempting. Her role, an actor's agent who signs three ageing broads - Joan Collins, Shirley Maclaine and Debbie Reynolds - in a musical special. The pay-off line was the prior knowledge that all the principals hated each other. The real-life reputation of this quartet of man-eating females was self-evident. Between them they have collected sixteen husbands, innumerable offspring and countless affairs with celebrities. For once Joan Collins finds herself outclassed in the achievement class. One Golden Globe award is no match for a string of Oscars. On the other hand, this ex-*Dynasty* star still has a rare gift for cutting down rivals with withering effect, though lacking Elizabeth's crude use of expletives. Their combined efforts will become an irreverent period-piece of self-mockery about feminine vanity, a classic of bitchiness. Rehearsals were hardly necessary.

CHAPTER THREE

GENIUS ON CANVAS AND STONE

~

EVERY GENUINE ARTIST has an individual speech, be it canvas or stone, a challenge to lazy habits of thought, the complacency of vision. In this chapter I have recalled artists who introduced new creative intelligence into sculptural vision; those whose iridescent colours, as elusive as oil spilt in a puddle, imprinted their work vividly on the imagination. At times it is difficult to grasp the significance of their message. The key maybe lies in Graham Sutherland's advice "I found that I could express what I felt by paraphrasing what I saw."

SALVADOR DALI

SALVADOR DALI . . . GENIUS OR CHARLATAN . . . so many contradictory assessments. After the death of Picasso, Spain rated Dali as one of their greatest artists. He did not approve the overall ranking-precedence. His revised table showed him fifth behind Jan Vermeer, Raffaello Sanzio (Raphael), Diego Velázquez and Leonardo da Vinci. Picasso came sixth.

Others were not so complimentary, like André Breton, Surrealist pioneer, who downgraded Dali as a poseur insinuating himself into the surrealist milieu. Such censure was biased. Even though Dali had experimented with Cubism and metaphysical painting, his conversion to surrealism did produce some spellbinding results.

No one could deny his ability to shock, but all too often subject-matters invited confusion. His own explanations hardly helped. Interpretation he described as a spontaneous method of understanding based on interpretative critical association of delirious phenomena. Dreams were fantasized with the jumbled disorder of the human unconscious.

He was a shameless provocateur, an exhibitionist self-condemned to the treadmill of his own silliness. The flamboyant absurdity of an emotionally turbulent life-style undoubtedly trivialised his talents. I can recall so many instances of his irrational behaviour, such as a dinner-party in Madrid when he monopolised the meal by indulging in boastful reminiscences. It was like a catalogue based on delirium tremens. How he inserted jewel-drawers in the stomach of a full-sized stuffed bear to satisfy the whims of Elsa Schiarelli; designed a sofa modelled on the voluptuous carmined lips of Mae West; created a fountain that spouted water from the innards of a grand piano suspended from the ceiling, an innovation that did not appeal to Helena Rubenstein. He even attempted to influence shoe design, arguing that given certain elastic qualities, it should be shaped like a rhinoceros' horn. The biological and aesthetic needs of a woman would be satisfied by a sensuous, airy gait. Somewhat surprisingly, he admitted some inventive hunches failed, like the attempt to add another dimension to ballet decor. Geometric forms would be made by liquid films of soapy water as the dancers dipped wire cubes into tanks, creating membranes of liquid in beautiful shapes. At least that was the theory. Sadly only pools of water trickled on the stage.

The ploy of introducing shock tactics surfaced when I took part in a television discussion with Dali and Sir Gerald Kelly, then President of the Royal Academy. The Spaniard arrived dressed in sombre black like an undertaker, pallid face, high white collar, black string tie, jet-black hair, gold lamé waistcoat and gold-topped cane. He reassured us straight away that he was different from the rest of mankind. Kelly did not disagree. For our edification Dali explained that the routine life of a genius was on a more exalted plane that embraced sleep-patterns, digestion, erotic experiences, life and death. Sir Gerald, often tactless and short-fused, snorted disbelief, that became audible when Dali said he had become the world's first atomic artist, inspiration coming from the heavens through the tips of the antenna-like waxed moustaches. It was no longer necessary for him to sleep in a black open coffin. It was too much for Kelly. Explicit higher criticisms were bleeped out. His later judicious assessment described Dali as an artificial denatured man with paranoic tendencies!

I have referred to a dinner-party in Madrid. Our guests that night were Francois Cervert, the French racing driver, and a very pretty girl; Dali accompanied by an oddly-clad female of uncertain age. The meal progressed, Dali's choice being a favourite dish of lobster and chocolate sauce, conversation dominated by the Spaniard's experiments already described. The floor-show was a welcome diversion. A raven-haired girl with clicking castanets, guitars throbbing in the background, began a passionate dance broken momentarily by the staccato tapping of heels as her arms wove slow patterns in the air before plunging into a corybantic frenzy. The performance was greeted with a volley of "*olé*"s. The spell was broken. Dali rose, bowed, expressed thanks, then beckoned Cervert's girl. Both departed into the night. The Frenchman was left with the weird female as a stand-in. The episode was a Dali "happening".

On a par with his braggadocio of arranging for his Russian-born wife, Gala, to be splashing about naked in their swimming-pool so guests could admire her finer points; or exploiting his own psychological abnormalities like the lecture delivered on a scorching hot summer afternoon clad in a diver's suit, carrying a billiard cue, accompanied by a pair of Russian wolfhounds.

His experiments in search of artistic truth were multi-faceted. His film of Luis Buñuel's surrealist *Un Chien Andalou* was informative. He enjoyed creating images with multiple erotic meanings, like the watches he painted with soft tongues which were flagrantly sexual symbols in *The Persistence of Memory* hanging in the Museum of Modern Art in New York; elephants on spindle legs; hallucinations in which he introduced strange, monstrous creatures and the supernatural into his canvases. The effect was disturbing as doubtless he intended.

The last time we met was in Madrid. He was suffering from

psychic depression. He had ceased play-acting and was obsessed by his own death and talked of nothing else. The fragility of life had been brought home after that night in June 1982 when his beloved wife died. After that he became a recluse in the 12th-century manor house that was a gift to her.

He waited for death, yearned for the release, refused to eat, but medical ethics delayed the moment by intravenous feeding. In accordance with his wishes, he is buried under a crystal dome in the museum of his work at Figueras on the Costa Brava. The art world became a duller place when he left the scene. As to his work, time alone will pass judgment. It will not be easy. Artistic diversification is distracting. He was such a notorious self-advertiser. He once told me that Jean Cocteau had sketched an amorous Adonis for Elizabeth Arden's My Love perfume, but had gone one better the following year by designing a unique Bird-in-Hand compact. It was commercial art, but remarkable for its exquisite perfection of detail. That was Dali's strength. In his paintings, real objects become involved in unrelated subjects. Images created emanate from the artist's unconscious mind understood only by himself. Whilst appreciating his skill, reminiscent of the early miniaturists, they are negative. At least not as pointless as the mindless exhibits by the Conceptual Art School in the 1999 Tate Gallery Exhibition. Dali may have been controversial but would have dismissed these poseurs as mindless. The influence of his Freudian dream symbolism was significant. Sadly I am not of their thinking. I prefer the period when Dali devoted himself to dramatic religious works. Posterity will remember *Christ of St. John of the Cross* that hangs in the Glasgow Museum.

DAME LAURA KNIGHT

MANY YEARS HAVE PASSED since Dame Laura Knight died, but her work is still appreciated and collected. Her career bridged many changes in taste, but right up to the end of a long life, she tried to fathom the mystery of form and colour. Mastery over materials resulted in iridescent shades vibrating the canvas. Every artist has an individual speech that challenges the eye. Laura was no exception. It was silent about her private life which was just that.

Inscrutable Somerset
Maugham, his lined
face the colour of
parchment. Harsh
reality affected his
outlook on life,
encouraged mordant
asceticism, and
created a personal
image of one vast
shrug of the
shoulders in human
shape.

To Louis Stanley
after racing to
the Dorchester
Norman Mailer
April 1965

ABOVE: The turbulent Norman Mailer and the inscription referring to the race from The Savoy to The Dorchester.

LEFT: The author with T. S. Eliot, one of the greatest literary figures of the last century.

BELOW LEFT: The author with J. B. Priestley in the Albany rooms, Piccadilly.

The author and W.H. Auden enjoy conversation in the sun-dappled garden of the Old Mill House.

LEFT: Robert Graves had a prodigious output, some 125 books written in longhand. He is probably the greatest love poet in English since Donne.

RIGHT: Compton Mackenzie, a romantic throw-back to the aesthetic days before the First World War.

BELOW LEFT: Frank Leavis, an acerbic academic and formidable opponent.

BELOW RIGHT: E.M. Forster, the most important novelist of his generation.

LEFT: A personal inscription to the author from Walter de la Mare.

BELOW: The author with Walter de la Mare. As a poet he ranks with Blake, Shelley and Bridges. His lyrical gift ranks him far above any contemporary.

RIGHT: With Gloria Swanson in a suite of the Hotel de Paris, Monte Carlo.

BELOW LEFT: The film director Alfred Hitchcock, maturely rotund. When asked for his views on the new breed of continental directors, he sidestepped by saying "I am not a moviegoer."

BELOW RIGHT: Tom Mix, always cast as the puritan of the plains, distracted neither by scheming women nor good whisky.

ABOVE: Louis Stanley with Orson Welles. The critics welcome a genius who excels in one thing. Orson's talents were too widespread and innovative . . . a huge potential wasted.

LEFT: The author with Ralph Richardson, the avuncular, pie-loving eccentric whose acting career spanned six decades.

RIGHT: If genius was influenced by looks, I would nominate Merle Oberon, whose transcendent beauty with her ever-widening eyes seemed to absorb everything.

ABOVE LEFT: Louis and
Jean Stanley with
Elizabeth Taylor in
Monte Carlo. The
most volatile actress
of the last century,
everything about her
has been
tempestuous, no half-
measures, and
conventions ignored.

ABOVE: Peter Sellers
was fascinated by
motor racing and the
thrill of speed under
control. He asked if
he could drive a BRM
during our test
session at Silverstone.

LEFT: Joan Collins has
become as ageless as
Marlene Dietrich.
Approaching 70, her
heart-shaped face is
still exquisite—no
lines, no wrinkles,
just expressive dark
eyes, high lip-gloss
and scarlet claws.

RIGHT: I recall Augustus John as a patriarchal figure with hunched shoulders, a deep voice, and hawk-like eyebrows conveying an impression of strength and enforced dignity. Direct and forcible in speech, he had a shrivelling contempt for pretence and was impatient of the pertinacious snob.

BELOW: Words can never explain Jacob Epstein. Like the sculptors of the Renaissance, he could carve marble, tackle metal, hew granite.

LEFT: The sculptor William Reid Dick with the familiar figure of Lady Godiva on horseback.

RIGHT: Salvador Dali, a genius or charlatan? There are so many contradictory assessments. After the death of Picasso, Spain rated Dali as one of their greatest artists.

BELOW: Dame Laura Knight, the first woman to be elected to the Royal Academy.

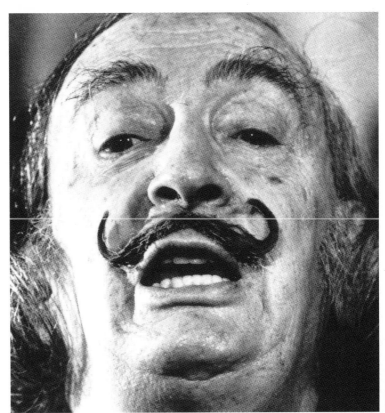

ABOVE: Barbara Hepworth converted the old St. Ives cinema into an imaginative museum for her work. Sadly it was gutted in a fire and Barbara perished in the flames.

LEFT: Stanley Spencer assumed guises that were hardly flattering: village idiot, rebel, recluse, and egotist.

RIGHT: Henry Moore, so modest and retiring, gave no hint that he ranked as one of the world's greatest sculptors.

RIGHT: The author with Sir Alfred Munnings. He was prone to vent his spleen on individuals and schools of thought that did not accord with his rigid guidelines.

BELOW: Sir Gerald Kelly. With false modesty, he played down his artistic skills. He once said that critics rated his taste in claret above his status as an artist.

I think of evenings in their St. John's Wood home, when Laura, rich in experience, would recall in that soft, enticing voice, episodes that had an influence on her life. In the early days she knew poverty and hardship when their lace-making family business declined: her marriage to Harold, a romance that lasted over 57 years: the public and private opprobrium when he became a conscientious objector in the First World War: the relief of the anonymity of London: the gradual rise to fame and recognition.

There were three traumatic happenings that affected her career. The introduction to the world of ballet came from the backstage experiences during the Diaghilev season at the Coliseum. The moment etched on her mind of watching a ballerina clutching the curtains after an inspired performance . . . breathless, exhausted, sweat trickling down her back . . . then the curtain call, regaining composure for an audience ovation. The acclaim happened night after night – vignettes waiting to be captured. The opportunity was made possible when Lydia Lopokova allowed her dressing-room to be used as a studio, providing Laura kept quiet.

This period brought her into contact with Anna Pavlova, one of the world's most celebrated exponents of classical ballet. Laura painted a word-picture of her technique: how she danced as simply as a stream flows – lost in a mist of whiteness: the motions of a *pas de deux*: the exactitude of musical phrasing. Looking through Laura's portfolio of sketches no one could say that Pavlova was photogenic. Her body was small with tapering limbs, but the emphasis was on the long, full throat. There were also sketches of Enrico Cecchetti, the legendary maestro, shown at his famous classes where he demanded perfection of balance and line, beating time with malacca cane.

The next period was influenced by the raucous atmosphere of circus life, when Laura lived the life of a Bohemian enjoying the unfettered freedom. To absorb the authentic feel she spent five seasons with Carmo's Road show, teaming up with Joe, a clown, and his wife Amy, keeping the same working hours and shared lodgings during the tours. Laura often recalled how after the evening show they would munch their suppers at the back of the stabling, sheltered only by a tent, interrupted by the thud of a horse's hoof on a plank in his loose-box or the roar of a sleepy but restless lion in the cages just behind them. She recalled the star-strewn depths of the sky through a gap in the tent-flap; the shadow of the great dome of canvas, the wagon rumbling on and on through towns and villages and the countryside; chattering and dreaming over the reins.

This experience was heightened by the fairground atmosphere; primitive pugilists in the boxing ring; clowns, acrobats, circus characters well captured in the large canvas *Charivari* that was exhibited in the Royal Academy in 1929. Laura had an acute eye for the points of a horse away from the circus, sketching the sweating power of plough horses working over ploughland. Encouraged by Sir Alfred Munnings, she turned to racehorses. He suggested visits to Epsom and Ascot, putting at her disposal his vintage Rolls. Laura packed easel and canvas, but forgot the horses. Instead Cockney humour, jellied eels, bookies and gypsies offered wider artistic scope.

The third compelling experience was when Laura sat for ten months on the Tribunal of judges drawn from the major Allies to hear evidence against eighteen leading Nazis. The legal basis for the trial was questioned, but such was the revulsion of the people that doubts were swept away by an emotional demand that the perpetrators of such evil should be punished for the atrocities. Such were the details described of cruelty in the extermination camps that Laura was granted leave and returned home in a troop carrier for a few weeks. She never forgot the horror: how Jews were pictured as the incarnation of evil: how some 5,750,000 were exterminated; the total loss of life being about 54,800,000. The fact that the accused in the dock were instrumental in such destruction left chilling memories. Sketches froze the scene . . . Rudolf Hess, staring into the distance with glazed eyes; Julius Streicher sweating profusely; Ribbentrop overwhelmed by his pending fate; Hermann Göering's unrepentant defence of the Nazi actions. Laura's one regret was that Adolf Hitler escaped the ultimate humiliation.

Harold, in fragile health, died in Colwall, Cornwall in 1961. His attitude to painting was unlike Laura's. His taste was the old masters, especially Vermeer. Some of his portraits were outstanding, one in particular of W. H. Davies, the Welsh poet, whose *Autobiography of a Super-Tramp* was one of Harold's favourite books. Laura died in London in 1970. A rare spirit had passed away. She was the first woman to be elected to the Royal Academy. I recall a tribute that gave her immense pleasure: the retrospective Exhibition at the Royal Academy in 1965; also the imaginative *75 Years of Painting* in the Upper Grosvenor Galleries four years later. It was the public's appreciation of delicately observed actualities: work that held the key to her artistic personality and private world.

SIR ALFRED MUNNINGS

SIR ALFRED MUNNINGS WAS PRONE to vent his spleen on individuals and schools of thought that did not accord with his rigid guidelines. An artist who experienced the rough edge of his tongue was Stanley Spencer. An instance of this occurred on Newmarket Heath. I had accompanied Munnings to see the start of the Cesarewitch, the long-distance race on the Rowley Mile Course, which he aptly described as "hanging-about in Suffolk to see a race run in Cambridgeshire." Very few were watching, for the grandstands and bookie enclosures are far away. It is like being at a private race with horses circling round, no starting-stalls, jockeys chattering. It was Munning's favourite viewing-place, scene of some of his best known paintings.

I mentioned that the previous day I had been with Stanley Spencer at Cookham. The race was forgotten. Munnings pulled out a wallet and produced a number of photographs. "Look at this charlatan who calls himself the ecclesiastical painter of the decade. He produces the controversial *Resurrection and Christ Preaching at Cookham* whilst indulging in pornographic filth like these." It was no exaggeration. Erotic self-portraits showed Spencer, naked, clearly sexually aroused with virility enhanced. These explicit poses reflected the twisted mind of a nasty little man. When we looked up the horses were disappearing in the distance.

Munnings disliked Spencer. He was an unpleasant piece of work. No opportunity was missed to attack him. He noticed a Spencer painting in a dealer's gallery. Obscene in nature, he checked how the dealer had obtained it. Zwemmer had purchased it with a number of Spencer's drawings. Munnings took the painting and drawings on approval, had them photographed then asked the police to prosecute under the obscenity laws. The Director of Public Prosecutions sanctioned the charge. Intervention came from Sir Gerald Kelly who had succeeded Munnings as President of the Royal Academy. Returning from America, he checked the facts, saw the DPP and the case was dropped.

Munnings had his quota of critics. The reluctance of the Royal Academy to recognise any virtue in sporting art faltered in 1868 when Sir Edwin Landseer was offered the presidency. He declined the honour. Landseer was an animal painter rather than a sporting artist. Breakthrough came when Munnings was elected the Royal Academy's first sporting president. The gusto of his paintings made him a figure that could not be ignored. His work was not an intellectual absorption but a spontaneous admission of his personality. It was not everybody's taste. Preference was given to the individual iconography of Jean Miro based on Surrealistic theories of automation; grotesque satirical etchings of Paul Klee; the sensuous Cubist-based style of George Braque. Alongside, Munnings work was like English fresh air. He captured the atmosphere of the Heath, the sheen of horses and natural rhythm of their movements.

BARBARA HEPWORTH

BARBARA HEPWORTH, WITHOUT DOUBT, was the idealistic English sculptor of the century. Her work was influenced by the Cornish landscape, moorland megalithic remains, weird coastline rock formations and restless movement of tides. She was infatuated by mythological legends, her life being shaped by two contrasting influences. As a child she knew the Yorkshire background of cobbled streets, forbidding warehouses, slag-heaps, foundries, dreary houses in identical rows, filth, odours, smoke and grime. Brief intervals in an artistic clique in Hampstead interrupted by air-raid destruction, and refuge in Cornwall where she was to spend the rest of her life.

Her home in St. Ives had a cell-like calm, but outside she came to life. On the granite moors of Bodmin she was fascinated by the atmosphere of desolation; the strange standing monolithic dolmen *Chun Quoit*; *Lanyon Quoit*, finest cromlech in England; sea-forest of isolated rocks at Kynance Cove; *Cheesewring Rock* balancing on the lip of a quarry; *Men-an-Pol* on Bosporthennis moor. All these natural phenomena influenced her approach to the important commission *Single Form* that stands outside the United Nations building in New York as a memorial to Dag Hammarskjöld.

Not only was Barbara sensitive to the Cornish atmosphere, but she identified with the everyday life of the community. St. Ives out of season is unspoilt. Slippery cobblestones, cats prowling in alleyways, evocative names like Teetotal Street, Virgin Street and Salubrious Place. The area known as the Stennards and Down-along, the invisible partition that separated miners from fishermen, who lived in Down-along by the wharf. Barbara always commented on the blue translucence of the sea, a feature that attracted Whistler and Walter Sickert and inspired the vibrant colony of creative artists. Barbara Hepworth was their inspiration.

I remember planning the conversion of the old St. Ives cinema into an imaginative museum for her work. Sadly it was gutted in a fire and Barbara perished in the flames.

SIR GERALD KELLY

SIR GERALD KELLY, LIKE MUNNINGS, had a mischievous streak that delighted in flaunting convention. I remember him as a President with an aggressive intelligence, not always marked by good humour. Short, fleshy and bull-necked, he had a habit of backing into the limelight like a man-eating dove. With false modesty, he played down his artistic skills. He once said that critics rated his taste in claret above his status as an artist. Self-derision ignored the meticulous precision in detail. He took six years to complete the State portraits of George VI and Queen Elizabeth.

Always outspoken, Kelly was naively frank about the early years. He never forgot a broken romance when a rival walked off with his girl . . . "very pretty with all the qualities I admired, but fidelity was not a strong point." He took an escapist trip to Burma on the strength of two snapshots taken by a friend of the Burmese dancers. In his studio in London I watched him producing yet another of the familiar Burmese beauties aided by a photograph clipped on the corner of the canvas.

In Cambodia, Kelly obtained permission to paint the leading members of the Royal Corps de Ballet in their gold-encrusted costumes, but restrictions were imposed. As the girls were also the King's concubines, the sittings in the palace had to be supervised by chaperones. No photography was allowed. Unfortunately the French Ambassador, ignorant of the ban, used his camera over the artist's shoulder. Official protests ended Kelly's concession. Kelly's output was a yearly average of six portraits and a couple of nudes. One canvas was special. His wife was a regular sitter. Each painting captioned *Jane* with a serial number. A complete set was 80. My preference was due to good fortune. He met Somerset Maugham in Paris. Immediate empathy. Eleven striking portraits resulted.

Jacob Epstein

Jacob Epstein had a unique distinction. No other twentieth-century sculptor so stimulated controversy and opposition to his work. Normally an Englishman does not get excited about sculpture. He just ignores it. Epstein could not be ignored. The reason was simple. It is impossible to examine his work without a definite reaction. The sense of beauty of the artistically lazy became atrophied by the banal. Epstein made them readjust their values, which was resented.

When Epstein was named as the sculptor of a memorial statue of Lloyd George, there was a mixed reception in the House of Commons. The reaction was anticipated by the sculptor.

He told me he never met the statesman, but Megan had given him innumerable word-portraits and photographic likenesses. What impressed him most was Lloyd George's leonine head. He was determined not to spoil the effect by sculpting a figure in robes. "All statues in robes look the same. Lloyd George would be in a standing position, in the everyday clothes of his political life."

Epstein was accused of handling religious subjects with irreverent realism. The public expected to see a conventional Christ, a pale abstraction of a late Renaissance model. Epstein refused to accept this formula. He created his own conception. The giant study of Christ – *Behold the Man* – was one example. His crucified Christ in Llandall Cathedral was another. I saw this work at an early stage in his studio. The complete work infused a new creative intelligence into sculptural vision. Many critics named the Cavendish Square *Madonna* as his greatest work, but it was surpassed by the strikingly conceived figure of *St. Michael overcoming the Devil* at the entrance to Coventry Cathedral.

I was with the sculptor in his studio at Hyde Park Gate when he was working on the Bowater Group. Although desperately ill, he worked against the life-clock. A few days later he talked about the casting with his bronze moulder. He died the same night.

Words can never explain Epstein. Like the sculptors of the Renaissance, he was a complete sculptor. He could carve marble, tackle metal, hew granite, and handle his material with sensitive thought and technical mastery. I remember him as a compassionate, cultivated man with the conversation of a scholar who talked in a strong American accent.

SIR STANLEY SPENCER

STANLEY SPENCER ATTEMPTED TO RECREATE the Christian narrative in a Cookham setting. He described the theme in detail. Listening to paintings is an acquired taste. It was as unconvincing as the figures he drew. They fell through the crust of ordinary experience into a bloodless world of stark unreality. Looking at them induced a sensation of revulsion. They are nasty, earthy creatures, goblinesque, ghoulish, though they confirmed Spencer's reputation as a brilliant colourist, skilful at composition, but basically he was a troubled man. Inner worries and fears affected his work, but he found inspiration in the community of Cookham. It provided material for everyday life. He assumed guises that were hardly flattering: village idiot, rebel, recluse, and egotist, invariably obsessed by religion and eroticism, emotionally involved with women, caught up with sexual problems and infected with a chatterbox complex.

This dwarf-sized, bespectacled man, innocuously pallid, used to argue that all problems could be solved through sexual indulgence, that nothing the Church had to offer, be it prayer or meditation, could match the spiritual renewal induced by the physical act of love. He believed that erotic paintings conveyed something of the purpose of living. So spoke the artist who was masochistically dominated by grotesque women.

GRAHAM SUTHERLAND

COULD BE DISTURBING. Influenced by Matisse and Picasso, Sutherland was hailed as the *avant-garde* leader of English painters. Portraits often controversial, almost caricatures, like Lord Beaverbrook and Somerset Maugham but falling short of the likeness of Churchill commissioned by both Houses of Parliament. Winston detested it. Lady Churchill went one better. She destroyed it. I prefer to remember Sutherland by the tapestry he designed, *Christ in Glory*, for the rebuilt Coventry Cathedral.

WILLIAM REID DICK

THIS SCULPTOR LEFT many reminders of conventional skill. I think of President Roosevelt in Grosvenor Square; Lord Leverhulme at Port Sunlight; the chiselled recumbent figure of George V on the tomb in St. George's Chapel in Windsor; the impressive statue of David Livingstone by Victoria Falls; and the famous statue in bronze of Lady Godiva in Coventry. She is an illusion. Reid told me in his studio that she was a composite of four young ladies, but was silent about the anatomical division.

L. S. LOWRY

L. S. LOWRY WAS ONCE DESCRIBED as an entomologist who stalked human insects with a butterfly net. In that sense he was a collector of people. His stalk-like figures, solitary houses, colourless streets, black churches, slab-sided mills and terrace rows, reflected the social predicament of a Lancashire industrial scene now vanished along with iron railings, wheelbarrows and figures in fat boots.

A sensitive eccentric, Lowry's life was as dreary as the grey squat house in Mottram-in-Longendale that was his home for many years. Alcohol and smoking were shunned. On the two occasions we met, he sipped orange juice. Foreign travel was not for him. Unlike Stanley Spencer who was obsessed by sexual urges and pornographic satisfaction, Lowry never married, partly by choice but partly influenced by his ugliness. He had a long nose, a squint and a flabby, loose body. Only three women featured in his life. His mother to whom he was devoted, nursing her through her last illness; Anne Holder, his model for single paintings; Carol Ann, claimed by her mother as a relative of the painter. The relationship was denied, but over a period of years Lowry became very fond of the girl. In his will she benefited by being left the bulk of his estate. The reason for this emotional tie has never been found.

For some forty years Lowry's paintings were ignored by the public. He used to say that such apathy never bothered him. If critics were bitchy, let them get on with it. If the images he drew were grotesque, that was how he viewed life. He was attracted by the old and odd and contrived to record life in the industrial north as it used to be, a visual record of reality.

Fashions changed. Prices soared. Recognition had come. Lowry was appointed an official artist at the Coronation in 1953. Two years later the Royal Academy elected him an Associate. Seven years on a full Member. Harold Wilson offered him a knighthood, Edward Heath a Companion of Honour. Both were declined, but an Honorary Degree from Manchester University was accepted. It was different . . . recognition from home.

Lowry was not a genius, but he recorded something of the life in the industrial north, an era that is no more. His paintings form an atmospheric historical record. He has been likened to Pirandello, Beckett, D. H. Lawrence and Ionesco. I prefer to put him in the English satirist school of Hogarth, Gilray and Rowlandson.

In retrospect I think the recognition that gave him immense pleasure was when in 1967 the General Post Office issued a postage stamp showing one of his industrial scenes

HENRY MOORE

HENRY MOORE AND HIS ATTRACTIVE Russian wife, Irina, were frequent guests at the Old Mill House. Seventh son of a Yorkshire miner, Henry retained a slight regional accent, looked like a farmer, so modest and retiring that strangers had no hint that he ranked as one of the world's greatest sculptors. Our dinner parties usually had guests distinguished in many walks of life. Henry ignored his own reputation and had naive interest in the achievements of others. He enjoyed social contacts with other cultures. After marriage, the Moores became established in a studio in Hampstead and formed a circle that exercised immense influence in modern interpretation of the visual arts. Close neighbours were the poets Geoffrey Grigson and Herbert Read, painters Ivon Hitchens and Paul Nash, the author Adrian Stokes, and Barbara Hepworth who was living with Ben Nicholson in The Mall Studios. This côterie of inventive originality was fragmented through the bombing raids of 1940. Henry moved to the seclusion of a sixteenth-century cottage at Perry Green, a hamlet in Hertfordshire.

The homely qualities of that county appealed, living there until his death. He was absorbed by the rounded, solid shapes into which life builds itself. His ideas were seen in the hand-sized plaster maquettes that could be shaped and altered, enlarged to human dimensions or even on a monumental scale. Prolific in output, the Moore catalogue of his sculptures is more than 6,000. His drawings, water-colours and graphic works of rocks, roots and landscapes portrayed various aspects of the natural world. Critics in learned fashion analysed the reasoning behind the sculpture. We were assured that he discovered forms within the block that were always there. He merely stripped away the concealing shell to reveal them in all their stoniness. It sounded profound. Moore was not convinced. He never trusted metaphysical jargon. He followed his own muse.

It is true that his work does not appeal to everyone. Some regarded it as artistic gallimaufry that scoffed at the conventional way of looking at nature, but the fact remains that Henry Moore was the first English sculptor to find new contents, new forms and new combinations for the human figure. His huge statue in front of the UNESCO building in Paris has sympathetic company . . . a mosaic mural by Miró, a bronze relief by Arp, a mural by Picasso and a mobile by Calder. Of all his successes I asked him which gave the greatest satisfaction. After reflection, he said that high on such a list would be the pleasure of being the first British artist to be given a whole floor for a show at the New York Museum of Modern Art and the material satisfaction of being the only British artist to win the

500,000-lire award at the Venice Biennale Exhibition. Times changed. In the seventies his tax liabilities came to more than a million pounds a year.

I asked if the criticisms sometimes levelled against him by the Royal Academy ever tempted replies. The answer summed it up, "After all, you don't ask T. S. Eliot what he thinks of Ethel M. Dell."

AUGUSTUS JOHN

RUSKIN ONCE SAID THAT A WORK OF ART, in addition to looking well, must also speak well. The artist was attempting to say something; above all, he was trying to say something which could not be expressed in words. In that sense, art communicates to us in its own language. It can be through the pseudo-Gothic strangeness of John Piper's work with its owl-hooted, bat-haunted landscapes, or the world of wiry lines and flat patterns of Graham Sutherland, or a montage of ways by other distinguished painters. In this respect, Augustus John was vividly articulate in paint, appealing directly to the emotions by visual means. Admittedly it is possible not to like his art – that is a matter of taste – but impossible not to respect it. Strong reactions are the test of all great art. Eccentricity itself does not have that effect.

This is true of John's unrestrained originality in conceptions. In his world of famous portraits he was the artist first and only secondly the portraitist. It was not of primary importance to him that the likeness should express the sitter, but that the painter expressed the painter. His approach was never grandiose. He thought such treatment boring, even intimidating, arguing that truth is spoken in a still, small voice. Great mystics were not long-winded: great poetry was not sustained beyond a page or two of print: likewise the greatest paintings could be contained within a square foot of canvas. Much of John's work comes in that category. It was the lyric, not the epic: Chopin not Wagner. When inspired, all the stops would be pulled out, resulting in scenes of passion, mystically imaginative, super-sensual, tinctured with melodrama, but never a drop of sentiment.

Vignettes of personal memory are linked with Freyern Court, John's home in Hampshire, yielding idyllic, almost timeless glimpses of a world gone by. The tone was set by the front door painted pink with startling designs. The ideal time was in the Spring when the orchards were in bloom and daffodils fluttered in the breeze. The garden had a wild appearance, box-hedges overgrown, paths mossy and a tall Elizabethan wall with swelling bays. At the rear of the house were goats in stalls, their milk churned into butter by a maid. It was a perfect setting for a remarkable group of Bohemians with a hint of Romany days.

I think of Dorelia, John's favourite model, as striking as her husband. I question whether anyone had so many paintings and drawings of herself in so many galleries. Presiding over tea at the head of a long table, Dorelia sat very erect, still beautiful and wearing the flowing pleated skirt made famous by John's portraits of her before the First World War, becoming a fashion in Chelsea circles. The room itself had character. I remember a Welsh dresser crowded with choice pottery. Over the fireplace hung a vigorous portrait of a youth. "One of my boys, Caspar, destined to be a future First Sea Lord." Another son, who nearly became a Jesuit, was drowned off the Cornish coast. John's canvases of his children are rightly praised. Full of life, naked, effervescent and mischievous, they were imaginatively captured with exquisite draughtsmanship. His daughter, sitting next to me, showed how a gauche youngster could blossom into such an attractive woman. The library was impressive. Augustus John chain-smoking and grumbling that since a librarian had been entrusted with the task of cataloguing his extensive collection of volume, he had not been able to find any particular book. In relaxed mood, he talked about his sister Gwen, and the relationship with Rodin, who was infatuated with her. John recalled finding an outstanding figure of Gwen in the Musée Rodin intended to be a London memorial to Whistler. Its fate was decided when an official rejected it because one arm was unfinished. Instead the Burghers of Calais were substituted. John was still indignant. "Bloody stupid. Any idiot could see it was a mistaken choice." Gwen loved France and lived there most of her life. She tried to persuade her brother to buy a castle in Brittany, but it was too pricey. Instead John suggested an interesting house in Galway owned by a community of nuns. The bid was vetoed by the local priest. He told these women of God that John would probably use his studio to draw naked women, unlike Gwen whose paintings often depicted young nuns, after her conversion to Catholicism in 1913.

John often spoke of artists he had known, people like Sickert, Derain, Conder and Modigliani: how he sipped maraschino with Oscar Wilde: met Steer and William Orphen at the Slade with Ida Nettleton, who became his first wife. Celebrities patronised his studio, anxious to identify with his fame in Chelsea and Galway, Montparnasse and Mayfair. He was elected to the Royal Academy in 1948, resigned because of the rejection of a sculpture by Epstein, but re-elected two years later. An Exhibition of his works filled the four rooms of the upper floor of what used to be known as the Gibson and Diploma Galleries. The space was needed. It had to house 460 exhibits. The honour was appreciated, but he still remembered his naive pride when his *Moses and the Brazen Spirit* won the Slade prize for composition in 1898.

Such enthusiasms never deserted John. We walked down a long path to his studios at Freyern Court. One was little more than a garden shed. It was packed with rejected canvases, many of sensuous nudes. Nearby was a modern studio where he indulged in a late conversion to sculpture. Eight works had been completed, all portraits of women, except for a head of W. B. Yeats executed from memory: each had touches of John's vitality.

Background had formative influences. Of Celtic origin, John was born in Tenby, Wales in 1878; mother died when he was a child: father, a lawyer, lived to be 91: two aunts, prominent officers in the Salvation Army at the height of the Movement's glory days, were responsible for his early upbringing, but did not deter him from indulging a nomadic life-existence in Ireland, Dorset and Wales where he produced so many poetic small oil paintings of figures in landscapes.

In retrospect I recall Augustus John as a patriarchal figure, hunched shoulders, deep-voiced, hawklike eyebrows, conveying an impression of strength and enforced dignity. Direct and forcible in speech, he had a shrivelling contempt for pretence, impatient of the pertinacious snob. In the closing years of his life, many friends were in awe of him. Augustus John was a law until himself, but not a harsh disciplinarian. In 1942, he received the Order of Merit.

I end on a lighter note. John enjoyed shove-ha'penny and

limbered up his fingers every morning by playing on the smooth board he had owned for twenty-five years. After work was done and before dinner, he would throw-down a challenge and invariably won. I recall such an occasion. Smoking the inevitable short clay pipe, he found himself on the losing side. Exasperated, he colloquially announced he was going to get away from all this, emphasising the point with a sweep of his arm. "Not Galway, but Easter Island, where there is only one post a year, brought in by a Brazilian man-of-war". By brandy time he had changed his mind.

PABLO PICASSO

I REGRET NEVER HAVING MET THIS LEGEND. Instead word-pictures by those who knew him well have to suffice. Some were biased like Salvadori and W. H. Auden, but the composite figure that emerges is a capricious character, fatalistic, superstitious and an atheist. Plenty of idiosyncrasies. Weakness for hats, self-conscious about his lack of inches and bull-like chest. As an artist indulged in erotic themes and sexual pleasures that seeped into everyday life. Curious kink: liked his attractive wife, Francoise, forty years his junior, to pad about naked.

As an artist, Picasso was an innovator; a loner who preferred to work in solitude. Cubist double-imagery is an acquired taste. I prefer the dramatic canvas of *Guernica* that mirrors the tortures of war and human suffering.

VIGNETTES OF MEMORY must include the painting in the Royal Academy Summer Exhibition, James Gunn's haunting *Pauline in the Yellow Dress,* on a par with Pietro Annigoni's study of Queen Elizabeth in a long flowing blue robe. It was a commission that nearly didn't happen. The request came from The Worshipful Company of Fishmongers. The Italian thought it was a hoax. The letter was thrown into a wastepaper basket, but retrieved with superb results, in spite of the sitter being very fidgety. Princess Margaret submitted herself to 32 sittings. The result lacked vibrance.

I think of the rugged naturalistic bronzes by Elizabeth Frink. Her last commission was a bronze Christ for Liverpool Cathedral unveiled only a few weeks before her death; of pastel paintings by Eric Kennington that enlightened T. E. Lawrence's *Seven Pillars of Wisdom* and other examples of his work in the Imperial War Museum. His sculptures were noteworthy, particularly the bronze head of Thomas Hardy and the decorations on the facade of the Shakespeare Memorial Theatre.

An unusual artist was Meredith Frampton. Late recognition came with a one-man Exhibition at the age of 88. It was what he wanted. For 45 years he lived in a house he designed on the brow of a hill in Wiltshire, but no recluse. Elegant in appearance, casually dressed, duffel-coat, wire-rimmed spectacles, he preferred orthodoxy to modern art.

He was fascinated by glass, particularly test-tubes. This was brought to my attention by Sir Gowland Hopkins, the biochemist whose research into the nature of amino-acids and the necessity of experimenting with a diet of unknown substances led to the identification of vitamins. When he was appointed President of the Royal Society, Frampton was commissioned to paint the official portrait. The scientist is shown at his desk surrounded by glass instruments. He holds a test-tube in which is the pigmentation of colours from the wing of a butterfly which he established affected the treatment of leukaemia. Frampton missed no detail in the photographic resemblance of the glass and test-tube. The effect was extraordinary. I saw the original with Hopkins and his daughter, Jacquetta, wife of J. B. Priestley. The scientist's verdict was that his portrait was of secondary importance, but the glassware was outstanding. At least the artist would have been pleased.

Cultural Art invites criticism, always recognising that tastes do vary, even among poseurs, but, in other spheres, unbiased scrutiny is essential, though at times the result is embarassing.

I experienced such a moment when Anglia Television presented a self-profile featuring the roles I had in motor-racing and industry as well as as a collector of ceramics. Sotheby's of London co-operated by giving permission for an important ceramic sale to be filmed. The catalogue had six full-length illustrations of the main items. I told the producer that I would buy the one just before the end of the sale as it had special interest.

In those days a horseshoe table was in front of the rostrum for serious bidders. Just before this particular lot was called, televison arc lights were switched on and cameras began to roll. A porter with the item on a tray moved round the table for inspection. By the time he reached me, brisk bidding had already reached four figures. I examined it closely, had doubts, sought an opinion from ceramic specialist Mannheim who was sitting next to me. The auctioneer, Tim Clark, asked if all was well. I said I was uneasy. Immediately the lot was withdrawn. The dilemma was that something had to be bought, otherwise the programme would be upset. Only six lots remained. In desperation I became the owner of a piece I did not want. The doubts were confirmed. The suspect piece was comparatively modern of modest value! It proved one's peers are not always infallible.

In retrospect I find the current trend depressing. I am not in sympathy with the protoplasmic abortions called Modern Art. They are just vulgar and vulgarity is the antithesis of Art. Christopher Smith, speaking as Cultural Secretary in the Blair administration, criticised the 1999 nominations for the £20,000 Turner Prize. Alleged to be representative of British art, he could not appreciate the entry of a bed with dirty sheets, soiled underwear and discarded condoms. Conceptual art such as this should be relegated to the privies of the mind. I prefer to define Art as being both simple and profound, a language understandable across the decades – preferably with delicately observed actualities.

CHAPTER FOUR

REMARKABLE WOMEN

~

IT IS DIFFICULT OVER-DRAMATISING the private lives of personalities exposed to the glare of hyped publicity, but these three women were internationally famous and gifted. They shared in common the inevitability that death was near, yet continued to work to the last. They are examples of stoical courage and dedication.

The first was tall, attractive, cascading blonde hair, bronzed skin, over-loaded with jewellery and radiating self-confidence . . . Jean Rook, highest paid writer in Fleet Street, luxurious life-style, son at Eton, and proud of the sobriquet *First Bitch of Fleet Street,* earned by her vicious pen and ebullient attitude that castigated every section of society. Initial interest came when asked if I would submit to an interrogation by this lady for a *Daily Express* profile. Hesitation was understandable after scanning a resumé of previous encounters, proof, if such was needed, that the scribe had scant respect for rank or convention. The royal family did not escape. Prince Philip . . . "hawk-nosed, slit-mouth tetchy old devil". Prince Edward . . . "unready, unsteady, unemployed Eddie" . . . choice vignette of an eminent film star . . . "thoroughly unpleasant, style-less, vain and self-orbiting". On the credit side, Margaret Thatcher had given ten interviews at No.10 in fifteen years.

Apprehensive, I agreed to lunch at the *Ritz.* It began with a tape-recorder being placed in front of my plate. I declined to listen to myself eating. As a compromise the interview began over coffee.

Surprisingly, contentious issues were avoided. The result in print was generous. Afterwards we had several meetings. At heart I found Jean considerate, out-going, with a shrewd eye for detail. University-trained, her thesis on the influence of T. S. Eliot on English drama was scholarly. She came with Alan Frame, *Daily Express* editor, and his wife Ann to the re-opening of The Dorchester, then, shortly afterwards, everything went wrong.

Violent robbery in her Kent home, dragged down the stairs by her hair, bound and assaulted by masked men; jewellery and money taken. The shock contributed to her husband's breakdown and early death. Specialists diagnosed that Jean had inoperable cancer. Remission was short. The decision to continue work was courageous acceptance of the inevitable. Her last column was written a few days before she died. I remember Jean Rook as a true and brave professional.

The second woman was a Hollywood legend. Audrey Hepburn epitomised the glamour of make-believe in films like *Roman Holiday, Breakfast at Tiffany's* and *My Fair Lady* in particular with her role as the flower girl transformed by Ascot finery. As I write I look at Cecil Beaton's painting on the wall capturing Audrey as a fashion icon. Then, like Jean Rook, her career was shattered. At the Cedars Sinai Medical Centre in Los Angeles, cancer was diagnosed. The illness took its toll. Chemotherapy left her thin, gaunt and emaciated. Refusing to be hospitalised, she became Special Ambassador to UNICEF, drawing attention to the plight of the starving children, influenced by personal memories of hardship in German-occupied Europe. Stamina alone was not enough. Friends gave support. Givenchy flew her home in his private Gulfstream jet so she could spend her last Christmas with family. Shortly afterwards, Audrey died at La Paisible and is buried in Tolochenaz. It was the homecoming of a courageous star.

The third is Ingrid Bergman, whose natural beauty will never be forgotten. Interpretative acting won Oscars in films like *Casablanca, For Whom the Bell Tolls, Stromboli, Murder on the Orient Express, Gaslight*, with stars like Humphrey Bogart and Gary Cooper. Her friends included such names as Howard Hughes, Ernest Hemingway and George Bernard Shaw. Her career hit the heights, yet the drama surrounding Ingrid's private life outstripped any storyline. It began when she left husband and child for the Italian director, Roberto Rossellini. Reaction in Tinsel City was a wave of sanctimonious hypocrisy. Socially ostracised, Ingrid and Roberto came to Europe and made the film *Anastasia* in Britain. Box office success led to re-establishment in Hollywood, renewed international stardom and further Oscar recognition.

Ingrid's resilience to adversity never wavered, but was put on hold when cancer was diagnosed. Double operation for breast cancer and prolonged radiation treatment left her weak and frail. She appeared in *Joan of Arc at the Stake,* a major production directed by Roberto Rossellini, oratorio by Arthur Honegger, written by Paul Claudel. I was invited to the first night at the *Stoll*. Reaction was mixed. Some critics were bitchy, others bewildered. I was complimentary. The aftermath came later. The terminal disease was in its final stages. Ingrid left her Cheyne Gardens flat and came to lunch at *The Dorchester.* She looked tired and weary, the right arm supported by a sling. Not once did she talk of the throbbing pain. Instead she recalled the *Stoll* play. I was surprised that the adverse criticisms had hurt, but remembered words I had written expressed what she had tried to portray. Alan Burgess included these lines in his *Bergman Story.* I quote them as my tribute to the memory of an actress whose beauty was almost luminous and her stoical courage:

> In the engulfing darkness and piercing shafts of light at the *Stoll* she suggests the spiritual statuesque calm of one who has climbed to the summit high above the gross world. She evokes the sadness of things supremely well . . . the quality she possesses is more than beauty: it is strangeness in beauty.

DAME NINETTE DE VALOIS

BALLET-LOVERS HAVE REASON TO BE GRATEFUL to Ninette de Valois, a dancer turned choreographer. She founded, fostered, directed and held together the Sadler's Wells Company. She was influenced by the stern discipline, almost monastic in its rigidness, imposed by Diaghilev during her years with his company. She described their status as factory serfs. Rules were clear-cut. Dancers were not allowed at rehearsals to sit on one chair and put their feet up at another; fined ten francs if the morning class was missed; fined if shoes came off on stage; hair had to be in the set style of each ballet; practice tunics to be regulation length; no ornamentation allowed on dresses. De Valois adopted these disciplines with brilliant results.

Her career began in her teens. Billed as the miniature Pavlova, she toured English seaside resorts with a troupe of *Wonder Children*. "I have danced the *Dying Swan* on every pier in the British Isles; was the first to put on a curtain-raiser ballet at the Old Vic and devised ingredient dances for opera and plays." In her formative years, she danced for Diaghilev, then went her own way, independent but parallel, to become his equivalent in England.

Her Ballet School found the talent and schooled it. Her authority was total. What Madame decreed was final. She founded the Academy of Choreographic Art, later the Royal Ballet School, and as choreographer created seventeen of the Company's first twenty-two ballets; talked Lilian Bayliss into giving her the Sadler's Wells Theatre, engaged Constant Lambert as musical director, and persuaded Frederick Ashton to leave the Marie Lambert group. The ground plan was complete. After lacking any balletic tradition, the Royal Ballet emerged with an unmistakable English style, all achieved by a shy, reserved woman who shunned self-publicity and personal limelight.

I recall an occasion at the Opera House when preparations were in progress for an evening performance of *Le Lac des Cygnets*. Rehearsal was in full swing under de Valois' directions. A pianist played the strains of the Mazurka; a sylph-like girl unbuttoned her skirt, shook it off and joined several other faun-like creatures who danced as if blown together by the music. At the evening performance, a bell summoned us to stalls and boxes. Every tier of the amphitheatre was packed. Lights faded like dying glow-worms. Applause greeted Constant Lambert. He bowed, tapped the stand with his baton, and the theatre welled to familiar chords. The magic moment as the vast curtain parted and delicate wraiths of grace floated across the stage.

Ninette de Valois once described the scene as the ectoplasm of music . . . when ballet and music fuse and lead us to the edge of infinity.

In a box by the stage sat Madame, ever watchful, ever critical. At the time of writing she was celebrating her 102nd birthday, but her spirit still watches from that box.

CLEMENTINE CHURCHILL

LADY CHURCHILL WAS A REMARKABLE WOMAN endowed with rare genius, a genius of temper in the sense we speak of steel having a fine temper. In conversation, everything became exciting; equally stimulating as talker and listener. An astute brain lay behind the slightly irregular face of this tall, handsome woman. Shrewd judge of people, adept in the arts of feminine manoeuvre in the political field.

Such acumen is an invaluable asset for the hostess of Number 10, noticeably absent over the past few years. The house has a dual personality. Since 1735 it has been, though spasmodically, the domicile of the Prime Minister and, with each successive Premier, has housed two personalities at one and the same time . . . the man in his Cabinet and the man in his home. Under Blair a supplementary use as nursery has been added for blatant vote-catching potential.

Recollections of her life must be equated with the career of the man she married and to whose welfare she devoted her energies. No light responsibility. It was one long fight. During the Second World War, all three political parties accepted him unanimously as His Majesty's First Minister, yet it took him forty years to realise his ambition. At times he was mistrusted by each political party. Three times his political career lay in ruins; three times he made a comeback. In the days of the Lloyd George Budget and the House of Lords Reform, Winston was virtually ostracized, yet in 1940 he was hailed as the man supremely equipped to command the battle.

It is one thing to pay deference to an Elder Statesman; it is another to live with one. At times it was like living with a volcano, for Churchill was a man of many facets; preoccupied and moody; aggressive and tactless; had a habit of bruising sensibilities without realising he had done so. I wonder what Clementine Hoxier's reactions would have been as a young girl had she glimpsed the years ahead in a crystal ball. She was twenty-three when they first met. By her photographs, she had large, expressive eyes set in an oval face. Her hair parted in the middle accentuated classic features. There was no questioning the natural beauty of this daughter of Colonel H. H. Hozier and Lady Blanche Hozier. The girl was intelligent, vivacious, interested in politics with strong liberal flavour. The initial meeting with Winston took place during his 1908 election campaign in Dundee. Shortly after, he proposed. The news was approved by this American mother; no hesitation on the part of the girl's parent. Churchill was a brilliant catch. He was the grandson of a Duke of Marlborough, son of Lord Randolph Churchill; a national figure in his own right through Boer War exploits, and, at thirty-four, President of the Board of Trade. In a letter to Wilfred Blunt, his future mother-in-law wrote, "He is gentle and tender, affectionate to those he loves, much hated by those who have not come under his personal charm."

They were married in St. Margaret's, Westminster, on September 8th the same year. It was the society wedding of the season. Lord Hugh Cecil, a staunch Tory, was best man. Balfour and both Chamberlains, his bitterest opponents, sent wedding presents. Wilfred Blunt recorded in his diary . . . "The bride was pale, as was the bridegroom. He has gained in appearance since I saw him last, and has a powerful, if ugly face. Winston's responses were clearly made in a pleasant voice, Clementine's inaudible." I have also come across an entry in Mrs. Sidney Webb's diary when she approvingly wrote, "On Sunday we lunched with Winston Churchill and his bride – a charming lady, well-bred and pretty, and earnest withal – but not rich, by no means a good match, which is to Winston's credit."

The young bride had more than her share of early worries, for they experienced Conservative party ostracism. Fortunately such were her Liberal views that Tory wrath was like a compliment. Blenheim was virtually the only Tory house to welcome them. Bitter opposition was met by the Churchillian fighting spirit, but it hurt. He once complained, "I have never joined an intrigue. Everything that I have got I have fought for, and yet I have been more hated than anybody." It is true to say that he was genuinely astonished by the animosity he stirred. There were compensations. They seldom moved in social circles, a form of relaxation that never appealed to them. They were content with their small group of intimate friends, ensuring a sound foundation for their partnership. At the end of a long life, Winston paid this tribute to his wife . . . "We were married in 1908 and lived happy ever after."

DAPHNE DU MAURIER

LADY BROWNING WAS PART of that national institution, the French family of Du Maurier. The founder of this eminence was George Du Maurier, grandson of the aristocratic emigré who escaped from France during the Reign of Terror. He bequeathed his striking personality to two generations, his son, Sir Gerald, the Edwardian stage idol, and Daphne, his granddaughter.

Daphne Du Maurier, born in 1907, educated in Paris, returned to work in England. From the outset she had a love of words. Her vocabulary, copious, expressive, charged with spirit and colour, was that of someone who had read widely, and, in reading, learnt what some greater writers but worse masters of English had not, that any word is good enough so long as it is the one word wanted.

She created her own world, a world that bore a vital relation to experience, as all fiction must if it is to bewitch and move us; the characters in that world exist in a medium which is not the atmosphere we ordinarily breathe. That medium was her own mind. Just as there was a world called Galsworthy, another called Greene, so there was a world called Du Maurier. It may have been a bubble world, but it held together.

Her home in Cornwall was a perfect shell for her sensibility. The charm of Menabilly could hardly escape anyone; so quiet, dignified, and *gemütlich* was it, within and without. The little wooden hut overlooking the sea always reminded me of its counterpart in Ayot St. Lawrence where George Bernard Shaw found inspiration. It was similar at Menabilly where Daphne wrote the majority of her books.

I remember Daphne as an attractive woman, slender, blonde hair with piercing blue eyes. Complex, introspective, anti-social, at times almost reclusive, she took refuge in the safe fantasy world of her novels, often identifying with characters and situations, invariably against a Cornish background. It would be true to say that her life, real and fictional, was influenced by Menabilly.

Psychologically Daphne's life was clouded by an unsettled marriage due to her husband's military career with its professional duties and social implications. In 1937 Frederick Arthur Montague ("Boy") Browning was commanding officer of the Second Battalion Grenadier Guards, stationed in Alexandria, an appointment that brought little joy to Daphne who was bored by the endless cocktail parties enjoyed by officer's wives. Aldershot followed at Greyfriars, a rented house in Fleet, with similar stereotyped social contacts. In 1944 "Boy" was given command of the newly created 1st Airborne Corps – blending of 1st and 6th Airborne Divisions and the Special Air Service Brigade that supervised the 6th Airborne landing on the left flank of the invasion of Normandy, with Field Marshall Montgomery as Commander of the ground forces.

In 1948 Browning resigned from the army, and, on Lord Mountbatten's recommendation, was appointed Comptroller of the Household of Princess Elizabeth, then newly married. Four years later she became Queen, and Browning moved to Buckingham Palace as Treasurer and Comptroller to the Duke of Edinburgh.

It was all heady stuff, but left Daphne with a marriage only in name. She had genuine love for her husband, but emotions were stifled by a way of life that did not appeal. There was no magic in visits to Balmoral, Sandringham and Buckingham Palace with their protocol trappings. All she wanted was the reassuring existence of Menabilly with writing a form of escapism. She felt left out, insecure with nagging worries of her husband's peccadilloes and resentment at the thought of his former fiancée, Jean Regardo. The concern occasionally surfaced, as in her dedication to *The King's General* . . . "To my husband, also a General, but, I trust, a more discreet one." Had she been a conventional army wife, such doubts would have been swept aside. Instead the antipathy made her decline invitations to accompany him to Buckingham Palace.

It was sad that such barriers existed. Browning was a handsome man, charismatic, with zest for living, qualities that appealed to the Queen and Prince Philip. I remember Browning describing how on the first official tour by the Princess, she had an expensive camera with every sophisticated gadget to ensure photographic perfection. Unfortunately the results were disastrous. The only record came from Browning's box-Brownie snapshots. It is impossible to judge from external observations, but I feel that Browning was selfish and insensitive to have left his wife isolated in Cornwall. On the other hand, when I saw them together at Menabilly, they seemed reconciled and on the same wavelength.

Daphne's obsession with Menabilly was understandable, its elegant white-walled drawing-room with long windows overlooking lawns. Inevitably it was linked with the haunting Manderley of *Rebecca*.

Daphne's literary output was prolific with novels like *The Loving Spirit, Jamaica Inn, Frenchman's Creek, The King's General, My Cousin Rachel,* and *The House on the Strand* . . . all set in Cornwall. For me none match the mysterious, sinister narrative of *Rebecca* that engulfed the haunting mission which in reality was a blending of two houses . . . Menabilly, which was the Rashleigh family seat, and Milton, near Peterborough, the ancestral home of the Fitzwilliam family. The composite building was given global recognition by the directing skills of Hollywood and the initial portrayal of the heroine by Joan Fontaine, bringing her stardom and Oscar nomination.

The theme lingers. Daphne's opening lines set the tone . . . "Last night I dreamt I went to Manderley again." The spirit of the dead Rebecca is ever-present; never leaves the second Mrs de Winter; the inferred lesbian relationship between Mrs Danver and Rebecca; the glimpse of the deranged woman at the top of the stairs; the scene when Maxim and his wife drive through the night and see the red streak in the sky as Manderley blazes. It is a gripping piece of writing.

During a visit to Menabilly, Daphne talked of the richness of material she found in Cornish lore. I took the opportunity to mention some research I had carried out, an intriguing narrative of fact that defied fiction, also in a Cornish setting. I gave an outline to Mary Webb, then Managing Director of the publishers Hutchinsons. Without hesitation she asked me to sign a contract giving them first refusal of publication and film rights.

Daphne asked I could give a resumé. I arrived in Breage, a quiet, rather solemn Cornish village dominated by a fifteenth-century granite church, for one purpose, to see the tomb of Margaret Godolphin. I found it in front of the altar in the south aisle beneath which she lay. Lifting the carpet I read this inscription:

> Beneath this brass repose the mortal
> remains of Margaret Godolphin, daughter
> of Colonel Blague, of Horningsheath,
> Groom of the Bedchamber of King Charles I;
> the wife of Sidney Godolphin, afterwards
> Earle of Godolphin; and the friend of John
> Evelyn, who was told the story of her noble
> life. She wished to rest at Breage, the cradle
> of her husband's race. Born 2nd
> August, 1652. She died in London 9th September,
> 1678. This brass was placed to
> her memory by George Godolphin Osborne,
> 10th Duke of Leeds.

At the base of the altar is the Latin epitaph written by Evelyn. The same inscription was placed upon her coffin. It is followed by her favourite motto: *Un Dieu, Un amy,* "One God, one friend."

Daphne asked if I had details of this Margaret. Referring to my notes, I gave her a descriptive vignette. Margaret Godolphin had great physical attraction – young, elegant, charming, beautiful. Possessing all the pretty arts, she came to the Court of Charles II as a Maid of Honour, demure and pure, a tempting subject for the influence of the hypocritical John Evelyn, confirming an extraordinary rite of friendship symbolized by an altar drawn in his Diary with a heart upon it surrounded by a halo of stars. On the altar Evelyn wrote, "Be this the symbol of inviolable friendship," and presented it to Margaret, with the pen, which she took, and subscribed: "Be it so: Margaret Blagge, 16 October, 1672."

The relationship between this man of fifty-two and a girl of twenty developed in subtle fashion, until a complication arose in the rival attraction of Sidney Godolphin, the future Lord Treasurer of England. Margaret had to resolve her triple alliance . . . love for the spiritual, love for Godolphin, and the hypnotized fascination for Evelyn.

The complexity of Margaret's nature was such that, while shrinking from the physical ties of marriage, she had become so deeply involved with a married man. She deplored the pleasures of the world to such an extent that plans were made to enter a strict religious Order. At the same time Louis XIV was so intrigued by reports of her physical beauty and wit, he invited her to St. Germain.

Margaret persisted in her spiritual devotions under the scheming Evelyn, but married Godolphin secretly. Emotional clashes of conscience followed as the triangle developed. Godolphin was away for long periods on Court duties. Her infatuation for Evelyn began to slip from its pseudo-ethereal plane. Mrs Evelyn's suspicions quickened. Promptings of conscience on religious matters left Margaret remote and introspective. Pregnancy led to the final tragic chapter.

Evelyn's influence was possessive. He had persuaded her to be painted by Matthew Dixon, insisting there should be no sparkle. Setting to be drab. Tombstone used for a seat. Funeral urn as background. Courtly curls tied back. Result looked plain, dismal, uninteresting. Lady Berkeley, determined that Sidney Godolphin should not see his fiancée in such a light, arranged for a painting by Mary Beale, insisting it should be the portrayal of a potential wife. We see her in silks and curls – and a cupid.

The story was played to its close in London "at halfe a houre after one" on the afternoon of 9 September 1678, yet Margaret Godolphin was buried in the remote Cornish village. The explanation is supplied in Evelyn's Diary:

> The Fees to the Physicians, the intire Care of her funeral was wholly committed to me, so as having closed the Eyes, and drop'd a teare upon the Cheake of my blessed Saint, Lovely in death and like an Angel, I caused her Corps to be embalmed, and wrap'd in Lead with a plate of Brass sothered on it, with an Inscription and other Circumstances due to her worth, with as much diligence and care as my grieved heart would permit me; being so full of sorrow and tir'd with it, that retiring home for two daies I spent it in solitude, and sad reflections.

At her special request they carried her to Godolphin to be laid with her husband's ancestors. The wish was expressed in her last letter which she left with her sister-on-law, Jael Boscawen, in the event of her death. Over three hundred years have passed since this letter was written, yet even now its pathos makes sad reading. It was as if she knew she would die in child-birth. She wrote:

> For my Funeral, I desire there may be no Cost bestow'd upon it all. But (if I might) I would begg, that my body might Lie, where I had had such a mind to go my selfe (at Godolphin), among your Friends: I believe, if I were caryed by Sea, The Expense would not be very greate

On the 17th they set forth:

> an herse with 6 horses, and two other Coaches of as many, and with about 30 people of her relations and servants . . .

Evelyn himself "waited on the companies as far as Hounslow Heath, with a sad heart," but "was oblig'd to returne upon some indispensable affaires," to retrieve his letters before Godolphin could read them. Among her effects was a sealed packet which she directed to be burnt unopened. It may have been the six letters to Evelyn which she recovered just before her marriage and refused to return.

The cortege went on its long journey to Cornwall without Evelyn or the grief-stricken husband, though the latter had recovered sufficiently to be looking through her effects when Evelyn returned post-haste.

Evelyn tells us . . . "The Corps was ordered to be taken out of the hearse, and decently placed in the house with tapers about it, and her servants attending, every night during all the way to the foote of Cornwall, neare 300 miles, and then as honourably interred in the Parish Church of Godolphin. The funeral cost not much less than £1000."

A few weeks later Sidney Godolphin left London and followed his wife's body to Godolphin where he remained near the grave until the following January.

After visiting the church, I went to Godolphin, through fields to a long drive, thickly wooded, to the entrance to Godolphin Hall. The setting was perfect. The castellated north side with a loggia of seven bays, heavy Tuscan pillars, windows mullioned and transomed. Here it was that Margaret Godolphin felt she would be among friends when death had finally resolved the strange triangle of love, friendship and deceit. I tried to imagine the scene when the cortege with its coaches and eighteen horses drew up by this courtyard and the coffin was slowly carried through the archway.

Daphne was amazed that such a drama had been enacted so close to her countryside of legends and traditions. She offered support and went with me to Breage church; had access to examine the church register. The entries were faded, the ink turned brown, but the writing was clear. We found two mistakes. The date was wrong and an error had been made as to the identity of the corpse. The wrong Godolphin had been entered. The slips had been corrected later. Unofficially we had the crypt opened. On the lead coffin was a plaque bearing John Evelyn's signature. Even in death he had the last word.

I prefer not to recall Daphne's closing years. Frail with no urge to write. Nursed by Esther Rowe, she died in her sleep, and is buried in the ground of Kilmarth, the dower house to Menabilly.

ECCENTRICITY MADE RESPECTABLE

THE SITWELL TRIUMVIRATE of Osbert, Sacheverell and Edith was the essence of the *avant-garde*. Edith went through life like a pre-Raphaelite ghost, dramatic dress-sense, flowing dresses embroidered with Florentine flowers, gold turban hats, peacock feathers, rings with semi-precious stones. Her personality matched, dramatic and startling. It was therefore with a degree of apprehension that I awaited her arrival for lunch. It was like entertaining a living Holbein. Grey-green eyes peered out of recessed sockets, aristocratic features, but her hands were fascinating with several garish rings and two large gold Urim and Thummims. Virginia Woolf had been fascinated by their beauty. I understood why.

In conversation she was surprisingly animated, contrary to her reputation of being witheringly cold. A chance remark about Frank Leavis revived a long-running literary feud. Time had mellowed her vitriol: she wistfully observed that Leavis had gone over the top in his attack on C. P. Snow; after all, Charles did write good English. I was interested to hear her views of *Façade*, the series of instrumental pieces designed to be played in conjunction with the recitation of her surrealist poems. I found them not easy to understand. She agreed that others shared my view, but on this occasion they tried it out at a private performance at her brother's house in Chelsea. Reaction was so encouraging that Osbert agreed to arrange a public performance at the Aeolian Hall. The result was near disaster, partly because the presentation was so bizarre. To make sure that their personalities did not distract audience attention, three primitive archways were painted on a curtain; two of them had masks with stentophones fitted to their mouths; the centre one showed a female with closed eyes and open mouth. That was Edith's position. Osbert was stationed behind the smaller mask. The format was simple. Osbert gave explanations; Edith recited, accompanied by Walton's music. Audience reaction was chaotic. Time is a healer. 29 years later *Façade* was staged at the Royal Festival Hall in London. Edith was given a standing ovation: admitted quiet satisfaction for she felt her verse had an imaginative and rhythmic intensity.

I was asked which were my favourites. I named *The Little Ghost Who Died for Love,* the elegy with its haunting sadness; the ironic note of *Serenade* and *The Sleeping Beauty* with its elegiac metre. When I asked if any of her poems had particular appeal, she thought hard and picked one written during the air-raids and quoted five lines:

> Still falls the Rain
> Dark as the world of man, black is our loss
> Blind as the nineteen hundred and forty nails
> Upon the cross.
> Still falls the Rain . . .

Her interpretation of the falling of the bombs represented by the falling of blood from the side of Christ . . . the analogy of redemption through suffering. As in many poems, there was preoccupation with issues of life and death.

On a more personal note, Edith recalled her unhappy childhood. It was a mistake to have been born a girl, with a love for books and music. Her mother, blasé and bored, would have preferred a pretty, conventional-type debutante; her father Sir George, resented an ugly duckling. The social milieu at Renshaw Hall was not for her. She found solace with Helen Rootham, the governess who encouraged her artistic talents. From 1914 to 1938 life in London and later Paris was frugal, money was short, but poems flowed from her pen. Paris brought sadness. She nursed Helen Rootham in her terminal illness. Unhappiness came from a relationship with Pavel Tchelitchew, a white Russian homosexual artist. In maturity her Plantagenet appearance became accepted as poetic exhibitionism even though at times reaching a point of absurdity.

For Edith Sitwell, poetry was a lonely companion. Her poetic sisters hunted the Infinite in packs, she made the journey alone.

ELEANOR ROOSEVELT

THE FIRST LADY OF THE WHITE HOUSE plays a backstage role that has varied over the years. It is not politically influential, nor socially glamorous. The idea that Washington is a glittering whirl is false. It is an essentially provincial town. New York is the principal metropolis, social capital and cultural centre of the United States. Consequently the First Lady of the White House does not set the social tone of the nation. Her role is formidable to anybody not accustomed to large-scale housekeeping and entertainment. The White House has 102 rooms; employs 72 servants; Americans tramp through it except for a surprisingly small private portion, under the pretext that the place is really theirs.

Martha Washington, wife of the first President, set stiff standards of etiquette based on the European courts. Since President Jefferson was a widower, Dolley Madison, as the wife of his Secretary of State, acted as First Lady from 1801 onwards, becoming mistress of the White House in her own right when her husband James Madison, principal author of the constitution, succeeded Jefferson, who wrote the *Declaration of Independence* in 1809. Her parties were famous, likewise her courage in staying in Washington until the last minute as the British approached the undefended gates during the war of 1812-14, and rescuing the official portrait of George Washington before the British burnt down the White House.

Since then a First Lady has every right to make of the job what she pleases. Each had her own finger-prints of style. Pat Nixon was particularly effective on the receiving line; Jacqueline Kennedy, icon of fashion editors and society columnists. Both had the misfortune to be wives of flawed men, the latter being as notorious a womaniser as the perjured reputation of sex-obsessed Bill Clinton, which Hillary matrimonially ignored . . . Nancy Reagan was a strong, astute figure determining to secure the President's place in history as a man of peace and weed out right-wing ideologues from the Government. She was the most effective First Lady in 40 years. With Ronald, they were a highly effective team. She made tough decisions, took the heat, and let her husband still be the nice guy. Her natural diplomatic and political gifts gave her extraordinary strength in adversity . . . the assassination attempt in 1981 when a bullet came within three inches of the President's heart; her fight against breast cancer; and her caring love coping with Ronald's Alzheimer's disease. Nancy Reagan has become the *grande dame* of the Grand Old Party.

The only other First Ladies to play a substantial political role were Mrs Woodrow Wilson and Eleanor Roosevelt, but their roles and motivations were very different. Woodrow Wilson, for the last 17 months of his second term, was almost totally incapacitated, mentally and physically, yet remained sufficiently aware of his surroundings to obstruct any attempt to make proper provision for the conduct of government and even had hopes of nomination for a third term. Throughout this period, Mrs Wilson alone decided what documents he should see, what political decisions should be referred to him and what Bills he should sign in person. She had no real political motives nor desire for personal power, it was to strengthen her husband's hold on life and will to recover.

Eleanor Roosevelt's career as First Lady stands completely on its own, a major political personality in her own right. Almost immediately after entering the White House she began a newspaper column and was the only First Lady to hold her own Press Conferences. There was never anything covert about her influence. She entered fields of controversy and did not expect to be protected from criticism.

On a personal note, I recall my meeting with Eleanor. Invited to breakfast in her New York apartment, her reminiscences were far-ranging. The room was small, almost claustrophobic. Steel grilles over the windows were off-putting. A photograph of Franklin in full health presided. She talked of her childhood, how at sixteen she went to a finishing school in England; of her gratitude to Louie Howe, the wizened, untidy Albany journalist, who guided her in the quirky world of politicians and pressmen; how the first ten years of her marriage revolved round the births and worries of having six children. Then came the shattering blow of Franklin's infantile paralysis. She concentrated on combating the crippling disease, relying on the stimulus of friends and excitement of political life. For eight years the anxiety lasted; partial recovery helped; by then her self-confidence had stabilised her public life; learnt to speak well and to the point. Her newspaper column – My Day – carried candid comments without regard to the official views of the Establishment; opposed dictators, appeasement and defended the young. Her energy was incredible. She recalled how one editor refused to believe her published schedule, sent young reporters with her, only to be shattered by the day's killing pace. I went with her to the Grand Central Terminal, that magnificent central concourse with vaulted blue ceiling – about 10 storeys high – with 48 acres of railroad tracks underground; milling hordes of people. On all sides there were smiles and greetings from a cross-section of New York's fusion of races. Eleanor Roosevelt was a loved figure in this melting pot. When I said farewell to this remarkable American, I recalled a conversation with Greer Garson. In 1942 she won the Oscar for her portrayal of a well-heeled housewife experiencing the rigours of the home front in *Mrs Miniver*, Hollywood's tribute to British indomitability. She described how President Roosevelt had urged the producers to get it before the public as a morale booster – a role that Eleanor had played throughout her life.

HAUNTED BY FRIENDLY SHADES

GIVEN SENSITIVITY, THE PAST IS NEVER FAR AWAY in Cambridge, but it needs a sprinkling of knowledge of what has gone before. The scene by the Mill has immediate appeal, but aesthetic pleasures alone are impersonal. Look across Lamas Land and the Little Island and you see an attractive house with adjoining granaries, a site that has been in continual use for some 500 years. This is now Darwin College, founded in 1964 by the two Colleges of Caius, St John's and Trinity. It was so named because of the association with Cambridge of Dr. Erasmus Darwin and his grandson, Charles Darwin, and the fact that Newnham Grange was the home of Sir Charles Darwin's son, Sir George Darwin, and his family.

It has interesting associations, many captured by Gwen Raverat, daughter of Sir George, in a charming book called *Period Piece*, compulsory reading for anyone seeking the charisma of the place. This talented writer and artist was sadly stricken by a stroke, but though severely handicapped she could still sketch and write. For several years she was a familiar figure on the river-path, slumped in a wheelchair, wrapped in an old rug and dark cloak with a black, wide-brimmed clergyman's hat rammed on her head, sketching in all kinds of weather until a Swiss nurse took her back to Newnham Grange for lunch.

If ever a place is haunted by friendly shades that of Gwen Raverat must surely return to the Grange. Her home was equally evocative and was loved by such figures as Bertrand Russell, Arthur Clough, Rupert Brooke and Augustus John, whose horse-drawn gaudy caravan with Dorelia in gypsy-looking clothes would cross Silver Street bridge on the way to Grantchester, invariably pausing for a while at Newnham Grange.

MICHAELA DENIS

IT IS UNUSUAL TO FIND an elegant young woman drinking gin-and-tonic in a London West End flat who has lived with the Aborigines in Central Australia, had journeyed to New Guinea to make friends with the Chimbu, a Stone Age people, who trekked through Africa on a journey to King Solomon's Mines. Such were some of the things that Michaela Denis had done with her husband, Armand. They had recorded photographically some of the remote places of the world and captured with their cameras strange sights, primitive peoples, and rare animals.

I asked about the danger of catching a tropical disease in some remote jungle. Michaela described an occasion when this happened. She and her husband stood for a whole day in a swamp waiting to photograph a rare creature. The sun was unbearably hot on their heads; the muddy water, which was up to their necks, was icy cold. The stench frightful. Some hours later Armand developed a feverish temperature. He had caught the dreaded tropical disease, tick typhus. In less than three weeks, antibiotics had cured him, without leaving the usual weak heart.

On one safari in Central Africa, their team, which included Tom Stobart of Everest renown, captured a wild 800 lb sealion. In a reptile-infested Australia pool, they netted 68 crocodiles. The point about such feats was that no member of their party ever carried a lethal weapon. They never killed an animal. The only shooting was with a camera.

Michaela Denis was one of those rare women that appear but once or twice in a century. She was born with the most reliable prophylactic against tedium – consuming curiosity which took her to some of the world's strangest places. She was the only woman I have known who had a vulture as a pet.

MARGOT FONTEYN

BALLET IS A SYNTHESIS OF MUSIC, choreography, and interpretation. In that world Margot Fonteyn occupied a transcendent place combining personal beauty with superb technique, emotional range, dramatic powers, and an ability to become the character she danced. I watched many integrated performances of breath-taking beauty . . . the wraithlike lightness of her Giselle that became the spirit of light in mist, whilst *Lac des Cygnes* became a memorable vehicle, the roles of Odette and Odile ending in the apotheosis of the closing scene in which light gradually returns and the swan-girls, evermore to be swans, are seen in two diagonal lines. In the distance there glides into view over the dark waters a shell-like barque of gold bearing the Swan Queen and Siegfried, reunited in an eternal world after Siegfried had given his life for love of Odette.

Her role in ballet was recognised in the 1956 New Year's Honours when as Dame Margot Fonteyn, she became the first dancer to be so honoured by the Sovereign while still dancing.

Her private life was emotionally traumatic. When just sixteen, and already a soloist, she came under the influence of Constant Lambert, musical director and composer, twenty years her senior and married. It was a bizarre Svengali-type relationship with a raffish, heavy-drinking man handicapped by a limp from childhood polio. He wrote a ballet *Horoscope* based on their affair with the man, energetic and full-blooded, born under Leo and the young woman born under Virgo, fused together by mutual moonsigns. The affair lasted eight years, succeeded by an interlude with the young choreographer Roland Petit in Paris.

Emotionally frustrated there was a spell with Roberto 'Tito' Arias, terminated by his playboy womanizing, to be rekindled years later when, obese and with three children, Arias felt flattered, proposed marriage within a week, promising a divorce. It was unrealistic. Here was a world-famous ballerina shacking-up with a notorious gambler, criminal record for bootlegging and shady dealings. Fonteyn became a passport to respectability and hostess in London when he became Panamanian Ambassador. The next stage was to persuade her to bankroll his political ambitions to the extent of raising revolutionary funds for an abortive coup in 1959. Arias consoled himself with a string of women. Fonteyn found herself overwhelmed by the charismatic Rudolf Nureyev, a wild, untamed dancer with a sexual urge for men and women alike. Of Tartar parents on both sides of his family, he joined the Kirov Ballet School at seventeen, a spartan experience, nine sharing a room. He refused to conform, would not wear the Kirov uniform, had unkempt hair, and became an objectionable rebel. Further trouble came when Stalinist informers reported Nureyev's sexual deviations. Kremlin decreed that homosexuality was a crime with minimum sentence of seven years hard labour. When the Kirov was on tour in Paris, he slipped the Russian guards at Le Bourget as the troupe was about to embark for London, asked the French police for political asylum – literally in French custody and a free man.

He brought to Covent Garden a smouldering, untamed, whirling performance like a predatory dervish, an obsessive force that fascinated audiences and critics. Margot Fonteyn sent for him to be her partner. Though seventeen years his senior, they fused into the perfect partnership, fire and light commingling. Under her tuition Nureyev controlled his tantrums. Margot became more feminine, even relaxed, ignored Rudolf's homosexual preferences, decided to divorce Arias. Once again it was not to be. The Panamanian's car was stopped at traffic lights, anarchists shot him five times. Her sense of duty meant she could not abandon her quadriplegic husband. She tended the wastrel until death released them both.

Margot passed away on February 21, 1991. Nureyev retired to his Italian island, one of his seven homes. His grief was profound. It was a wonderful partnership. She used to recall with pleasure their reception at Vienna Staatsoper after the performance of *Swan Lake* in 1964 when they advanced for a record 89 curtain calls. Rudolf's tribute said it all . . . "there was an absolute musical quality in her beautiful body and phrasing. For me she represented eternal youth." . . . sentiments I echo.

Nureyev's life ended ignominiously: his lifestyle exacted its toll as he succumbed to the disease of Aids. In October 1992 he was awarded France's highest cultural honour, the rank of Commander of Arts and Letters in the Legion d'Honneur. On January 6, 1993, the greatest male dancer the world has ever known, joined our greatest ballerina, reunited like Odette and Siegfried.

The women I have singled out as *remarkable* are just that. Each outstanding, icons in their own field, untouched by fads and fashions that affect the majority of females.

During the century I have seen many changes, each one relevant to the spirit of that particular era. Changes were not arbitrary. Victorians took shelter behind crinolines, chaperons, convention and swooning. Ostensibly on the retreat, sly young women encouraged men by a fleeting glimpse of an ankle. Men assumed the natural role of a pursuer. The interim period between two world wars saw women of marriageable age in the majority. Roles became reverses. Emancipated, independent and unmarried, women became the hunters. Equality of opportunity made females more masculine. Short-haired, flat-chested, chain-smoking girls tried everything to beguile men. The effect made them effeminate by reaction. The war halted that. Masculine virility was re-established. The last twenty years have witnessed revolutionary changes. Marriage as such is naff. Single-parents accepted. Drug addiction commonplace. Age-of-consent reduced. Lesbian and homosexual relationships legalised. "Aids" part of the biological scene. Moral values outdated. One characteristic remains the same. I understand on good authority that the face of the world would have been different had Cleopatra's nose been shorter. That being so, I am interested to see how the whims of designers exercise our social economy. Sloane Street and Bond Street suggest little has changed. Fashionably dressed women are not interested in the appraisal of men. With microscopic carefulness their eyes are for ever upon other women. In theory, women dress for men: in reality, women dress for women.

From personal observation, I isolate icons of different eras, Twiggy was in her own category. Wide-eyed, pale, orphan-boy alertness, the starved child-woman, Cockney accent, unsophisticated and vulnerable, half-innocent, half-wanton, she cornered the market. Jean Shrimpton was another. A fashion model at the top of a highly competitive tree, chameleon expression, brown-black hair and endless legs made her a valuable property. Mark McCormack came into my *Dorchester* suite, picked up a glossy magazine, looked at the beauty on the cover, and identified Jean as one of his girls – such is the clientele of promotion entrepreneurs.

Appearances were all-important. In France the norm of the Sixties was typified by Francoise Hardy. Like Twiggy, she was tall, thin, with thick black hair framing a beautiful face, vibrant green-grey eyes. She wrote all her own songs, played a guitar as she sang the ballads with winsome simplicity. The MGM film *Grand Prix* confirmed the quality of her acting, but the effect was always low-beat. Conversation over meals was usually quiet but invariably thoughtful. She seemed to light up in front of the camera.

It was with such girls in mind that a thousand imitations were launched and Mary Quant came into her own. Skinny clothes for skinny girls, a generation of youth that needed to express itself on its own terms. Mary Quant was ideal for the role. She too was skinny, leggy, with pale lipstick, upper and lower lashes emphasised with a heavy black liner, soup-bowl bangs, cut heavy, shiny and dead straight. She lunched in the Grill with her tall husband, Alexander Plunket Greene, and talked of future projects, of fashion trends, emphasising that women dress for women and undress for men. I was tempted to ask whether the rumour was true that she shaved her pubic hair into a heart shape, but somehow over coffee it seemed somewhat indelicate, if not bad taste. The opportunity never occurred again.

So much for superficial reality, a scene in which man is made to feel like a stranger on a butterfly farm.

I prefer the world in which my nominated women lived their "remarkable" lives.

CHAPTER FIVE

STATESMEN
AND POLITICIANS

~

I T HAS BEEN SAID THAT A STATESMAN'S PLACE in history depends upon the fate of the policies and the institutions with which he is identified. It is certainly true today when to an exceptional extent international relations depend upon the interacting characters and psychology of a few individuals. The technical apparatus of government has changed, and not for the better. It is difficult to differentiate between statesmen and politicians; the former would never become so had they not first been politicians. Few today qualify for this elitist role. Compared with the past, we have Second-Eleven Members. Operative words are spin and sleaze. Overwhelming majority in the House means that controversial Bills are hustled on the Statute Book with scant attention to dissenting voices or reasoned debate. Clichés and sound-bites substitute policy. No. 10 is littered with banana-skins. The Constitution dismantled; the United Kingdom fragmented. Our legal system can be over-ruled by the Court of Appeal in The Hague; Monarchy threatened by a Republican group; the Lords stripped of its traditional function as the Second Chamber; Franco-German alliance clique seeks to create a Federal Europe in which this country will be relegated to minor membership. The pound to be abolished in favour of the euro, in spite of opposition from a majority of public expression in a referendum. Socialist whips control the Commons. In such an atmosphere, democracy is substituted by dictatorship aping a Presidential state.

Aspirations of New Labour denigrate our past, dumb-down achievements, wipe the slate and start afresh. This is The Millennium. The past never happened. Society is reborn.

Such an attitude is flawed. Politicians must learn from the past. Our way of life is an absorbing canvas. Would-be legislators must remember that hard-fought progress is not to be ignored. Let me recall how events took shape after the First World War of world light-years away. Police were giving permission for cars to be used in London instead of horses. Car-tax was levied at £1-per-horsepower. Traffic lights appeared for the first time in Piccadilly. Our economic problems were minor compared with the Germans at 4-trillion to the dollar, a loaf of bread in Berlin costing more than 200 billion marks. There was the Wall Street crash and the General Strike, whilst our unemployment exceeded two million. Certain news items had a familiar note. Seventy nine years ago six policemen were murdered by the IRA, whilst Sinn Fein declared that an arson campaign would make government of Ireland by Britain impossible. Proposals for a Channel Tunnel were rejected by the Government. The Greenhouse Effect seemed anticipated when rain ended a 100-day drought followed by the worst summer since 1879.

There was no Andrew Lloyd Webber, but three plays were running in London's West End from the imaginative pen of Edgar Wallace. Petrol soared to 1/1d a gallon. Public vehicles circulated in Hyde Park for the first time since 1836. An American State introduced a bizarre punishment that might appeal to Jack Straw. . . motorists who killed a pedestrian had to spend an hour alone with the corpse – it is easy for a later generation to ignore such facts. For the majority even the world of the 'Thirties' belongs to history. It was a decade of paradoxes and extremes, marking the end of an era. On one side: the aftermath of a world of certainties; on the other, the nuclear age.

Emancipation of women made a big impact. It meant that four million between the ages of twenty-one and thirty were added to the Register by the Equal Franchise Act. Threat of national bankruptcy led to an All-Party Government endorsed by 554 votes against 56. Labour only won three out of twenty-eight London boroughs in local elections. Britain was forced off the Gold Standard. The *Star Spangled Banner* became the official American anthem. *It* was the vogue word for sex-appeal, not *Tara*. Women wore sheath dresses. Thousands joined the publicised Women's League of Health and Beauty. £3-a-week was the living wage for the father of a family; £10-a-week meant luxury. Butter 1/- per pound; eggs 1/- a dozen; tea 10d per pound. Thomas Cook advertised eight days on the French Riviera for less than £9. Return sea passage on the Orient Line to Australia cost £124 first-class and £57 third-class. Jim Mollison gave hope to those in a hurry with a record flight from Australia to this country in 214 hours.

Cinemas were wired for sound. Talking-films produced classics like *The Taming of the Shrew* with Mary Pickford and Douglas Fairbanks; *Disraeli* with George Arliss; *Untamed* with Joan Crawford; *Broadway Melody* with Bessie Love; Charlie Chaplin was silent in *City Lights;* Greta Garbo was still without a voice; Erich Maria Remarque's anti-war *All Quiet on the Western Front* commanded attention. Cricket purists were upset because wickets were one inch higher and wider. Golfers objected to steel-shafted clubs. President Hoover opened the world's tallest building, the Empire State Building with 86 floors, 1245 feet high. George Bernard Shaw met Stalin. Rupert Murdoch was born. Wall Street collapsed, with fortunes on paper disappearing. The world's first atom-smashing machine was tested in Cambridge. Unemployment topped the 2.3-million mark.

In retrospect each decade had historical and political significance. So much happened in the Forties. Everything developed so quickly. Blackouts, evacuation, food rationing; the frontiers of Europe redrawn by the horrors of the Second World War; invasion of Denmark, Norway, Holland and Belgium; Dunkirk retreat; surrender of France; German devastation of Coventry and London; Pearl Harbor and America at war with Japan; the atomic era beginning with Hiroshima and Nagasaki; Japan surrendering; Nazi war criminals hanged at Nuremberg. After 2000 nights of darkness, we were again ablaze with light. The price of victory was 55 million dead.

Such is the political correctness of our era of New Labour that this sombre record is set aside as unimportant. Such facts are excluded from the history of our nation. Purblind critics express the mood of a vocal minority. Their numbers include many members of Parliament.

We returned to near normality with the news that the pound was devalued by 30 per cent against the dollar; petrol rose to 2/3d (11p). a gallon; car tax was proposed at a flat rate of £10 a year; railways were nationalised; Civil Servants were suspended for holding Communist and Fascist views; the Derby was run at Epsom after a break of six years. The social pattern was taking shape, alternating between deep depression and high prosperity. It was a decade of extremes.

In the Fifties our lifestyle changed more drastically than in any other decade of the century, except for the fragmentation of the Constitution by Blair, of which more later. The General Election of February 1950 saw Clement Attlee's Labour Party retain power with a majority cut to six. Twenty months later the Conservatives became the Government, with Winston Churchill again Prime Minister.

It was the time of the Korean War, with British and Commonwealth forces involved and anti-British rioting in Egypt, factors that underlined the need for a rearmament programme. The first test-explosion of a British atom bomb took place off the coast of Australia. In July 1953 the Korean War ended. In April 1955 Churchill resigned as Premier and was replaced by Anthony Eden, an appointment confirmed a month later by a General Election and increased majority. Escalation of the EOKA terrorist campaign in Cyprus and Egyptian seizure of the Suez Canal in July 1956 led to a political pressure from other countries, British forces were withdrawn. Eden resigned in 1957 and was replaced by Harold Macmillan with majority increased to 100 at the next election.

Whilst the political merry-go-round held the headlines of world affairs, everyday life slowly assumed a familiar pattern. Petrol was 3s (15p) a gallon and we still complained. Tea rationing ended. 1951 had the wettest February since 1870. Television licences were raised to £3. Parking meters were introduced in London. Radar speed checks came into use. Unemployment was in the region of 620,000. In their wisdom, British Rail closed 230 stations. The Berlin Airlift ended. Liberals lost a record 314 election deposits.

Identity cards were abolished. The Queen made her first Christmas broadcast. Hillary and Tensing conquered Mount Everest. Gordon Richards won his first Derby. The Boat Race was called off after the Oxford boat sank. To take our minds off political abstractions, we had the first-ever pictures of the dark side of the moon from a Soviet rocket.

Surveying the political scene against this absorbing background, I have picked out political figures who touched the fringe of statesmanship; others who failed to make the grade; an élite who achieved greatness. Comparisons are difficult when standards of conduct have deteriorated. Gone are the days when illicit affairs, if discovered, led to resignations. John Profumo's adultery with Christine Keeler would be swept under the carpet like Alan Clarke's torrid affairs. Governments do not fall because of Members' misdemeanours. In the past Robin Cook might have left the Foreign Office because of his marriage break-up over his relationship with Gaynor Regan. He must have taken comfort from the French, who regard sexual matters as private. François Mitterand kept his mistress and illegitimate daughter at public expense, whilst the cavortings of Bill Clinton became extra-mural biological exercises. All fall short of the fact of the French President, Félix Faure, who died in the arms of a whore inside the Elysée palace.

So much for human frailties. Now the task of picking our Labour politicians whose efforts were significant. Aneurin Bevan is remembered as a stormy petrel, always vehement, ill-tempered, married to Jennie Lee, miner's daughter and staunch left-wing. Elected to the national executive and appointed Minister of Health and Housing in the 1945 Labour Government. His greatest achievement was the introduction of the Health Service in 1948, after painstaking negotiations with doctors and dentists. Little did he realise that the ideal would become a crippling financial commitment fifty years on. It was never anticipated by that social reformer and economist, Lord Beveridge, whose Report formed the basis of the post-war Welfare State. In committee I found this Oxford don meticulous in detail. He was conscious that the Welfare State was established by the Liberals in 1906, but hoped to foster self-reliance on the insurance principle, arguing that the State should help those who helped themselves. In his home he would talk about the abolition of Want. In the sphere of economics it was tempting to compare him with Lord Keynes. They made an interesting contrast, approaching the subject from different angles. Keynes was the deductive economist, beginning always from first principles, Beveridge inductively. Both men had covered a wide range of achievements; in Beveridge's case it began in those distant days when Winston Churchill, as Home Secretary, brought in the younger Beveridge at the suggestion of Sidney Webb, the social reformer and historian, to introduce the Labour Exchanges and unemployment insurance. Janet Beveridge, formidable Scottish lady, was an ardent supporter of his welfare views. I opposed her in an Oxford Union debate on education and was relieved to gain a close victory. From the Bevan era of flower power, Carnaby Street fashions, the Beatles and the oral contraceptive pill we have progressed to satellite communication, the Internet and the World Wide Web, Dolly the cloned sheep; science fiction has become fact, yet the basic problems that Nye tried to solve remain. Maybe Brown's windfall will provide the answer, but there will be no short-cut. Ethical and moral dilemmas will increase as science leaps forward. Technology gives more information, but we have to learn how to use it. Nye's dream intended that the Health Service must be for everybody, mainly funded from taxation, voluntary and local authority hospitals to be taken over, the sale and purchase of medical practice ended. That was his main contribution. He put them into the bill and never wavered from the principles. Rich or poor, anyone could use it or any part of it. It was a worthwhile epitaph to a distinguished political career.

At this point it is interesting to recall how the Labour Party came into existence. Its first two leaders were James Keir Hardie and James Ramsay MacDonald, both illegitimate sons of Scottish servant girls and reared in the poorest sections of Victorian society. Keir Hardie grew up in the slums of Glasgow, his stepfather working at Napier's shipyard. He never attended school and in mid-teens could not read or write. The family moved to Quarter, a colliery village, and the lad became a miner. Cured illiteracy; fellow miners elected him to Union office; at 24, sacked for being an agitator. Aim was to harness the trade unions to the new doctrine of Socialism;

founded the Scottish Labour Party, then the Independent Labour Party and became the first Labour M.P.

In many ways eccentric. Believed in re-incarnation and second sight. In 1900 the unions allied themselves with the Socialists to form the Labour Representation Committee. Six years later the committee returned 28 MPs who became a separate parliamentary party, the Labour Party.

As leaders of the new Labour Party, Hardie was a disaster. Details of policy bewildered him; at 54 gave up the parliamentary party chairmanship. His successor, Ramsay MacDonald, was a more astute character; in 1900 became secretary of the Labour Representation Committee with biological theories of Socialism, believing that an industrial society could grow towards collectivism. From 1906 he became the automatic front-bencher who challenged Ministers. 1911 elected chairman of the Labour Party. In 1924 became Prime Minister, the only manual worker to reach that position. As a minority administration dependent on Liberal support, there was no Socialist legislation, but he proved that Labour was fit to rule. His second Government in 1929, again relying on Liberal support, was a failure. Economic crisis led to a National Government with Conservatives and Liberals.

The stop-gap leader was George Lansbury; aged 72, the only Cabinet Minister to survive the 1931 landslide. The Party had only 46 MPs but formed a useful opposition. Pacifism caused a break. When delegates voted in favour of military sanctions against Mussolini's invasion of Abyssinia, Lansbury resigned.

As a stop-gap measure, Clement Attlee, Lansbury's deputy, was selected, the intention being it would be short-term. Instead he held the position, defeating Morrison and Greenwood in a ballot, and was never formally challenged again. Not only that, Attlee was to become an elder statesman of immense wisdom, experience and compassion. His six years as Prime Minister were a watershed in British political history; as Deputy Prime Minister during the war, his personality and administrative skill proved invaluable in steadying the nation's aim. Had few of the superficial qualities of leadership, not an orator, but was a skilful parliamentary debater with dry wit and said a lot in a few words. Opponents misjudged his cryptic realism. Sheep in sheep's clothing can produce a keen bite.

His manner was reserved, at times brusque, with great intellectual power, quiet judgement, making rapid decisions untroubled by afterthought. His Cabinet included dominating men like Ernest Bevin, Stafford Cripps and Herbert Morrison, but his authority, when he chose to exercise it, was total.

Clement Attlee is the only senior *statesman* of international standing the Labour Party has produced. No one in New Labour can equal that role.

Taking stock of other Labour politicians, there was Harold Wilson, who, forgetting childhood ambitions to become an undertaker, became at 48 the youngest Premier since Lord Rosebery. He was a mixture of extremes. Cultivated a pipe-smoking image; developed a sharp tongue in debate. He did not discourage the rumour that poverty as a boy meant he went to school without boots, to which Harold Macmillan had disarmingly replied, "If Harold Wilson ever went to school without boots, it was only because he was too big for them!"

Tony Blair imitated his bid to capture the young vote by inviting pop groups to No. 10 in the same way that Wilson wooed the support of the Beatles. The Member for Huyton liked the working-class image approach. He joined me at the Adelphi Hotel in Liverpool wearing a dirty DOM raincoat. Views could be contradictory. He opposed Britain's application to join the European Economic Community, then changed his mind. Membership was a priority, but he failed in successive attempts to join the Common Market. After visiting America in 1966, he announced that Britain and America shared common agreement in foreign policy, then a year later denied we had any special relationship with the United States. He announced that the remedy for our economic problems did not depend on devaluation, then unexpectedly devalued £-sterling by 14.3 per cent to 2.40 dollars, the third devaluation in three Labour Governments. He had the misfortune to have George Brown as Foreign Secretary, a man with as much gravitas as Robin Cook. Other similarities included the Gallup Poll of 1968 that showed Wilson's popularity lower than Neville Chamberlain's in 1940. Sir Alex Douglas-Home's comment has a familiar tone . . . "On the record of promise and performance, no one can any longer believe anything that the Prime Minister or his Ministers say." Leopards are reluctant to change their spots.

Ernest Bevin, trade-union leader and politician, illegitimate son of Mercy Bevin, a village midwife, had a tough childhood. Kitchen-boy, van-boy, page-boy, later conductor on a horse-drawn tram, he had much in common with John Prescot in his ambition to become a Member of Parliament. It was a long trail, but reactions after reaching the Commons were different. Prescot enjoys flaunting his temporary importance, urges restraint by motorists but owns two Jaguars; reluctant to walk a few yards to a Conference Hall in case his wife's hair is disturbed by the wind. Bevin by contrast disliked the charade of *nouveau riche,* but on one occasion tried deception. Due to speak at a meeting in the Cambridge Guildhall, he arrived at the University Arms Hotel in a large limousine, then changed to a clapped-out Baby Austin and drove to the market-place, politically correct. The main difference is that as Minister of Transport, Prescot is a failure, whereas Bevin, in spite of mistakes, was a great Foreign Secretary and strong man of the Attlee Government. His role as Minister of Labour and National Service in Churchill's wartime Government of 1940 was a pivotal post. As a member of the War Cabinet he was responsible for an enormous re-deployment of industrial workers with the minimum of trade union opposition. By 1943 almost a million workers had been transferred to industries vital to the war effort. Typical of the man, he refused the CH when offered it by Churchill as a reward for this work, saying it was just part of the job. He was a genuine Labour politician.

Emmanuel Shinwell's life spanned a century of change and the emergence of the Labour Party. Born in Spitalfields in the East End of London when Queen Victoria still had 17 years to reign, Marx had died the year before in 1883, and Bismarck was the first Chancellor of the German Empire, his life coincided with social and political upheaval. A link with today was Gladstone's preparations to deal with the Irish question – still unresolved, but Shinwell's first taste of politics came when he led the Clydeside dock strike in 1911, and he continued to be involved throughout the decades ahead.

Highlights were 2 months in jail for inciting a riot; elected to Parliament in 1922; Minister of Mines 1922; re-elected in 1928, the year when women were given the vote; 1930 Financial Secretary to the War Office; refused to join the alliance when Ramsay MacDonald formed the coalition National Government so as to keep the Premiership; offered the post of Minister of Food in Churchill's War Cabinet, but declined and remained in opposition; became Chairman of the Parliamentary Labour Party, 1950, aged 66, and Minister of Defence; Labour lost office in 1951. Steel had been nationalised; warned Hugh Gaitskill that the Labour Party could be split over the issue of the nuclear deterrent; Harold Wilson elected Prime Minister with a majority of 4.

Shinwell revolted when the Labour Government talked of entering the Common Market, a policy he vigorously opposed. Life peer in 1970, an honour coinciding with the first Russian spacecraft landing on the moon; resigned the Labour Whip in 1982 over the increased left-wing militancy in the Party; celebrated his century in 1984; died aged 101.

Shinwell had a full life in momentous years. No one could say he was a passive colleague. He quarrelled with most of his colleagues over policies. After giving support to Ramsay MacDonald, he became a fierce opponent, defeating him at Seaham Harbour in 1935; antagonised Sir William Connor of the *Daily Mirror* who, under the pen-name of *Cassandra*, castigated him as being . . . tetchy, testy, irritable, petulant, hasty, cautious, choleric and churlish. My last meeting with him was at Lord Edwin McAlpine's invitation. He assured the Labour peer he would also top the century-mark. Sadly it was not to be.

Winston Churchill, a great admirer of Emmanuel Shinwell, called him a great patriot.

Harold Macmillan was an enigma. Elected member of Parliament for Stockton-on-Tees in 1924. It was hardly a new experience: sixteen relatives were already in the House. Conscious of belonging to a ruling class, strengthened by marriage to Lady Dorothy Cavendish, talented daughter of the 9th Duke of Devonshire, he was offhand with Labour members. Even so, Harold Wilson considered him as the cleverest politician of our age with two provisos: not a statesman, nor a great Prime Minister. The put-down did not bother Macmillan, who once remarked that dealing with foreign affairs at home, he was regarded as a politician; handling the same problems abroad, his dealings were the findings of a statesman. Never short, like William Hague, of firing a broadside at Labour, he once described Socialist finance as reminiscent of a bucket shop, confidence man and three-card trickster.

He had a self-confident touch and rapport with the public. His record as Premier had many successes and few lows. About Britain's historic role in the world he would be eloquent, and had an absorbing interest in international affairs. I had several meetings, one in particular being different. I was present at the 10th Anniversary of the United Nations in San Francisco, attended by Harold Macmillan as our Foreign Secretary. The return flight entailed two refuelling stops – at Winnipeg and the American base on the North Pole. Scorching heat became Arctic temperatures. On landing we were taken to a Nissan-type canteen that matched a runway carved out of a glacier. Macmillan ordered a gin-and-tonic *with no ice*, talked in a relaxed way, automatically brushed down the side of his moustache, and talked in a detached way about the cold war and possible *détente* between East and West, the Common Market and the Atlantic Alliance. History remembers him by his speech in 1960 before the South African Parliament . . . "The wind of change is blowing through this continent and, whether we like it or not, the growth of national consciousness is a political fact. We must all accept it, and our national policies must take account of it." South African policy of apartheid was incompatible with continued membership of the Commonwealth and led to the decision not to re-apply for that status, but voluntary continuance within the British family of the nations about to attain independence vindicated Macmillan's policy.

I think of Alec Douglas-Home, whose leadership, disingenuous to professionals, nevertheless led to a marked Conservative recovery. The fourth successive Conservative leader in four General Elections, he did not fit into the pattern of his predecessors. Not cast in the classic mould of Churchill, unlike Eden who emerged unexpectedly out of crisis, and dissimilar to Macmillan, the supremo in the science of politics; Home never pretended to be anything but the disinterested amateur reluctantly called to high office.

He became Prime Minister with the party racked by dissensions and feuds bordering on civil war, transformed morale and unity. His open-minded qualities of honesty, sincerity and integrity appealed to the electorate. He promised to tell the public everything the Government was doing in simple language. He never pretended to be a deep or original thinker, but disarming simplicity masked a shrewd operator. As a psychologist he adopted Couéism with its repetitive slogan of "getting better and better every day" hoping for miracle cures. We have a copy-book parallel today with the fatuous parrot-cry of "education, education, education" – at least Home was able to claim positive results.

Two more Commons politicians. Enoch Powell, more prophet than politician; devoted Parliamentarian; vehement opponent of European integration, resisted any suggestion of surrender of national Sovereignty; never invited consensus; his misjudged and misquoted speech damned his political future when he warned there could be rivers of blood in this land if the tide of immigration was not reversed. Jack Straw, faced with this problem, must acknowledge the wisdom of the prophecy in less racist terms. It was not in Powell's nature to play the Party game; better to remember him as scholar, soldier and poet.

Jo Grimond is a forgotten leader, yet, at one stage, it looked as if his ideal was within sight. With Labour in total disarray and the Conservatives suffering disastrous electoral losses, the conditions seemed well set for the creation of a progressive, radical, non-Socialist party of the Left, of which the Liberals would form the nucleus and the inspiration. Such prospects had to be trimmed back and once again the Party faced yet another challenge to survival.

Nobody knew better than Jo Grimond how tough the role is for a Third Man in British politics, conditioned by its two-party system. Fighting on two fronts simultaneously, constantly facing the threat of total encirclement, only a high morale and a determined faith could ever hope to keep the party going.

We met on many occasions in London. He was confident that the Liberals would emerge with a substantially increased vote and more MPs. His optimism was justified. The spadework continued through the efforts of Steel and Ashcroft, but neither matched the rumbustious campaigning of Grimond. As a platform performer he was a rousing speaker and spirited orator, with an evangelical fervour which he seldom captured at Westminster. In conversation he projected a youthful image of Liberalism that appealed to a new generation of voters.

As leader he made his party a more progressive force, resolved their internal conflict between blue Whiggery and pink Radicalism, the end product being a tougher-muscled party. His main objective was to strengthen and enlarge the political Centre-to-Left. In the event of a dead heat, he would decide the balance of power. With today's Liberal leaders such muscle has become a pipe-dream with a Scottish accent. It is impossible to turn a selling-plater into a thoroughbred.

Looking across the Atlantic, I think of the leader of the Liberal Party in Canada, Lester Pearson, whom all Canadians and most foreigners knew as 'Mike'. As recipient of the Nobel Peace Prize, he was a source of pride to all Canadians regardless of party. Always boyish in appearance, there was secret iron behind the outward geniality. I was interested in his interpretation of Canada's position amid the changing problems of the world. It was a simple creed. He felt that Canada could always take a disinterested stand, in the sense that she could do what was right irrespective of what anybody else did. It was easier for Canadians because they had no national interests that were continually under examination or challenge at the United Nations. There was no need to feel superior or smugly virtuous. The importance of co-operating with their friends had always to be taken into consideration. Mike Pearson's middle-of-the-road philosophy still prevails.

Now two Americans . . . one controversial, the other outstanding. John Foster Dulles was America's most controversial Secretary of State. To some he was the original misguided missile, travelling fast, making lots of noise, and never hitting the target. His conduct of foreign affairs policy left the question unanswered whether he shaped events or adjusted himself to them. At times he was more preoccupied with the record of JFD on the pages of history than with history itself. Gregarious and sociable by nature, he was a genial dinner-table companion, lucid in exposition, open-minded in discussion. He was proud of his "brink of war" doctrine as evidence of mastery of the technique of foreign relationships: that he deliberately took America to the brink of war and saved the peace by his boldness. I believe there was an alternative motive. With Machiavellian skill he kept the Senate war-wing happy by his public pronouncements, while quietly paving the way for a settlement with the Communist world by his actual operations. Be that as it may, technically he initiated only two new policies . . . the Treaty of Alliance with Chiang Kai-shek and the Northern Tier policy in the Middle East which the British converted into the Baghdad Pact.

On a lighter note I remember flying back from New York on a Monarch aircraft. In those days the extended flight entailed two refuelling stops, in St. John's and Shannon. It was civilised in that we slept in bunks, undressed and relaxed. I had dinner with Claire Dulles, an attractive young lady, niece of JFD, then we retired to our respective beds. Lights dimmed, curtains drawn, when peace was disturbed by a passenger who had drunk too much. His bunk was above Claire's. To get in bed required a degree of dexterity even with the aid of steps. The drunk ignored such aids, swung himself up, missed the mark, parted the bunk curtains, both legs landing of Claire's chest. Losing his grip, the fellow collapsed on the floor and was escorted away by stewards. Steam-age-travel had its drawbacks. It was personal brinkmanship.

Adlai Stevenson was probably the most famous loser of all time. Two defeats by Eisenhower in the American Presidency Elections of 1952 and 1956 denied us the chance of what could well have been America's greatest President. The tone was set in his speech accepting the Democratic nomination in 1952 . . . "Better to lose the election than mislead the people; better lose than misgovern the people." In the classical sense, he was the finest orator America produced, eloquent in Churchillian manner. We met in Chicago; after lunch we drove round the city with an informative commentary. His clean-up in Illinois politics must have been instinctive. During that afternoon it was clear he was that rare phenomenon in public life, an active leader, by which I mean a practising statesman who was always thinking. Civilised, witty and profound, he talked of a world tour when he visited thirty countries in six months to broaden his education by meeting everyone from "cobblers to kings"; felt that possibly he had raised the standard of debate in America on domestic as well as foreign issues; recalled how after the war he headed the first economics mission sent by President Roosevelt to Italy after the landings at Salerno and the invasion of Sicily. The objective was to restore the economic well-being of the Italian people, a practical gesture for he felt the Italians had suffered twenty years of Fascism, trauma from the retreats of the German army. He found them in dire misery, poverty, malnutrition and hunger, often in appalling living conditions. He said it sounded pious, but someone had to do it.

It was refreshing to listen to such practical attitudes, unlike today where in the Commons we are indoctrinated to prefabricated clichés invented by spin doctors. On the evening of July 14th, 1965, Stevenson, then United States Ambassador to the United Nations, collapsed in Upper Grosvenor Street, Mayfair, on the pavement outside the International Sportsmen's Club. A doctor called out of the Club gave an injection and cardiac massage, but he died before reaching St. George's Hospital.

So passed a very great gentleman with one ambition unfulfilled. Both President John Kennedy and President Johnson passed him over as Secretary of State. It was faulty hypothetical judgement. Instead he accepted the post of United Nations Ambassador and was a significant voice in moulding foreign policy.

The name *Adlai* came from the Bible. It means *the Just* . . . a fitting epitaph to a most just man.

JULIUS RAAB

JULIUS RAAB WAS UTTERLY UNEMOTIONAL without the slightest trace of humour. He was a tough man. I met him in the Chancellery in Vienna a few hours before the Treaty of Independence was signed. At that time he had re-orientated Austrian policy. Three years earlier, Dr. Figl, then Chancellor and later Minister of Foreign Affairs, referred to Austria as "a fortress, a wedge driven into the Eastern front". Eighteen months later Vice-Chancellor Scharf, leader of the socialists, declared, "a so-called policy neutrality – a courtship with Russia – will not bring us nearer to liberty. That is why we refuse all invitations to such escapades". Julius Raab went further. He announced that the Austrian Government would adopt a neutrality as complete as that of Switzerland. His bargaining with

Russia received unanimous endorsement by the Lower House.

When I questioned the policy reversal, the Chancellor argued that the Austrian electorate was no less anti-Communist than before, nor had he forgotten how his country's recovery was largely due to Western aid, but he knew on which side Austria's bread was buttered. I suggested that the "neutrality" visualised in the Treaty might become a passive condition. The Chancellor disagreed. He stressed that the role of mediator was not new to Austria. His aim was to develop goodwill on both sides of the frontiers and he was convinced that the Austrian action had lessened the threat of war in Europe. He emphasised that Austria would not join any military coalition, or permit the use of bases or admit foreign troops on her soil. Obviously Raab expected a boon for Austria as a trading-post with the East.

Years have passed since this Treaty. It is interesting to take stock. Raab was a patriot-Shylock exacting for his country the last ounce of flesh and blood. Coldly realistic, he ignored short-term advantages, but was no seer. Little could he have imagined that the European Union would one day threaten to suspend Austrian membership if it breached the EU's founding principles of democracy, liberty and respect for human rights. He would have been shocked to hear Louis Michel, Belgian Foreign Minister, argue for the expulsion of Austria . . . "I think that Europe can very well do without Austria, We don't need it."

The reason for such spleen was the inclusion in 2000 of Jorg Haider's far-Right Freedom Party in a coalition Government. In Raab's time, Haider would have been ostracised because of Nazi sympathies. His father, Robert Haider, was a prominent member of the Nazi Party; mother, Dorothea, an official in the League of German Girls, counterpart of the Hitler Youth. When the Americans came, Horder was forced to supervise execution of mass graves in which thousands of slave labourers were buried after digging a network of defensive tunnels. Alarmed by the reaction of the European Union, Jorg Haider backtracked, apologised and withdrew from the Government, but still has ambitions to be Austrian Chancellor leading a Government with far-Right Freedom Party majority . . . so much for Austrian neutrality in the Millennium.

Turning back the clock, I recall that memorable day in Vienna.

I stood in the Belvedere Palace during the signing of the Treaty of Independence restoring the freedom that died in March 1938, when German troops goose-stepped into Austria. After the ceremony, the bells of Vienna pealed as Herr Figl, Austrian Minister for Foreign Affairs, appeared on the balcony and joined hands with Molotov, Pinay, Harold Macmillan and Foster Dulles in a symbolic gesture. During drinks afterwards, Molotov went on the balcony to resounding cheers from thousands of Communist supporters. Foster Dulles, in our group, realising what was happening, went to the next balcony, waved a handkerchief, but had muted response.

The official banquet held in the Schoenbrunn Palace – the Versailles of Vienna – was attended by guests resplendent with uniforms, decorations and exquisite gowns. In the Great Gallery, where Mozart once played, I listened to *The Blue Danube* played by the Vienna Philharmonic Symphony Orchestra conducted by Kurt Bohm, also the *Radetzky March* played with unbelievable gusto. In the flood-lit grounds, the Austrian National Ballet performed against a backcloth of cascading fountains. Thousands of Viennese celebrated in the streets. Bands played in the Stalinplatz. It was a night of nationalistic pride. There was one discordant note. The Soviet delegation were reluctant to attend the function. Diplomacy won the day. The double-doors of the Great Gallery opened. Grim-faced Russians entered in wedge-formation with Molotov in the centre, guests brushed aside as the cavalcade exited through the opposite doors. No word spoken. Protocol had been observed.

On that occasion, there was no chance of meeting Molotov. That opportunity came at the Tenth Anniversary of the United Nations in San Francisco. Molotov occupied a large house some thirty miles from San Francisco protected by razor-wire, bodyguards and roaming guard-dogs. Only with help from the Russian Embassy did I enter the citadel. Meeting the most evil man of this century was thought-provoking. Vyacheslav Mihailovitch Scriabin was his real name, but the seventeen-year-old nephew of the composer preferred the *nom de guerre* translated *The Hammer,* later becoming *Molotov.* Initial reaction was anti-climax. Instead of a menacing figure, this trafficker in torture and death came into the room, pallid, stocky, in nondescript suit, rimless glasses, gunmetal wristwatch, typical suburban nonentity of anonymity, yet he was a mass murderer. There was no warmth, glacial, every answer guarded, almost monosyllabic.

His record was extraordinary. He had held the high offices of Prime Minister, Chairman of the Council of People's Commissars and Commissar for Foreign Affairs. He implemented the ruthless Five-Year Plan that turned Russia from an agricultural State into an industrial nation by collectivizing the farms, the transformation leaving a trail of 10,000,000 victims who died from floggings, torture and murder. Never has one man committed such crimes against humanity. Molotov was a survivor. He condoned Trotsky's banishment to Mexico, where Stalin's agent murdered him with an ice-axe; lived through Litvinov's reign; saw dictators like Lenin and Stalin fall from grace; watched as their embalmed bodies were reinterred at the foot of the Kremlin Wall. Molotov continued to hold the reins of power, carrying out the Central Party purges that included the Secret Police. Even after Malenkov lost favour, Molotov still held office under Khrushchev. Nothing weakened his image as symbol of Soviet power.

Touching on incidents in this catalogue of intrigue and murder, left Molotov unconcerned. Routine tasks were carried out. Only twice did he have positive reactions. His dislike of Lenin led to a diatribe about his flawed policies. The second was the feeling of betrayal when Hitler tore up the Molotov Ribbentrop Pact of 1939 that led to German troops marching into Moscow suburbs, precipitating the Russians lining-up with the Allied Forces. It was all academic stuff, but never was there any suggestion of remorse for atrocities he had sanctioned.

Eventually Molotov was exiled to Siberia. An ailing nonagenarian, he waited for death. If justice has any meaning for the Almighty, the gates of purgatory and hell should have opened. Maybe they were . . . I sincerely hope so.

BEN-GURION

Ben-Gurion, the man who established his people in their Promised Land, never relinquished his role as a visionary or allowed himself to forget the horror of Hitler's rule in Europe. Nothing blurred the memory of the *Einstzkommandos,* the gas-wagons or the slaughterhouses. But the campaign exacted a toll on his health. Thrombosis symptoms led to frequent private visits to England and the recommended calm of a Cotswold inn. It was the doctor's order and gave him an opportunity to indulge with his wife, Paula, their absorbing hobby as bibliophiles. It was books – books – and more books, plus the joy of being able to browse, away from the press in bookshops, sometimes in the Charing Cross Road, but mostly Blackwell's in Oxford. Subject-matter was varied, including Greek, Roman, Hebrew and ancient philosophers. I suggested Heffer's of Cambridge could match the Blackwell shelves. He put it to the test, found Reuben Heffer more than helpful, but the "discoveries" disappointing by comparison with Oxford.

Only once did Ben-Gurion voice thoughts on his homeland. On the journey to Cambridge, he expressed fears that the next generation, who had never known Hitler, would take the State of Israel for granted and forget that there were still enemies demanding its destruction. Those doubts have since proved only too true. He talked like the Founding Father, but once back in the Inn all became forgotten as the purchases were examined.

ABDUL AZIZ

PRINCE SULTAN BIN ABDUL AZIZ, Servant of the Mighty One, was one of the most powerful figures in the Middle East. In his capacity as Minister of Defence and Deputy Prime Minister of Saudi Arabia, he accompanied King Faisal, King Khaled and King Fahd on all State visits abroad. I had occasion to visit him at his Geneva house, stronghold would be a more apt description, overlooking the lake. He was to inspect a Mobile Hospital that I had designed and produced, the brain-child of the combined planning and experience of English and American surgeons and doctors. The brief was to incorporate facilities adequate to deal with any emergency, the result was the equivalent of St. Thomas' Hospital on wheels.

The reason for the check-inspection was for possible use by King Khaled, whose two concerns in life were hunting and a heart condition. Medical and surgical facilities in the hospital would enable the King to enjoy hunting with the reassuring thought that in the wings would be the unit staffed by specialists, doctors and nurses . . . naturally all the fittings and trim would be in gold.

The Sultan showed particular interest in the surgical equipment. Surrounded by entourage, military and medical, he turned to one of his minions, took the unfortunate man's ear, twisted it and asked the surgeon if he cut it off, could it be sewn back. Being told it would be possible, he picked up a scalpel and went through the motions of performing the operation. Everyone laughed except the unfortunate victim, who, pale and upset, clearly thought the experiment was for real . . . such is Arabic humour. Afterwards, over the inevitable tea with Prince Turki, the liquid poured out of the teapot was gin, with tonic in a jug – rigid observance of Islamic laws sidepassed. Later that night over dinner, I suggested it could be possible to design a mobile mortuary suitably equipped with gold fittings as a back-up vehicle. The Sultan expressed the hope that the thought was premature. It did not prove so.

Prince Turki, who became Commander-in-Chief of the Saudi Airforce and the first Royal prince to pilot sub-sonic jets, stayed for a time in London during fighter-bombing training. His house in Sussex Gardens bristled with electronic safety devices. Inside it was furnished in typical Saudi fashion. Main lounge had twelve-seater settee with wings, centre cushion raised to indicate royal status, dominated by large painting of Prince Sultan. His daughter, a very pretty girl, was married to Prince Turki. On a tour of the house, the main bedroom had a massive bed with headboard lined with royal suede with intricate switch-board on a side table. Each had a gadget-purpose. One in particular caused a large television set to rise at the foot of the bed.

As Prince Turki's wife was expecting her first baby, he showed us the nursery which he had planned, centre-piece being an elaborate cot costing several thousand pounds. When Jean suggested this should be her choice, he pointed out that in Saudi women had an inferior role. The top floor had elaborate decor with countless cushions strewn over the floor, setting for a thousand-and-one-nights! One final personal note. We had a visitation from Prince Turki and entourage to the Old Mill House. Walking in the grounds, they went into a Gothic-style Orangery. The trees were heavy with oranges. Turki picked one, took off the peel and ate it. As the fruit of these trees, like the lemons, are regarded as ornamental not for consumption, I waited for him to collapse. All was well, but it seemed like cannibalism.

ONE FINAL VIGNETTE. Had it not been for the Second World War, judgement on Winston Churchill would have been different . . . different in degree rather than substance. At the outbreak of hostilities he was on the verge of seventy-five years of age. Then occurred one of those rare moments in history when the hour called for a man of unique qualities. That man was at hand. There was almost historic propriety when the Prime Minister kissed hands.

Churchill's power was oratory. Here was a torrent of words that the Elizabethans would have relished. His speeches alone perpetuate the memory. Those who came after us can never know what they meant to those who listened. In moments close to defeat, they assumed the dimensions of an act for those who were powerless to act themselves . . . *I have nothing to offer but blood, toil, tears and sweat* . . . It was a touch of psychological genius. And again . . . *What General Weygand called the Battle of France is over. I expect that the Battle of Britain is about to begin. Let us therefore brace ourselves to our duty and so bear ourselves that if the British Commonwealth and Empire lasts for a thousand years men will say "this was their finest hour."*

His leadership was undoubtedly aided by the experience from innumerable departments. He had presided over each of the Fighting Services, Board of Trade, Home Office, Admiralty, Ministry of Munitions, Secretary of War, Colonial Office, Air Ministry, the Treasury, and Prime Minister. Apart from Robert Peel and Chatham, no one has possessed such comprehensive knowledge of the tasks of so many departments of government.

Winston Churchill deserved well of England. He epitomised an age. His departure echoed that national feeling. For three bitterly cold and very grey days in January 1965, Sir Winston Churchill lay in state in Westminster Hall in the heart of the Houses of Parliament. Thousands filed past the coffin by day and all through the night. With a chosen few, we entered the Hall and watched quietly in the wings. The silence was audible. The Service Chiefs of Staff as their own mark of respect had taken over the watch at the catafalque. It was the most poignant moment of the decade.

CHAPTER SIX

PIONEERS

~

HE SCOTT POLAR RESEARCH INSTITUTE in Cambridge is packed with interest. Over the main entrance is a bust of Scott, modelled by his widow, Kathleen, Lady Scott (later Lady Kennet). Along the roof balustrade is the inscription *Quaesivit arcana Poli videt dei* – "He sought the secrets of the Pole: he found the hidden face of God." On the left of the entrance, as a memorial to Scott's polar party, is a statue by the same sculptor of a boy with arms outstretched, titled *Aspiration*. "The front of the building is composed of two large arches suggesting the two poles. Small balls lie behind the arches vaulted with domes of the same arc as the polar regions of the globe" – such was the description of the architect, Sir Herbert Barker. Inside, coloured diagrammatic maps of the two polar regions are encircled by the names of their explorers. Below the domes, stars are set in the marble floor in the polar constellation, the Southern Cross for the Antarctic, the Great Bear for the Arctic.

The Institute was founded as a memorial to Captain Robert Falcon Scott and his companions who perished on their return from the South Pole in March 1912. The emotional reaction to that tragic journey and Scott's last letter to the Lord Mayor of London was the opening of an appeal fund at the Mansion House. The response was so overwhelming that, after the needs of the surviving dependants had been met, a substantial balance remained. Frank Debenham, a member of Scott's last expedition, and the first Professor of

Geography at Cambridge, proposed that an Institute of Polar Research should be founded in Cambridge to encourage polar exploration and research, and act as a centre where polar explorers could meet, exchange views and plan future research projects. His ambition was realised. In November 1934, the Institute was officially opened by Stanley Baldwin, then Prime Minister and Chancellor of the University.

The relics are part of history. The diaries of Scott and Wilson record the day's work in firm, legible handwriting, a glimpse of a life completely cut off from the rest of the world. Equally revealing are the diaries of Lady Franklin, Sir John Franklin's second wife. We see the sleeping-bag of Captain Oates, with one leg cut where he was frostbitten, and the statue of Fridtjof Nansen, the Norwegian explorer and statesman, who in 1893 sailed for the Arctic with Johansen in the *Fram* and reached 86° 14'N on foot. There are examples of the art and cultures of the Eskimos: water-colour sketches made by Wilson during Scott's two Antarctic Expeditions and a signed photograph of the Queen which Vivian Fuchs took with him on the South Pole Expedition.

The Institute is Frank Debenham's dream come true. He was a remarkable man. During his years at Cambridge, he became something of a folk legend, a role that appealed to his Australian temperament. During term he would often hold court in an upstairs cafe in Regent Street that produced excellent coffee and crisp rolls. Occasionally Edward Welbourne, the Master of Emmanuel College, would join us and invariably act as Devil's Advocate in any discussion – being bloody-minded was second nature. The only one to take the bait would be Gordon Manley, President of the Royal Meteorological Society and an expert on polar climatology. One of Welbourne's snide remarks was that Debenham only joined Scott by the back door. There was a grain of truth about it. When Scott and Dr Wilson visited Sydney on their way south for the journey to the Pole, Debenham was a sociologist at Sydney University working on the results of the Shackleton Expedition. Scott, anxious to involve Australia in the project to strengthen the scientific side, invited Debenham to join the team. The recollection of those days never left Debenham. He used to say that stay-at-homes could never visualise the hazards. Antarctica is a continent larger than Europe

LEFT: Jean Rook, then the highest paid journalist in Fleet Street, with Alan Frame, editor of the *Daily Express*, and his wife Ann.

BELOW: Louis Stanley in conversation with Edith Sitwell. It was like entertaining a living Holbein.

ABOVE: Ingrid Bergman. "She evokes the sadness of things supremely well . . . the quality she possesses is more than beauty: it is strangeness in beauty."

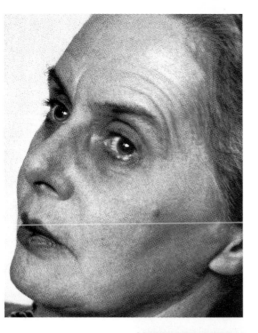

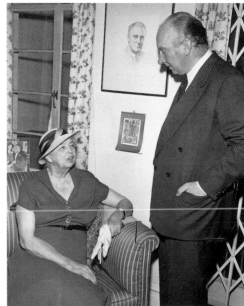

ABOVE: Ninette de Valois, a dancer turned choreographer. She founded, fostered, directed and held together the Sadler's Wells Company.

ABOVE RIGHT: Eleanor Roosevelt, the only First Lady to hold her own Press Conferences.

RIGHT: Louis Stanley with Daphne du Maurier. Menabilly can be seen in the background—linked with the haunting Manderley of *Rebecca*.

RIGHT: Clement Attlee who become an elder statesman of immense wisdom, experience and compassion. His six years as Prime Minister were a watershed in British political history.

BELOW: John Foster Dulles, America's most controversial Secretary of State.

BELOW RIGHT: Ernest Bevin disliked the charade of the *nouveau riche*.

ABOVE: The author with social reformer and economist, Lord Beveridge, whose Report formed the basis of the post-war Welfare State.

ABOVE: Harold Macmillan who had a self-confident touch and rapport with the public. His record as Premier had many successes and few lows.

LEFT: The author with Adlai Stevenson, the most famous loser of all time, with two defeats by Eisenhower in the American presidency.

RIGHT: Ben Gurion, the man who established his people in their Promised Land, never relinquished his role as a visionary or allowed himself to forget the horror of Hitler's rule in Europe.

BELOW: Louis Stanley with Julius Raab in the Chancellerey in Vienna. Coldly realistic, the Chancellor ignored short-term advantages, but was no seer.

ABOVE: The Cold War thaws as Ronald Reagan and Mikhail Gorbachev enjoy conversation.

LEFT: Winston Churchill whose speeches perpetuate his memory. Those who came after can never know what those speeches meant to those who listened.

RIGHT: Martin Ryle, Astronomer Royal, became a dominant figure in the controversy between the Big Bang and Steady State schools of cosmology.

ABOVE: Louis Stanley about to embark on the first commercial flight from Los Angeles over the North Pole to Europe.

BELOW AND RIGHT: Sir Malcolm Campbell and his son Donald broke speed records for over 42 years.

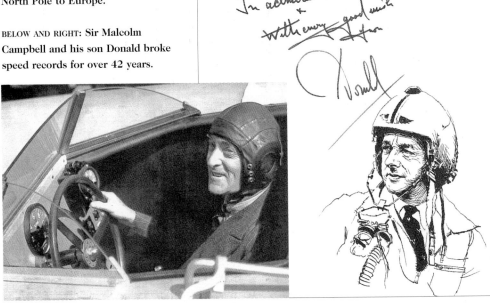

RIGHT: The architect Ove Arup whose imaginative flair was responsible for the Sydney Opera House.

BELOW: The mountaineer Harry Tilman. Together with Noel Odell he conquered Nanda Devi (below right), a 26,640 foot Himalayan mountain, and for 14 years the highest climbed by man.

LEFT: King George VI greeting Frank Stranahan during the 1948 Open Golf Championship.

RIGHT: The author with Peter Townsend.

BELOW: Louis and Jean Stanley talking to Prince Edward with Stirling Moss outside The Dorchester Hotel at the Park Lane Grand Prix.

ABOVE: Queen Elizabeth II and Prince Philip. Their partnership has been a blending of constancy and mutual affection, lightened at times by Prince Philip's honest gaffes.

LEFT: The author about to shake hands with Prince Philip. Mohamed Al Fayed is in the immediate background.

ABOVE: The author and his wife Jean in convivial
conversation with Prince Charles.

RIGHT: The Queen and Princess Margaret leave Skye for the royal yacht *Britannia*.

RIGHT: Princess Margaret awaits the delights of a masked ball.

with an area of some 5,400 square miles, or sixty times the size of Britain. On that score the Fuchs Expedition was a source of irritation. He felt the coverage by the media over-dramatised the situation when questions were raised whether the journey back could be made within the safety time-scale. Sir Leslie Martin, the architect, asked over dinner at the Old Mill House if such fears were justified and how the situation compared with Scott's plight. Debenham pointed out that such a comparison was difficult because conditions were so different.

He felt that Fuchs' expedition was feather-bedded. It only had to take equipment and provisions to the Pole. There it found shelter at an American research station, mechanical snowcats, tracked vehicles, radio links, even plane-surveillance. As regards the return journey, once the polar plateau and the formidable Beardsmore Glacier had been conquered, everything was plain sailing. He outlined the route in detail with the aid of cruets on the dining-table, like plotting a journey from Liverpool along the M6, coping with Spaghetti Junction, then the M1 and home.

The Scott Expedition set off on the 2nd November 1911 on a round journey of more than 1,700 miles without radio links and largely without maps. Beyond the Beardsmore Glacier, supply caches had to be established en route. The men were on foot because the dog parties had been sent back. Then came the terrible disappointment. They reached the Pole on the 17th January, 1912, to find the Norwegian flag had been planted a month earlier. They retraced their steps in worsening weather, had to reduce rations and suffered appallingly in blizzards that never lessened. There was an accident to Evans that led to his death through injuries, gangrene and frostbite and caused Oates to leave his tent during a blizzard to certain death, and the weakness that sapped the strength of Scott, Wilson and Bowers when only 11 miles from the One Ton Camp. The storm that never abated for 10 days led the three men to perish.

To Frank Debenham that saga was engraved in letters of gold. On many scores he felt the Fuch's Expedition fell short of what Scott's men had achieved. Even so, Scott would have acknowledged that the Fuchs Expedition was a significant feat.

The large bright orange motorised vehicles weighed between three and four tons and carried 22 tons of fuel, and almost cost

Fuchs his life. During the trek, his Sno-cat almost plunged down a crevasse. Miraculously each end of its caterpillar tracks clung to the top of the crevasse's ice walls, otherwise it would have fallen into oblivion. The rescue operation was complex and involved five other vehicles. Forty years later such recollections were relived at a reunion dinner in Cambridge. Six members were still alive, but widows of the others were also present. I often saw Vivien in Cambridge, 97 years of age, quietly doing domestic shopping in Newnham. None of the assistants in a butcher's corner shop had any idea of his identity or exploits, but he was happy with anonymity. After he died, a Memorial Service was held in St. John's College Chapel.

Returning to the Scott Polar Institute, I referred to the statue of the boy by the entrance, a lifesize naked figure with arms outstretched of the explorer's son. For many years we had a nanny who confessed that such was her modesty she always averted her gaze when passing it. The boy grew up to be Sir Peter Scott, the painter, conservationist, naturalist, sportsmaster and writer. In his last message home before he died, Scott had urged Kathleen to make his son interested in natural history, which was better than sport. It was in connection with the Wildfowl and Wetlands Trust at Slimbridge that he dined in the Old Mill House, sitting in the chair where Debenham described his father's expedition. I mentioned about our nanny's shyness at seeing him in the buff. They met for a few minutes, happily before the full Monty trend.

Peter Scott felt the Polar explorers were a race apart – men who seek the secrets of this vast continent. My interest was sharpened by being on the first commercial flight from Los Angeles to the magnetic North Pole. The SAS prop-engined plane refuelled at Winnipeg, eventually landing on a runway carved out of a glacier, just walls of ice on either side. The flight lasted over 24 hours – from scorching heat to below-zero temperature.

One postscript about 'Bunny' Fuchs. Although in his 90s, he overcame physical disability. A stroke left his right side partially paralysed so he taught himself to write with his left hand. He told me it was a throwback to polar experience. The Antarctic is a totally unfriendly place and you needed discipline to cope. That determination survived.

LORD BRABAZON OF TARA

LORD BRABAZON WAS ANOTHER MAN who achieved so much in so many fields. It is hard to describe his influence to anyone who did not feel the impact of his personality. Much of what he achieved has vanished through the sieve of memory. He held the Aviator's Certificate No.1 of the *Fédération Aeronautique Internationale,* dated 8 March 1910. Some thirty years later he marked that occasion by securing a personal car number, FLY 1. He won the £1000 prize offered by the *Daily Mail* for a circular flight of one mile by flying a hotch-potch of a flying machine at an average height of 40 feet. He won the *Circuit des Ardennes* in 1907 in a Minetva, and was not only one of the earliest riders on the Cresta toboggan run but the oldest when in his seventies. During the war he was Minister of Transport, then in charge of Aircraft Production. At the English Golf Union Executive Meetings the routine became almost standard. He offered me a cigar, then a cigarette, followed by tobacco, and finally snuff before accepting the fact that I was a non-smoker. His fund of stories was constant, a favourite being his reference to the Opposition in the Commons as "a lot of inverted Micawbers waiting for something to turn up". The Blair set-up would have given more scope for vituperation.

DONALD CAMPBELL

SIR MALCOLM CAMPBELL and his son Donald made headline news for over 42 years, a span of remarkable achievements. Malcolm became one of the most successful speed record-breakers on both land and water. Between 1924 and 1935 he broke the land-speed record nine times, raising it to 301.13 mph. When he turned to boats, he broke the water-speed record three times, raising it to 141.75 mph. His son continued the record-breaking sequence and reached 328 mph in a last fatal attempt on the water-speed record.

Donald I knew better than his father, for, as a family, we were responsible for the design and build of both Bluebird I and II, as well as contributing to financing the quest for the world land-speed record.

Both men were different in many ways. Each had individual

marks of style and personal traits, but shared skill and courage. In the motor racing world where speed is the essence, the challenge at times left drivers frightened. Donald felt the same way. He once said that he doubted whether anyone who had to control tremendous speeds did not sometimes feel fear.

He raised the subject at a dinner party where one of our guests was Pedro Rodriguez, the little Mexican who was to become a BRM driver the following season. The prospect we felt was exciting, for he had the reputation of being utterly fearless, a dedicated professional who left nothing to chance, an assessment he confirmed in a big way. He was surprised to be asked if he felt fear in a racing car. After a few minutes thought, he replied that once the race started the only emotion was exhilaration, which increased if the car was competitive. The trying period was waiting on the grid once the mechanics had left the track. The seconds counted on the official board were like an eternity. The only feeling was of total isolation, of rising tension tantamount to a form of fear – purgatory would be a truer description – but once the flag dropped, it disappeared. Pedro returned the question. Donald thought there were differences. In his case the competitive element was missing. It was purely a technical challenge which still tested nerves up to the split-second. It was not so much fear, just a feeling of inevitability. He asked Pedro what were the psychological after-effects of a crash. He replied that provided there was no physical injury, it was essential to get out again as soon as possible in the spare car, which more than anything helped to restore confidence, but it was not always as simple as that if injuries were involved. The return to the track was critical. Sometimes mental reactions and judgement had been affected, often without the driver realising it. He was no longer in contention. The competitive urge had lessened. In extreme cases it was advisable to quit before it was too late. At this point the counsel of an experienced team manager could help.

In Donald's case it was again difficult to make comparisons. Crashes at such speeds meant survival was largely a matter of luck. Donald recalled the horrific accident at Utah that should have killed him but was miraculously averted by designer skill in the build of the car. One of the hazards was the after-effects of a decelerating G-force from 400 mph to 0 in a matter of seconds, but the fear factor did not play a significant part. The language of strain came later – if there was an afterwards.

The subject of superstition came up. Pedro said that he had faith in the protective powers of a tiny gold cross that he always wore. Other drivers had a variety of quirks ranging from lucky and unlucky numbers; routine in dressing, colours, particularly green; even the misfortune of seeing only one magpie. Donald confessed to the belief that he was in touch with his father and relied on his approval for making vital decisions. I remember one such occasion when everything was set for a test run. Nothing happened. The thumbs-up sign was ignored. Donald announced that the test would have to be cancelled. He had received a communication from his father to that effect. That was that. I was tempted to say he might have had the wrong number. There was no point in arguing.

Pedro was asked if he feared dying. His reply was fatalistic. The death of his younger brother, Ricardo, in practice for the Mexican Grand Prix, had a traumatic effect on their family, but he decided to continue with his racing career. If he was killed, he did not believe it was the end. That faith was ever-present. Donald's attitude was an almost constitutional indifference to danger. He once told me he was not afraid of death. In the end it was the challenge that claimed their lives. Both lived more in their time than most men who survive many years longer.

The postscript to that dinner part was the funeral in Mexico City when thousands paid tribute to Pedro as the cortège went through the streets; and Donald's helmet and teddy bear mascot, Mr Woppy, taken from Coniston Water after the fatal water-speed record, the only physical reminders of that sad morning. I feel that tragedy might have been averted. He telephoned very early to say he was about to make the official run. Sleepily I asked had the course been swept. "As much as possible. It was imperative that a new record could be announced at the opening of the Boat Show later that morning. The odds against hitting floating debris would be 1000-to-1." Sadly that bet was lost.

SIR OVE ARUP

FOR OVER A CENTURY THE RIBA has recommended to the Sovereign that its annual Gold Medal for Architecture should be given to a specific architect. Only on two occasions has this tradition been broken. In 1960 it went to Pier Luigi Nervi, the Italian engineer, then a few years later the Award was given to Ove Arup, the consulting engineer, for significant contribution to modern architecture. The honour was deserved. This lean, ascetic-looking Dane with powerful profile and domed head had a rare facility for getting to the meat of any difficult problem. His views were always challenging. He would pose a series of rhetorical questions without giving an answer, ones that are never completely resolved. He queried what is the fundamental difference between an architect and engineer; at what point should they collaborate? The question of loyalty raised all sorts of difficulties – should it be to the client, to the architecture, to architecture with a capital A, or to his own engineering principles; should he look after stability and advise the architect about the cost of alternative solutions; were there occasions when the engineer ought to declare a project too silly for words, as assuredly Arup would have dismissed the Millennium Dome?

Whilst architects see themselves as master-builders, Arup worried that great architecture was often produced by people who didn't care a damn about sensible building. They become over-excited about Corbière visions, Miesian aesthetics and Louis Kahn's towers, but seem uninterested in according any consideration to the people condemned to live with and in their creations. Arup categorised architects into three categories . . . the Art-boys, the System-boys and the One-off boys. It is interesting to apply the test to the past.

I think of Sir Patrick Abercrombie, who campaigned for the Green Belt around London; Sir Ebenezer Howard, who originated the first Garden cities at Letchworth and Welwyn; Sir Edward Lutyens, who blended classical Renaissance style with Indian elements in the inspiring Viceroy's House in Delhi and the symbolic Cenotaph in Whitehall; Sir Basil Spence's architectural splendour in Coventry Cathedral when he commissioned Graham Sutherland,

John Piper to blend tapestry, glass and sculpture in his vision, adding the imaginative touch of bombed ruins of the old cathedral to recall past horrors. In stark contrast were the designs of Frank Lloyd Wright with the spiral ramp rising from a circular plan of the Guggenheim Museum, also the house in Falling Water, near Pittsburgh, with cantilevered terraces across a waterfall.

There is no shortage of imaginative choice but for flair Ove Arup takes pride of place for the Sydney Opera House with its series of forty-six concrete shells that hover over the auditoria like billowing sails. The build-up speaks for itself. Sixty engineers working in London spent 250,000 man-hours on the project. Computerised calculations drew the rounded shapes of the shells that rise as high as 179 feet. Arup devised a system of prefabricating the shells out of precast units by designing them as segments of one large theoretical sphere, broken into rib units like orange pieces. Simple but on a huge scale. The largest shell was vast enough to house a twelve-storey block of flats. It was architecturally advanced and ahead of its time.

Engineers often carry slide-rules in their breast pockets. Arup was different. Chop-sticks protruded. Whenever food lent itself to this custom, he preferred to eat with them and often insisted guests should so the same, wickedly enjoying their difficulties. On two occasions, I ducked out by using conventional table weapons.

A Scottish Pioneer

Sir Ian Stewart was an industrialist with wide-reaching interests, including BEA, Eagle Star Insurance, Royal Bank of Scotland, Beaverbrook Press, and the PR company, Industrial Connections. A keen golfer, he was a one-time Captain of the Royal and Ancient Golf Club. He enjoyed a rich life of action. Unassuming, with a rich Scottish accent, Stewart presided over innumerable meetings, business lunches and dinners, but few knew him well. It was only after playing golf with him on the Old Course at St. Andrews that I realised how in Scotland he was regarded as a revolutionary industrialist through his vigorous campaign to reduce unemployment and rejuvenate Clydeside. It was linked with his Fairfields Shipyard Plan, a five-year project that envisaged a labour-saving experiment to cut through crippling Trade Union regulations and encourage a worker's voice in management.

The scheme had been tried in England without success. Ian's aim was to bridge the gulf between the bosses and the workers, break down petty suspicions between Unions. He had carpenters doing painters' work when necessary and Union men sitting in the boardroom. The experiment won the approval of George Brown at the DEA, Jim Callaghan at the Treasury, and Ray Gunter at the Ministry of Labour. Unfortunately the plan was never put to a full test. Stewart admitted that a mistake was made by allowing Fairfields to enter the disastrous Upper Clyde Shipbuilders Merger. He agreed to serve as Deputy Chairman, given the assurance that the methods successfully used at Fairfields would be adopted, plus the recommendations of the industry's working party. This did not happen. Stewart resigned after two months, predicting failure. The scheme ended in bankruptcy fifteen months later.

It was an imaginative experiment that commanded considerable support, particularly from Sean Connery, who was so taken by Stewart's vision that he visited Glasgow to see for himself how it worked. He decided to make a documentary about Clydeside problems, producing *The Bowler and the Bunnet*. For the benefit of Sassenachs, a *bunnet* is the Lowland Scots equivalent of the flat cap. It was written and directed by Connery in a matter of weeks, but he failed to sell it to Regional Independent Television or the BBC. The documentary was good of its kind and highlighted the progress made by Stewart at Fairfields. Stewart and Connery next became involved in other interests with a Scottish flavour, like the establishment of a Merchant Bank, Dunbar and Company, in Pall Mall in 1971; after talking with Cubby Broccoli, Connery agreed to do another James Bond film for a fee of 1.2 million dollars, plus a percentage. Every cent earned would go to the newly-formed Scottish International Educational Trust, which had Sir Samuel Curran, Vice-Chancellor of Strathclyde University, as chairman and Ian Stewart among the trustees.

Such were some of the Scottish activities of this unassuming industrialist. I recall once, over a drink with Sean Connery and the Earl of Westmorland, Ian light-heartedly remarking how nice it was to own a bank. Tragically not long afterwards he died of cancer.

ACADEMIC PIONEERS

IN 1933 PUBLIC INTEREST WAS ROUSED through the unexpected purchase from the Russian Government of the oldest and most precious Biblical treasure in the world, the *Codex Sinaiticus,* for £100,000. Thousands viewed the manuscript when it was exhibited in the British Museum. Nor was it just idle curiosity. When the purchase was completed nearly £65,000 had been raised by public subscriptions – donations came from all over the country in pennies and pounds. In a very real way the *Codex* was a national treasure.

The first wave of excitement subsided to be succeeded by complete silence. Months passed into years. No mention was made of the *Codex*. There were rumours it had not come up to expectations: a facsimile reproduction would have been equally good; that it had been a waste of public money. Such criticisms upset those who had subscribed, but the silence did not mean inertia. Experts were engaged in scientific examination. I was asked to record the significance of their findings to answer sceptics.

Before relating these in detail, I recall the extraordinary way in which the *Codex* was introduced to the outside world. Credit must go to the German scholar, Dr. Tischendorf, a remarkable man whose life-interest was nosing out and studying ancient manuscripts of the Bible. His travels covered the East. Every library to which he could gain access was systematically inspected. Ironically, as often happens, his greatest discovery came by accident.

After prolonged negotiation, Dr. Tischendorf was given permission to visit the library of St. Catherine's Monastery at the foot of Mount Sinai. Investigations produced nothing of interest and he was about to leave when he noticed a large basket crammed with old parchments, waste material for lighting fires. On enquiry the librarian told him that two such heaps had already been burnt. Closer inspection of the basket showed that the sheets formed part of the Septuagint (Greek) Old Testament – the oldest manuscript he had ever seen. He obtained permission from the monks to take away a few sheets, in all about forty, but was so evidently delighted with the find that, becoming suspicious, the monks refused to give him any more. When Tischendorf returned to Germany the sheets created a sensation in the literary world, but he had learnt his lesson. The source of discovery was not disclosed. The caution was justified. The British Government deputed an eminent scholar to buy all valuable Greek manuscripts he could find – without marked success. Dr. Tischendorf next sought the aid of a friend at the Court of Egypt in an attempt to obtain the rest of the manuscript. It failed. The monks had learnt the real value of the parchments and refused to part with them at any price. In desperation he paid a second visit to Mount Sinai, but only found one sheet containing eleven lines of the Book of Genesis, thus proving that the manuscript originally consisted of the entire Old Testament.

Fifteen years passed without progress, until finally he succeeded in enlisting the sympathies of the Emperor of Russia, and off he went again to Sinai, this time with a commission from the Emperor. A long search revealed nothing. He decided to abandon the quest as hopeless. The evening before departure he was strolling in the grounds when a message came from the steward of the monks inviting Dr. Tischendorf to take refreshment in his cell. Scarcely had they sat down when the monk observed that he too had read a copy of the Septuagint and, going to a recess, produced a bulky bundle wrapped in red cloth which he laid on the table. Dr. Tischendorf opened the parcel and found not only the fragments he had seen fifteen years before, but other parts of the Old Testament, the New Testament complete, and some of the Apocryphal Books.

To cut a long story short, Tischendorf succeeded through the Emperor's influence in obtaining the manuscript, which was then stored in the Imperial Library, becoming the greatest treasure the Eastern Church possessed. For seventy years it remained there, jealously guarded and hidden from sight until the 1933 purchase restored it to the twentieth century.

When it first arrived in England it was in the same condition as the historic evening when Tischendorf saw it in the monk's cell – a mass of quires and loose leaves bound together in places by plentiful smearings of glue crudely applied by some careless binder of the Middle Ages. Exceptional care was taken to ensure that the task of reconditioning was as near perfect as possible. Innumerable samples of vellum, glue, thread, linen and other accessories were procured, compared and tested. Weeks were spent repairing tears and slits, but the greatest difficulty of all was how to straighten the leaves which were badly cockled. Eventually it was decided to employ a particularly ingenious device. Each leaf was hung in a humid atmosphere until limp. It was then fixed to a wooden frame by means of clips round the edges to which was attached a weighted string. This meant that each leaf was subjected to a pull equal at every point, and resulted in the sheet being perfectly straight when dry.

There was, of course, the risk of the strain being too great, for it had to be remembered that each sheet of vellum was only three-thousandths of an inch thick, besides being 1,000 years old. However no accidents occurred and the English oak boards and white morocco backs are supreme witnesses to the success of the binder's effort.

Regarding the contents of the *Codex*, the scholars were greatly helped by the use of mechanized aids, such as the ultra-violet lamp, which enabled them to shed fresh light on many textual obscurities. A classic instance occurred in the concluding lines of St. John's Gospel . . . There is something different about this verse in the Codex when compared with the others. The shape of the letters, the ink, and general appearance stamped it as obviously different from the rest of the page. So much is visible to the naked eye, but the application of the ultra-violet lamp accounts for the apparent variation. Traces of half-effaced writing appeared. These showed that the scribe had finished at the last verse but one, ending in the customary fashion by adding a *coronis* or tail-piece, and the heading "Gospel according to John" – which in those days was always placed at the end instead of at the beginning.

Apparently, however, he changed his mind, washed the vellum clean, added the final verse, and ended further down the page. The *Sinaiticus* is thus the only authority which in its first state omits the final verse, a discovery that played an important part in later discussions.

Each of Tichendorf's 15,000 critical notes on the *Codex* were compared against the original. The result was an endorsement of the German's scholarship. Considering the difficulties he had to tackle and the shortness of time at his disposal, it was an impressive effort. Another interesting result of the research work was that it proved the *Codex* was the work of three hands. This can be seen by the *coronis* or tail-pieces at the end of each section. When the scribes were engaged in writing the contents, they were careful to keep the lettering the same, but when the last line had been written, they allowed themselves the latitude of writing the *coronis* in their normal hand – the equivalent of a written signature at the end of a typewritten letter – and through these, three different styles of writing were discovered.

The question arose – why should more than one scribe have been engaged in the task of writing? This presented a problem to those who believe the Bible to be verbally inspired. First of all, it had to be realised that those who copied these books did not necessarily look upon their tasks as works of pious devotion. They were ordinary employees in matter-of-fact business houses. Book production in those days was on a strict commercial basis, and when the Emperor Constantine ordered Eusebius, Bishop of Caessarea, to provide fifty vellum bibles for the new churches of Constantinople, it was obvious that these huge volumes must have been published on a large scale. No customer, even a thousand years ago, was likely to wait a couple of years for one scribe to write out his order.

In the past there was controversy as to whether these early books were copied by eye from already existing manuscripts, or whether the scribes wrote them down from the dictation of a reader. This point was settled. As everyone knows, dictation is satisfactory as long as the writer's standard of spelling is high, otherwise confusion is inevitable. What happened during the writing of the *Codex* was a typical example. Scribe A was apparently an efficient and methodical writer; Scribe B was not so sure of himself and occasionally tripped up over his vowels; but Scribe C was in a class of his own. The surprise was that such a wretched speller and careless writer was ever chosen for the task. In all probability it was due to his errors that the *Codex* was never finished and quite likely never sold.

Among proofs in supporting the theory that the method was by dictation was one caused by the hesitancy on the part of the dictator. In the passage 1 Maccabees, vv 1,20, the scribe wrote instead of "8,000", the words "either 6 or 3,000". The reason for this could have been that when the reader came to this passage, he was uncertain of what was written, so he said "either 6 or 3,000", and the scribes writing automatically put the words down verbatim. One of the interesting things about the *Codex Sinaiticus* was the multitude of corrections that were written all over the text. Hundreds were to be found. Many corrections were transcriptional, mistakes such as would be made today in the proofing stage. Others were more interesting in that they altered the working by inserting or deleting certain passages. Far from detracting from the value of the *Codex,* they were perhaps its most important feature.

It was obvious that for the main part these corrections were inserted after reference had been made to the "master-copy" from which the *Codex* had been taken. In other words, it gave us a vital insight into the "*Codex* behind the *Codex*", which, on account of the purpose for which it was used, must have been the nearest it was then possible to get to the original writings for purposes of any documentary investigations. The old rule stood – the earlier the manuscript the more likely it is to be correct.

One final point. I have mentioned the criticism raised shortly after the *Codex* was purchased – that it was a waste of money when facsimile copies were available; such attacks were illogical and unfounded. In the first place, reproductions, however good, could never have recorded satisfactorily those important passages, indistinct through dirt and centuries of handling, or those sections made obscure through erasure and alteration. In every case, for final judgement, recourse had to be made to the original. In the *Codex Sinaiticus* the nation has one of the most valued literary treasures in the world, a unique link with an age long past. Praise is due to the pioneering enterprise and skills of our academics. It was an exciting experience.

CRICK AND WATSON

FRANCIS CRICK WHO, WITH JAMES WATSON, made a scientific discovery of the first magnitude, formed an ideal partnership. Crick, a physicist; Watson, an American geneticist: they complemented each other's strengths. Work-base was the Medical Research Council Unit in the Cavendish laboratories, then in Free School Lane. Their brief – to find the correct structure of deoxyribo-nucleic acid, or DNA, that determines how hereditary characteristics are passed from parents to children. Their leader was Nobel Prize-winner Dr. Max Perutz, who agreed with the Crick/Watson contention that there were two chains which ran in opposite direction, and probably linked together.

The answer was elusive. Perutz recalled his reactions . . . when he entered the laboratory, the structure was there . . . the double-helix model reaching from floor to ceiling, fully ten-feet high . . . the solution to one of life's greatest riddles . . . the most memorable moment of his career.

Crick and Watson were ecstatic. Watson, by nature reticent, at times moody, always found it difficult to show emotion. He had lodgings in Scroope Terrace, where Camille Prior, wife of a Professor of French and friend of Donald Beavis of King's, was landlady. She told me that Watson's glumness was due to his being the only male lodger with several pretty girl students. This time inhibitions were forgotten. It was the break-through to a process that began in 1869 when deoxyribo-nucleic acid was found.

Crick, more extrovert, rushed to his favourite pub, the *Eagle* in Bene't Street, announcing to bemused regulars that the secret of life had been discovered. Perutz described it as the greatest discovery in biology of the century. In 1952 Watson returned to America; Crick followed in 1976 to work as Distinguished Professor conducting research at the Salk Institute in California.

The BBC decided to dramatize the moment with a film in which Watson was played by Jeff Goldblum and Tim Piggot-Smith took the part of Crick. Much of the shooting took part in the old Addenbroke's hospital building with sets of a Chinese restaurant interior; replicas of Cavendish laboratory rooms, and Crick's top-floor flat in a medieval building called the Old Vicarage, a misnomer as it had been a chantry house. Later he moved to Portugal Place where the gold-coloured double-helix above the door became a landmark for tourists.

Research continued. In 1984 DNA fingerprinting became possible. Fifteen years later it still required time to isolate a single gene. Then came the startling announcement. Scientists had completed the first "working-draft" of the entire human genetic code, with the exception of the final ten per cent which would be added in a couple of years. This will complete the sequence of all the DNA bases present in the human body of 1,000 billion cells, arranged in the right order. This human genome map will contain both the geography of life and an evolutionary history stretching back some billion years.

It is a breathtaking moment. It will transform thinking of Creation as profoundly as Charles Darwin's evolution theory. To a layman it is a strange language without grammar, the genome is an instructional manual of life that passes on genetic traits and makes the proteins needed to build an organism – enzymes, cells, organs, skeleton or brain. But as yet, there is no theory which explains how it does that unimaginably complex job. This billion-character manual is followed by each human cell, but will take decades to decipher in its entirety. We are assured that the genetic roots of illness will be probed; new cures will be found; treatment of cancer caused by malfunctioning genes could be revolutionised; diagnostic tests improved.

When Francis Crick hurried into the *Eagle* and invited the regulars to drink with him to the unfolding of the secret of life, I wonder if he realised its future potential.

In 2000 he was awarded the Philadelphia Liberty Medal to be shared with James Watson in recognition of formulating this molecular model for DNA that has proved to be the building block of all life.

SIR MARTIN RYLE

IN THE EARLY YEARS OF RADIO-ASTRONOMY three British scientists were outstanding . . . Bernard Lovell, the man behind the Jodrell Bank telescope; Fred Hoyle, whose theories inspired academics to approve or disapprove; Martin Ryle's research produced significant results. I knew Martin from the outset of his career. Potential was obvious. His analytical mind helped the Cambridge radio-astronomy group to become second-to-none in the world. He always played down personal success, insisting they were shared achievements. No point in arguing. The Establishment corrected the impression by bestowing these honours: Fellow of the Royal Society, 1952: First Chair of Radio-Astronomy at Cambridge, 1964:

Gold Medal of Royal Astronomical Society, 1964: knighted, 1966.

When Sir Richard Woolley retired in 1972, Martin became Astronomer Royal. It was the first time this honour was given to someone not previously Director of the Royal Greenwich Observatory, a tradition observed for more than 300 years. In 1974 he was awarded the Nobel Prize for Physics, jointly with Anthony Hewish.

Background was scholarly. His father was a physicist at Guy's Hospital, later Regius Professor of Physics at Cambridge, and finally Professor of Social Medicine of Oxford. Martin graduated from Oxford with a First in Physics; invited by J. A. Ratcliffe to work at the Cavendish laboratory to study radio emissions observed from the sun, also the galaxy of stars of which our sun is a member. Such was Martin's introduction to radio-astronomy.

Outbreak of war disrupted plans. He went to the Air Ministry Research Establishment, joined one of the finest teams of electronic scientists, concentrating on radar systems in the Royal Air Force, became a specialist in radio-counter measures against German radar. Its importance was highlighted on 12th February when the German warships *Scharnhorst* and *Gneisenau* passed through the English Channel from Brest to Kiel, undetected on the English coastal radar defence because of massive jamming by Nazi transmitters on the French coast.

Returning to the Cavendish he became involved in analysing radio waves emanating from astronomical objects outside the earth. At the outset he used a simple device. Two large aerials several hundred yards apart with combined outputs, giving a receiving version of the Nichelson interferometer; then installed eight parabolic reflectors along a five-kilometre stretch of old railway line, developing aperture-synthesis simulating the performance of a reflector too large to be constructed. Results were recorded by signals from the reflectors in digital form. Computer-drawn images produced fine details of radio-galaxies.

Undoubtedly radio-synthesis aided the development of radio astronomy and led to the discovery of quasars. Throughout, Martin's enthusiasm never waned. He would recall how on a night in May 1948, he collaborated with Graham Smith and K. E. Machin in running the interferment-telescope for the first time, and discovering a radio source, *Cassiofieraz*, only the second ever found. It marked the beginning of the major task of cataloguing radio sources. Martin became the dominant figure in the controversy between the Big-Bang and Steady-State schools of cosmology. He favoured the Big-Bang theory by showing that very distant galaxies, whose light and radio waves had taken some 8 million years to reach us, were packed more closely together than those in the neighbourhood of our own galaxy. Media gossip suggested that Martin and Hoyle were enemies. On the contrary, they were scientific sparring partners that used to surface when we met occasionally in a Green Street coffee-shop.

In private, Martin's main interest was designing and building sail boats. Design techniques were a challenge. He would come with me to the BRM works in Lincolnshire, sit in the drawing-office and listen to discussions about designing a Formula One racing engine, one of the most complicated of engineering exercises, sometimes accompanying us to Silverstone or Brands Hatch to see the end-product in action. I recall his satisfaction when, after designing and building a 16-foot catamaran, it was exhibited at the International Boat Show, also the pleasure of sailing on the Solent in his 18-foot auxiliary sloop.

At the height of international scientific success, Martin began to have doubts. Maybe influenced by life-threatening lung cancer, he became disillusioned, feeling his scientific research had been misdirected, priorities had been wrong. In 1984 he died. I was given permission by his wife, Rowena, to quote from a letter he wrote to Professor Chagas of the Vatican Academy of Science and a handwritten note found in personal papers . . . "I am left at the end of my life with the feeling that it would have been better to have become a farmer in 1946. One of course can argue that somebody would have done it anyway and so we must face the most fundamental of questions, should fundamental science be stopped." Martin believed a nuclear holocaust was inevitable, the time was short. A handwritten sentence summarised these fears. "Our world is one . . . yet evolution has now reached the stage where as a species we may soon die . . . we as scientists should be able to see this more clearly and must use our influence to change the too-limited aspirations of governments."

Martin was right. Our cleverness has outgrown our wisdom.

THE CHALLENGE OF MOUNT EVEREST

THE SAGA OF MOUNT EVEREST reached its climax in 1953 when Edmund Hillary with Tenzing Norgay, the Nepalese Sherpa, stood on the summit of the world's highest peak, confirming the prediction of Sir Francis Younghusband, who was associated with previous attempts . . . "In the end man will prevail, another and another expedition will be sent to Mount Everest, and, with the certitude of mathematics, man will prevail." When he came to Cambridge for the celebrations marking "Bunny" Fuchs' 92nd birthday, Hillary looked older, more lined, but still rugged.

His link with Everest expeditions stretched back to 1921 when permission was granted by the Tibetan Government for a party to penetrate to the base and explore the approaches to Mount Everest, a move that led to the formation of the Mount Everest Committee, whose members came form the Royal Geographical Society and the Alpine Club.

Led by Lieut-Colonel Howard Bury, the first expedition discovered a possible route to the North Col at 23,000 feet, followed in 1922 and 1924 by expeditions led by General G.C. Bruce. At this point, Professor Noel Odell enters the picture. This Fellow-Commoner of Clare, later and honorary Fellow of the College, was a frequent visitor to the Old Mill House. The mystery of Mallory and Irvine was often discussed. It was interesting to listen to an eye-witness account of their final bid for the summit; how at 28,000 feet he watched Mallory and Irvine make their final bid for the summit. Clouds swallowed them. The rest was conjecture. He descended to Camp Four, several thousand feet below, quietly confident the climbers had made it, but became anxious at the absence of torch signals. He decided to go back, climbed to Camp Five, 2000 feet up and spent a turbulent night there with storms threatening to destroy the tent. The next morning, he returned to Camp Six, climbed higher, but still no sign of life. Acting on an agreed signal to those below, he laid out the sleeping bags in the shape of a "T" indicating the search had failed. The party returned to base. In London he recalled a private audience with King George V and the

Memorial Service in St. Paul's.

When I asked whether the mountain would ever reveal its secret, he thought it unlikely though in 1969 a body was found by a Chinese climber. It was Maurice Wilson. Dr. Charles Warren described how in 1935 he had found and buried the body of Wilson, who had perished on a solo attempt the previous year. The body found by the Chinese was almost certainly that of Wilson, which had reemerged from the ice at a lower point 25 years later.

Odell doubted it would happen to Mallory and Irvine. From where at least one of them was presumed to have died (and the only evidence was an ice axe identified as belonging to Irvine), they would have been swept by gales down a steep rocky slope and over a 12,000 feet precipice. The remains would have become buried in the glacier below, perhaps emerging briefly after 20 years or more, only to be hidden again by fresh snow.

The unlikely happened. The mountain revealed its secret. The bodies were found, but the uncertainty remains. One clue suggests that credit should be given to Mallory as the first man to reach the summit. He carried in his pocket a small Union Jack intended to be placed at the peak. The flag was missing. The inference is clear.

Years later we often met in Odell's Cambridge flat in Holbrook Road, sitting in a study packed with books, photographs, memorabilia, ice axes and a telescopic Tibetan horn. Although in his nineties, his powers of recall were incisive. He talked of the 1938 Everest expedition dogged by atrocious weather, they nevertheless reached 25,000 feet. On that trip he took a young Sherpa called Tensing. Links with Harry Tilman were often mentioned. Together they climbed Nanda Devi, a 26,640 feet Himalayan mountain, for 14 years the highest climbed by man. Like Hillary and Odell, Tilman in his own right was a pioneering legend. In 1934 with Eric Shipton and three Sherpa porters, he was the first to penetrate the inner Nanda Devi basin of twelve peaks of over 21,000 feet and the Richganga River that flowed through the terrifying gorge identified by Hindu mythology as the final earthly home of the Seven Rishis. They crossed the chasm and carried out a survey of glacier systems in this unknown territory, gaining the Royal Geographical Society Gill Memorial for mountain exploration. At his home in Cheshire, Tilman described how, after climbing the gorge, they found a pocket of rolling grass slopes with alpine flowers, like a scene from the film *Lost Horizons*. Tilman was impatient at restrictions imposed by age. On the study mantelpiece were three reminders of his prime. On a small base was a stone from the summit of Kilimanjaro, the highest mountain in Africa; on the second a piece of rock from the summit of Nanda Devi; the third, empty, intended for a stone from the Everest summit. Tilman said he would not die in bed. In his eighties he sailed in a yacht on another record-breaking venture. In the inhospitable, storm-wracked waters of the South Atlantic Tilman died alone as he predicted.

I feel the Everest myth should have ended when it was conquered. It has become tarnished, climbed by more than 900 people since it was first conquered 47 years ago, it is now a Himalayan environmental hazard. Tons of rubbish have accumulated; a team recently took away 632 oxygen bottles from the South Camp at 25,918 feet as well as 435 gas canisters, more than 1,000 batteries and tons of burnable trash. Water supplies at the base camp have been tested for contamination by biological waste, as well as snow samples to help climate research. No longer remote, thousands now trek to the region every year.

I asked Noel Odell why he took up the Everest challenge. His reply was an echo of Frank Smythe's words: "I wish I knew . . . only, in discomfort, in storm, in the beauty and grandeur of the mountains, I discovered something very much worthwhile, and, like a magnet, this indefinable something will draw adventuring pioneers back to the scene of former triumphs and disappointments . . . maybe to fresh conquests . . . maybe death." Simple words, but true in depth.

CHAPTER SEVEN

ORB AND SCEPTRE

~

QUEEN ELIZABETH THE QUEEN MOTHER is the Royal matriarch, symbol of national continuity with whom we could identify, as was demonstrated during the celebrations marking her hundredth birthday, a span of years synchronic with every stage of a changing world during those years. It is interesting to note what everyday life was like when Elizabeth Bowes-Lyons was born.

The Court Circular on that day read: "The Queen drove out yesterday afternoon, accompanied by their Royal Highnesses Princess Christian of Schleswig-Holstein and Princess Henry of Battenberg." Mafeking was relieved. Largesse was recorded in a news item that the Queen had sent £4 to a mother in Stoke Park Lodge, near Slough in recognition that her three sons were fighting under the British flag in South Africa. Oscar Wilde died.

Newspaper headlines predicted that the price of clothes, coal and food would escalate in the winter months ahead. A clerk earning 35s (£1.75) per week would be worse off than when he earned 28s (£1.40) the previous year. Families living in one room would have to pay ninepence extra for coal. Gas bills would rise from 2s (10p) a week to half-a-crown (12 ½ p). Wool prices having risen by 20 per cent meant suits would cost about 35s (£1.75).

A reluctant predecessor of Michael Fish misread weather portents. London experienced an unexpected hurricane. Torrential rain turned Piccadilly Circus into a lake; communications between

London, North-West of England, the whole of Scotland and parts of Ireland were interrupted. Only two wires worked between London and Glasgow. Such was her welcome.

Life thereafter followed a familiar pattern of her family background. Normal childhood into an attractive, vivacious young lady with many admirers. Choosy, she was reluctant to enter the Royal Family. The Duke of York had to wait two years before she consented to marriage. From that moment everything changed; most traumatic was the Abdication, succession passing to her husband, whose conscientious sense of duty conceivably shortened his life. Throughout their lives together she endeared herself to the nation at every level.

Her hundredth birthday celebrations had one discordant note. The *New Statesman* printed an anti-Monarch feature that included such phrases as *Long live the Republic; The Queen Mum is dead; 100 good reasons to be a Republican.*

Such gratuitous insults were disgraceful. The Queen Mother probably never read the trash, but it was significant that no attempt was made by the Labour Party to distance themselves from such an unwarranted attack. Pleading ignorance was impossible. After all, the social event of the Labour Conference is the annual party given by the *New Statesman*. On reflection the silence was not surprising. In spite of their obsequious fawning to the Queen and selected members of the Royal Family, Tony and Cherie Blair appear to see themselves as President and First Lady of the United Kingdom with the Prime Minister a Closet Republican.

Left-Wing anti-Monarchists agitate for immediate reform of the Royal system as a starter. On that point few would disagree. Modernisation is overdue. Prince Philip agreed in trenchant fashion . . . "No one wants to be like the brontosaurus who couldn't adapt and ended up in a museum." That does not mean changing into a Presidential Republic.

It is timely to look at history in retrospect. Our two great epochs were Elizabethan and Victorian, both owing their inspiration to the spirit of a woman. The England of Elizabeth Tudor can never be recaptured. It was a unique reign. Historians acclaim it as one of the greatest in our history, and yet in some ways foreign to our nature . . . an age of poverty and poets . . . the link with the

Catholic Church had been broken . . . an Empire was waiting to be founded. Edmund Spencer composed *The Faerie Queen* in celebration of a Monarch so absolute and personal with the right to name the succession.

Amid such a blaze of extremes, England gradually assumed greatness, yet the pattern was almost Machiavellian, Court environment Italian, atmosphere reminiscent of the Medici; cruel, almost sadistic, but triumphantly glorious. No Monarch had such a flexible intoxicating background. Its complexity was reflected in the character of Elizabeth Tudor. The chisel of the sculptor has preserved the enigma . . . mask-like features . . . inscrutable expression hiding the bitterness of knowing it was the Crown not the woman that held the affection of the people . . . tight lips . . . high cheek-bones . . . sensitive hands . . . all expressive of a frame that shook with the violence of inherited anger. No woman has commanded such respect and pity at the same time; victim of the Tudor physical heritage, she sublimated herself in the quest for Royal greatness. Possessing a tragic incapacity for love, solace came in classical learning, with a remarkable range of erudition, conversant with the Court languages of the day, able to speak Greek with ease.

It is difficult to reconcile these conflicting qualities, yet out of them Elizabeth Tudor achieved in her reign an impersonal magnificence never equalled. It belongs to history with glory that of a Shakespearean past.

Princess Victoria came to the throne at a period closely resembling the troubled inheritance of Elizabeth Tudor. The faith of the people in Kings and Queen had waned. Economic conditions were deplorable, trade was bad, wages low, food expensive, discontent rife, criminal law savage. It needed but a spark to fan feeling into a rising that could have overthrown the Throne and disrupted the Empire. To make matters worse, after the death of Prince Albert, the Queen went into a seclusion tantamount to retirement from State duties and played into the hands of ambitious Prime Ministers like Disraeli, Gladstone and Salisbury.

Her heir, Edward VII, accepted the loss of executive power, but found compensation in his remarkable influence on foreign policy, aided by family relationships with half of the crowned Heads of

Europe, fluency in languages and negotiating skills. George V and George VI were genuine constitutional monarchs, but were not silenced. George V could be blunt. Criticising the policy-handling of the 1914-18 war, he argued that advice from the military experts was more professional than political decisions. His argument was approved. On two occasions discretionary powers were exercised in the choice of candidate for the office of Prime Minister. Each time the man proffered had the full support of his Party in the Commons. George VI was more diffident. He too had to chose between Winston Churchill and Lord Halifax. He favoured the latter, but realised that the Labour Party would not serve under Halifax, so it had to be Winston.

The accession of Elizabeth II marked a more practical approach. Over the years she had proved that a constitutional monarch is not an anachronism. She drew on her vast experience in national and international affairs; in that area she had greater first-hand knowledge than her Premiers. All State Papers are read; each week she confers with the Prime Minister. During the reign she has dealt with Winston Churchill, Harold Wilson, Harold Macmillan, Douglas Home, James Callaghan, accepted Margaret Thatcher as our first woman Prime Minister, John Major and Tony Blair, but problems wait to be solved.

Questions have been raised in the Commons about the future role of the Monarchy; individual members of the Royal Family have been criticised; personal habits questioned; concern expressed about divorces and allegations about Royal Household extravagance.

The latter has been tackled by Sir Michael Peat, Keeper of the Privy Purse. The travel budget has been slashed from £20 million a year to £9.3 million with the pledge that "cost reductions, value for money, accountability and transparency" would be assured. Royal travel arrangements mean that the Queen uses the BAe airliner, whilst other Royals rely on smaller commercial aircraft and helicopters in preference to the pride of the Royal Air Force fleet. The cost of £8,000 an hour for use of the Royal Squadron was considered too expensive. These and other cut-backs were in line with modernising the system.

So far so good. These decisions were off-set by examples of the high opinion held by Blair that surfaced when the Blair family left for a summer holiday in Florence and Toulouse. When Prince Charles and Prince William had a skiing holiday they used scheduled flights on British Airways and Swissair. The Blairs in their wisdom were not so democratic. They used the Royal Squadron at a cost to the taxpayer of over £50,000, the cynical inference being that the Prime Minister considers himself more important than the Monarch. Such perquisites of power that the Premier grants himself indicates he is out of touch with the public, with Walter Mitty monarchical illusions at variance with the real world. Incidents like these were topical items for *Prime Minister's Question Time,* but nevertheless indicative of New Labour's attitude to the evolving role of Monarchy and the Constitution, a debate that ignores its ongoing historical importance.

I prefer to avoid biased political ideology, and recall that November morning in London in 1947, greyish, hint of fog and threatening rain clouds. The occasion . . . the marriage of the Heiress Presumptive to her chosen consort. Those of us who waited in the Abbey of Westminster will never forget the scene that belonged to history and heralded what we hoped would be a second Elizabethan era. So much was happening yet, as often happens, vignettes of memory tend to highlight fragmentary details.

I recall the arrival of notable guests as they went to seats in the choir. Cabinet Ministers filling the northern rows of stalls. Clement Attlee sat in the easternmost stall. Then came a riveting moment. As Winston Churchill passed up the nave, the entire assembly, as if it were one man, rose to their feet, a tribute accorded to no one else, as the Elder Statesman took his place next to the Canadian and South African Premiers.

Everything went like clockwork as colourful Processions followed one after the other. Members of the Royal Family were conducted to their seats in the Sanctuary by Minor Canons in capes of crimson and gold. The Queen Mother was received at the West Door by the Dean and Chapter; a few minutes later the Queen was escorted to the east end by the Sub-Dean and Chapter in capes of dark green silk. The Procession of the Visiting Prelates. Preceded by a Verger bearing a silver-headed mace, came the Moderator of the Church of Scotland, the Bishops of London and Norwich and the two Primates with attending Chaplains. I remember particularly the Dean of Westminster occupying the central position in the Procession with the Archbishop of Canterbury on his right, the Archbishop of York on his left, all three preceded by the Abbey Sacrist wearing a rich blue mantle. In the Abbey the Dean of Westminster is absolutely supreme, taking primacy over every Prelate in the entire Anglican Communion.

At that moment the bells of St. Margaret could be heard pealing, another ancient custom, jealously guarded by the parish church of Westminster, a privilege from Tudor times of "ringing the King by". I remember how, as quarter-to-eleven sounded from Big Ben, the first movement of Elgar's beautiful Sonata in G Minor crashed from the great organ played by Dr. Peasgood. On the stroke of half-past eleven, the Royal carriage drew up to the Abbey. The young girl appeared at the west door leaning on her father's arm. The whole Collegiate body faced westwards and bowed to the King, for the Sovereign is the Official Visitor of Westminster. All turned eastwards. Trumpets sounded a fanfare composed by the Master of the King's Musick and the Procession moved eastwards. While details of the ritualistic preliminaries have remained crystal clear, the actual ceremony is blurred because much was private and low key. The Primate of All England performed the actual ceremony; the Archbishop of York delivered a simple address. The impressive Service ended with the bridal couple entering St. Edward's Chapel to sign the Registers. After a graceful reverence to the Queen Mother, the couple, hand-in-hand, walked down the Nave to pealing bells and cheering crowds outside. So ended an epic occasion of colour and floods of glorious music. Unbelievably the actual ceremony had lasted only three-quarters-of-an-hour. We had watched history being made. Awareness of the task that lay ahead was shown in Elizabeth's 21st birthday broadcast from the youngest self-governing Dominion. Her words found an echo across the centuries in the utterance of Elizabeth Tudor at Tilbury on the eve of the Armada . . . "I know that I have but the body of a weak and feeble woman, but I have the heart of a King and a King of England."

Alongside that proud avowal I place the dignified simplicity of Princess Elizabeth's solemn act of dedication on the threshold of a Royal life . . . "I declare before you all that my whole life, whether it be long or short, shall be devoted to your service and the service of our great imperial family to which we all belong, but I shall not have the strength to carry out this resolution alone, unless you join in it with me, as I now invite you to do. I know that your support will be unfailingly given. God help me to make good my vow and God bless you all who are willing to share in it."

Fifty years on we look forward to the Golden Jubilee celebrations. The Royal couple will return to the Abbey after a life of service. The Queen's life has been beyond reproach. Her vows have been carried out. The partnership has been a blending of constancy and mutual affection, lightened at times by Prince Philip's honest gaffes. Their marriage has symbolised stability, continuity and endurance, strengthening the core meaning of our Constitutional Monarchy.

CHAPTER EIGHT

BRAINS AND BRAWN

~

"Here for everything there is a time and a season and then how does the glory of a thing pass from it even like the flower of the grass."

To recall sporting events and personalities of the century ought to be an agreeable trawl. Sadly it is not the case. Almost every sport has been prostituted by an excess of greed. The latest at the time of writing was the dismissal of Hansie Cronje as South African cricket captain for providing "information and forecasts" to an Indian bookmaker for a few thousand pounds. The whiteness of cricketer's flannels now seem grey. Accusations of corruption have involved Australian players as well as Pakistan and India. It reminds me of a character in *The Great Gatsby*, introduced as the man who fixed the 1919 baseball World Series in which "Shoeless" Joe Jackson allegedly lost games deliberately. In cynical mood I recall the football pools match-fixing scandal of the 1960s and the sabotaging of floodlights at Charlton and Wimbledon in 1998, part of a "fixing" ploy. As yet we have been spared machinations of Far Eastern betting syndicates, but it is bad enough. Another sport falling from grace is athletics, with instances of top performers accused of taking forbidden drugs that enhance performances. China ignored censure by shattering world records in quick succession. Routine tests can be inconclusive. Juan Antonio Samaranch, when President of the International Olympic Committee, appears to have thrown in the towel by implying that drugs will be allowed in athletic events, presumably to avoid upsetting vested sponsorship and television coverage. Such compromises make a mockery of the Olympic ideal. Police action is more forthright. In the 1999 *Tour de France*, the significance of the yellow jersey to sponsored deals led to drug-taking allegations. Police made arrests and uncovered the racket.

The worst instance of a national sport being affected by greed is Formula One motor-racing. Its traditions have been undermined and turned into a hyped commercial circus controlled in dictator fashion by Bernie Ecclestone. Chris Tarrant asks who wants to be a millionaire. Ecclestone's version is different. If you want that sort of money, just do what you're told and you too will go to the ball. Dangling this carrot before owners, engineers, drivers, officials and odds-and-sods of hangers-on has done the trick.The *Mail on Sunday* Report of the richest men in the country lists several racing figures from ordinary backgrounds and modest means who now have bank-rolls of millions.

It is pertinent to ask how, single-handed and in such a short space of time, Ecclestone has become Czar of motor-racing. In saying this I am conscious that too close a personal acquaintance can be inhibiting, but facts are facts. He is a remarkable man, small in stature, just over 5 feet tall, who compensated by marrying Slavica, an ex-Armani model who is over 6 feet.

Like many ambitious people, Ecclestone's provenance was frugal and cash-strapped. His father, a trawler skipper, pandered to the lad's interest in mechanics, let him work in a motor-cycle shop, try his hand at dirt-track racing, progressed to four wheels, eventually entering the Formula One world as business manager to Jochen Rindt. His business acumen was gained as an astute secondhand car dealer.

I recall walking down a long corridor of the Milan hospital after Rindt received terminal injuries in the Italian Grand Prix at Monza; having to break the news to his wife, Nina,that Jochen had died. As she waited in the corridor with Colin Chapman and Bernie, their quiet sympathy was an enormous help.

Ecclestone's tactical persistence paid off. He was not intimidated by the fact that the sport he had entered was dominated by rich, egotistical amateurs, a club for gentlemen with the right background and a taste for speed and glamour. They just wanted to race. The business side was tiresome. Ecclestone's offer to negotiate deals with circuit owners, handle travel arrangements and other chores for a fee was welcome. The strategy paid rich dividends. Ambitious coups secured the licence to fix the sale of world-wide television rights for all Formula One races. As head of the Formula One Constructors Association, he handled the interests of all the teams. As vice-president of the Fédération Internationale de l'Automobile, the sport's governing body, he was at the heart of the rule-making authority, plus numerous other commercial interest linked with sport. By the time this book is published, there could be a Stock Market flotation of his Formula One empire which could create a family fortune exceeding 2.5 billion.

On a more personal note, I have always found Bernie unpredictable. I recall when he had dinner with me in The Dorchester. Over coffee he suddenly asked what I thought of the Hyde Park Hotel. I replied I didn't know it well, but obviously 5-star rated. "Why the question?" 'Oh, I was thinking of buying it!" There was no obvious retort, so I asked if he would care for another coffee. Bernie's world is bizarre, but it happens to be real.

One final thought . . . if only motor-sport was governed with the dignity, integrity and impartiality of the Royal and Ancient, the Jockey Club and Lord's, things would have been different.

GOLF

THE WORLD OF GOLF IS ONE WHICH holds many memories, having known and played with many of the greatest players. I appreciated these comments written by Robert Halsall, for many years at the Royal Birkdale Club, as well as Professional at Monte Carlo with Henry Cotton:

> I remember vividly seeing Louis for the first time at his own great club, Royal Liverpool. It was April 1930. I had been invited by Harry Bently and his father, known as Pa. I was to caddy for Harry, who at that stage was one of the best amateur golfers in England. As we moved to the practise ground, we passed the first tee. There stood a tall,

elegant young man, possibly a couple of years older than myself, swinging a club with a great deal of panache. I thought to myself, if he could repeat the movement when the ball was there, it would be something and my God, he did. Rarely have I seen such power generated in a golf swing. I thought to myself, I shall walk up the fairway with him to see him play his second. This time, the same swing but with something like a seven or eight iron which was despatched to within six feet from the pin, and don't forget this was with a hickory shaft. I watched him play another fantastic tee shot from the second before heading back to the practise ground. I said, "You've got your work cut out today Harry – who is that player moving down the second fairway?" He said, "That's Louis Stanley, a member of Hoylake." What a glorious course Hoylake was at that time.

Allan Macfie won the first Amateur Championship, beating Horace Hutchinson in the 1885 final at Hoylake by the decisive margin of 7 and 6 from an entry of 44. Although handicapped by deafness, he showed a lively interest in the game up to the end of his life. A familiar figure in Hoylake, he would slowly cross the fairways, cap well down over the eyes, drooping moustaches, cleek in hand. Caddies arriving early often found the fairway littered with balls left behind after he had given up practising in the fading light of the previous evening. The first Amateur Champion was a member of the Royal and Ancient Golf Club for 61 years. Full of theories, I found one that worked in spite of seeming contradictory. He said that to make the ball rise abruptly, the eye had to be fixed on the ground immediately in front of the ball. It invited topping, but is effective.

JOHN BALL AND HAROLD HILTON

SINCE THE AMATEUR CHAMPIONSHIP was inaugurated, few golfers have held this title more than once. Of these, John Ball was outstanding. He won it no fewer than eight times: his double victory in both Open and Amateur Championships in 1890 was not equalled until Bobby

Jones swept the board 40 years later. His only rival was Harold Hilton, whose record of winning both the Open and Amateur Championships on two occasions and the American Amateur Championship once would have made him the outstanding player of his period had it not clashed with the Ball era.

I recall the last appearance of these grand old players. Both had 99 matches to their credit. Everybody hoped that the sweetness of one more victory might fall to their lot in their final appearance. It was not to be. Both were defeated and, having reached the century mark, their championship careers drew to a close. Both have gone from our midst but to an older generation the mention of John Ball recalls a silent golfer with a slight stoop and red-topped stockings, striding across the Hoylake links in the dusk of a summer evening followed by his wizened little caddie.

JAMES BRAID

JAMES BRAID STARTED LIFE AS A JOINER, first at Elie, then St. Andrews, later Edinburgh, and was working at his trade when J.H. Taylor and Harry Vardon were budding professionals. He won the Open title for the first time in 1901. In the short space of a decade claimed the Championship five times. Tall, powerfully built, unflappable temperament, I liked his pawky sense of humour, preferred monosyllabic conversation. Superb cleek player, but occasionally hesitant on the greens.

J.H. TAYLOR

I RECALL J.H. TAYLOR AS A DOUR FIGHTER on and off the course. He won five Open Championships and finished second many times. In 1951 the BBC planned a programme recording Taylor's reminiscences. Unwilling to leave the quiet of Westward Ho, so the unit travelled to Devon. Technicians converted the sitting-room into a studio. The microphone was installed on a desk which J.H. told me had been presented by the Artisans' Golfers' Association. During that afternoon he recalled the 1895 and 1900 Open victories. He was especially proud of being the first English-born professional to have won the title.

HARRY VARDON

HARRY VARDON WAS SLIM, quietly dressed in knickerbockers and tweed jacket. He knotched-up a record by winning the Open Championship six times, 1896, 1898, 1899, 1903, 1911 and 1914. He told me that the closing years of the 19th century were for him the golden age of the game. I wonder what he would have made of today.

SANDY HERD

SANDY HERD WAS A PRODUCT of St. Andrews. Born in a humble house in North Street, he used to say that his introduction to the game was not on the links, but in North Street, where holes were lamp-posts which had to be hit by balls made from discarded champagne corks found in the R. and A. dust-bins. Childish ambitions came true. His friend, Laurie Auchterlonie, went to America and won the U.S. title; Sandy the Open at Hoylake in 1902 and runner-up on four occasions. The last time I played with him was in a practice round before the 1936 Open Championship at Hoylake. The course was long with a strong wind blowing from the Dee. He found it tough; as he tired the famous waggles decreased, but his long game was impeccable, particularly the cunning hook. He once reminded me that he had to play against the best ball of Vardon, Taylor and Braid – the equivalent of Palmer, Player and Nicklaus.

WALTER HAGEN

WALTER HAGEN WAS THE PROTOTYPE of a new generation of golf professionals. He broke down social conventions that downgraded colleagues to second-class citizens. Access into clubhouses was denied. Infuriated at being refused entry into the Royal Cinque clubhouse at Deal during the Open Championship, Hagen retaliated by hiring a Rolls Royce, parked it opposite the main entrance and entertained friends with champagne and caviar.

Alongside homespun colleagues, he was a sartorial fashion-plate; well-cut suits, ready eye for feminine charm, unquestionably vain; would change his entire outfit between rounds on the same day. He enjoyed life, I recall many of his brittle comments like, "I don't want to die a millionaire, just to live like one." Golf success made that possible. He was the first to earn a million dollars winning two American Open Championships in 1914 and 1919; four British Open titles in 1922, 1924, 1928 and 1929, plus the remarkable feat of winning four American PGA Match-play Championships in a row.

When health began to fail, Hagen rarely left his home in Treverse City, Michigan. He died aged 77. An appropriate epitaph is one observation I heard him say on several occasions: "Never worry . . . take time and smell the flowers along the way."

FRANK STRANAHAN

AS A YOUNG MAN FRANK STRANAHAN had the self-assurance of a veteran sauntering with supreme indifference through life with a golf club in his hand. With the exception of Cotton and Faldo, no golfer in these islands or America, amateur or professional, has equalled his tournament experience. Even off the links, the urge to improve never left him. I remember after dinner in Claridges, London, we went up to his suite where he putted to an improvised ashtray hole for an hour whilst chatting on topical matters. He was also much quieter than critics believed. After winning the British Amateur Championship at St Andrews, there were no hectic celebrations. We went to a small hotel in Elie, near St Andrews, telephoned his father in the United States and then had a quiet dinner with the championship trophy in the middle of the table.

BOBBY JONES

THE OLD COURSE IS LINKED with one of the greatest golfers of all time. 1930 saw the unbelievable become fact and golfing history made when Bobby Jones won the Open Championship at Hoylake, the American Open Championship at Interlachen, the amateur Championship at St. Andrews and the American Championship at Merion, plus a clear 13-stroke victory at a professional tournament in Augusta, and his 36-hole Walker Cup match at Sandwich. Jones played competitive golf on both sides of the Atlantic from April to September and never finished below first place. To name him as the greatest golfer of all time might be queried by the skills of such men as Vardon, Hagen, Cotton, Hogan, Niclaus, Ballesteros, Faldo and Tiger Woods.

Comparisons are impossible. Champions of different generations use different equipment and compete under different conditions. I think Jones' comments were applicable. "I think we must agree that all a man can do is to beat people who are around at the same time that he is. He cannot win from those who came before, any more than he can win from those who come afterwards."

The seventeenth at St. Andrews in the Amateur Championship final against Cyril Tolley. Jones' second shot to the green was a talking-point for years. To appreciate its significance it must be remembered that spectator control then was more flexible than it is today. The gallery was not penned behind the famous road. Jones aimed deliberately to the left in the direction of the eighteenth tee. The ball struck a spectator and dropped safely out of trouble. I let Bernard Darwin's words take up the story: "Hundreds are prepared to take the oath that it would otherwise have been on the road, and an equal number of witnesses are quite certain that it would not." Tolley was not so fortunate. Obliged to go for the green, he found the dreaded Road bunker. The flag was between him and the road. He played a shot which Jones declared had "never been surpassed for exquisitely beautiful execution". Some years later Tolley told me that he thought Jones took a calculated decision and struck a low shot that was bound to hit a spectator with the obvious advantageous result. If that was so, the tactic was acceptable; then, with the help of a stymie, Jones won at the nineteenth and went on to make history.

SAM SNEAD

SAM SNEAD'S SWING HAD A NATURALNESS about the action that was flawless. The initial impact came in 1936. He never looked back. He won every major championship except, ironically, the United States Open, being runner-up five times and third once. The roll included the Open Championship, three PGA titles, Canadian Open, Western Open and three Masters. Altogether he won some 112 Open

Championships and tournaments.

Snead was a caricature of the true West Virginian, though I found his understated humour almost English. It moved between sharply defined monosyllables and shrewdly placed silences. He was never oleaginous. Whoever heard of a West Virginian being smug, smooth or smarmy?

HENRY COTTON

HENRY COTTON WAS A MAN OF FEW WORDS on a golf course. He earned the sobriquet given to him by Hagen of "Concentration Henry." Few golfers have subjected themselves to such ice-cold concentrated self-discipline.

For several years we had suites in the Dorchester Hotel. Often in the evening Henry would come down and argue about golfing theories. One thing we agreed upon. It is impossible to eliminate error. In every championship, he had two opponents – the course and himself. Mental tension took its toll. I ranked Henry Cotton head and shoulder above British professionals, past and present.

ARNOLD PALMER

NO INDIVIDUAL ELEVATED THE STATUS of a golf professional as much as Arnold Palmer. He took to the game in the Pittsburgh area, served in the United States Navy, took a degree at Wake Forest, went into business, preferred golf and proved the point by winning the US Amateur Championships in 1954, turned professional and never looked back. In all he collected four Masters, two Open Championships and one US Open title. The influence he exercised on the game is remarkable. It is only necessary to recall the scene as "Arnie's Army" swept across the fairways wherever he competed.

GARY PLAYER

GARY PLAYER'S RECORD is one long catalogue of success. It includes three Open titles – Muirfield 1959, Carnoustie 1968 and Lytham, 1974; the American Open 1965; two American PGA titles 1962 and 1972; and three wins in the Masters. He was only the third player to win the four major professional events.

On a personal note, I remember an evening in his home outside Johannesburg when we went upstairs to his tiny son's bedroom. Sleepily the lad produced a tooth from under the pillow and confided that by morning it would change into money.

JACK NICKLAUS

IF A GOLFER ENDOWED WITH powerful back and leg muscles and a pair of sturdy hands is looking for a model on which to base his game, he need seek no further than Jack Nicklaus. Here is power golf at its best. Jack Nicklaus, the first player to accumulate over £2 million in stake money, was a perpetual phenomenon. If he is not a genius the word has no meaning.

TIGER WOODS

THE SENSATIONAL WIN by Tiger Woods in the 1997 Masters at Augusta produced immediate reaction from the media. The twenty-one year old golfer had outplayed the world's greatest players. Mesmerized might have been a better description. His power-driving was impressive. Long holes became a drive-and-wedge. The spectacle upset everyone. And still does. He continues to dominate.

BEN HOGAN

BEN HOGAN ATTAINED A PEAK of perfection in his mastery of shot-making that has not been surpassed. In 1948 he won eleven tournaments, including the United States Open Championship with an all-time low of 276 and a second PGA title. Everything was set fair for domination of the golfing scene when a near-fatal accident, a head-on crash with a lorry in the fog, threatened to terminate his playing career in 1949. Recovery was miraculous. Later that year he came to England as non-playing captain of the American Ryder Cup team. At Southampton a fleet of Bentleys waited to take the party to the Savoy Hotel in London. I sat with Ben and Valerie in the first car, but it soon showed that his nerves were on edge. The memory of the crash and the fact that oncoming traffic seemed to be on the wrong side of the road caused such tension that I suggested dropping back in the car-cavalcade and reducing speed. The next morning, Ben had recovered his poise and we went by road to Scarborough via Oxford, where the team had coffee with the Fellows of Christ Church, then on to Stratford-upon-Avon for an official lunch.

In spite of being in constant pain and virtually encased in a rubber suit, Hogan led his team to a close victory. On returning to the States, grim determination brought him back to the tournament circuit, not token appearances, but victory in three National Championships in 1953. He finished first in the five events entered, including his second Masters Tournament, the fourth American Championship, and the Open Championship at his first attempt, plus a third PGA title. The extent of his recovery was a tribute to his incredible recuperative powers.

WOMEN GOLFERS

IN WOMEN'S GOLF LAURA DAVIES has introduced consistent power golf, winning over 40 titles including both British and American Opens in 1987. Like Pam Barton of an earlier, she personifies the good points of the game.

Mildred Zaharias upset the LGU opposition to women wearing trousers for golf, deeming them unsuitable. The American arrived at Gullane for the 1947 British Women's Championship having won fifteen tournament in a row. Trouser-clad, she outpowered opponents with the muscle of a professional. Steel-like wrists enabled her to lash the clubhead through. Few women had such powerful back and leg muscles. Mildred had married a well-known wrestler, George Zaharias. She confided it was a fortnight before he threw her! Her reputation was as America's star girl athlete. She covered the 80 metres Olympic hurdles in 11.3secs, hurled a javelin 143 feet: 4 inches, tossed a baseball 296 feet, high-jumped 5feet, 5¼ inches, and threw the shot 39 feet, ¾ inches.

Another rebel was Gloria Minoprio. I recall the LGU horror when she appeared in the English Championship dressed in black tight trousers, black polo-necked sweater, black turban, stark white make-up to protect her skin from the sun, and the innovation of only one club, carrying a cleek that she adapted for every shot.

Minoprio was a somewhat strange woman. Withdrawn and reserved, she seemed strangely reluctant to sit down. Henry Longhurst, always inquisitive, invited her to join us for a drink at the bar. She declined the stool, but explained. Her slacks were crease-free through a tight strap under her shoes. Additional strain might have had embarrassing consequences.

My choice for the women golfer of the century is Joyce Wethered. Few women hit the ball so straight with such flawless style. Her technique anticipated future trends. Playing against the great Bobby Jones, the American said afterwards she was the only female who could match him shot for shot with an ideal temperament.

THE BOAT RACE

THE UNIVERSITY BOAT RACE between Oxford and Cambridge is one of the last purely amateur events that attract unprecedented public appeal. People who have never handled an oar in their lives, and to whom a sliding seat might mean anything, regard it as part of the sporting calendar. Race preparation is tough. Both crews train intensively for twelve weeks, rowing over one thousand miles in practice sessions. The 4½-mile race hinges on three bends, two 90-degree right-hand bends and one 180-degree left-hand bend, everything depending on the inside station and the luck of the toss. The crew that holds sufficient lead to take their opponents' water has virtually won the race after one of the most gruelling tests of stamina in athletic events.

It has history on its side. I can give the exact time . . . 7.56pm on June 10th, 1829 . . . when both these universities sent a crew to Henley. The Master of Balliol tried to kill popular support by announcing a compulsory afternoon lecture on logic. The academic veto failed. By evening the roads were packed with enthusiasts. Contemporary chroniclers recorded that 20,000 people framed the Henley reaches. The Oxford crew took their colours from Christ Church, then Head of the River, and dressed in black straw hats, dark blue striped jerseys, blue handkerchiefs and canvas trousers. Cambridge had pink sashes over their shirts. Oxford won easily in 14 minutes, 30 seconds.

The appeal has never faltered. The first Boat Race of the Millennium saw 250,000 spectators packed on the riverbanks to see Oxford defy the odds. After seven successive defeats, the Dark Blues won by three lengths after a nail-biting fight. Stroke for stroke, and side by side for three miles, times at Chiswick Steps were identical. Oxford's final effort made a nonsense of the choppy waters. Now for next year!

THE FOURTH OF JUNE

APART FROM THE WEATHER, the same things happen every year according to tradition. The secret meeting of the Vikings in the morning. Those not admitted are scornful. Then the Speeches in the Upper School. Looking back, these always seem the same. In fact, the prospect of sitting on those terribly hard seats and having to listen to a score of items before luncheon seemed a grim prospect . . .unless it was raining . . . and then there was the consolation of having a roof over one's head. But it was not so bad once the Speeches started. But the seats were hard.

After luncheon, the Playing Fields. Agar's Plough. Whenever I am in love with cricket's grace, I think of the Fourth of June. Stumps standing upright behind the white line of the popping crease which Smith Minor has just broken as he takes his guard. Fieldsmen moving into their places. The kaleidoscopic effect of feminine colours fringing the ground, the sound of willow meeting leather . . . the pattern of the field breaks . . . two leisured runs are taken. Cricket indeed comes at the right moment of the year. It arrives with the spring, comes to full glory in the summer, and dies before the leaves of autumn fall. At Eton on the Fourth it seems to reach the crest of a wave of greater radiance.

Some spectators think it would be fun to throw off the years just for this afternoon. And that is what they do. Much to filial embarrassment they become even younger than their shiny-faced sons, who do their best to restore family dignity. But those little dark-coated youngsters with ridiculously big silk hats have little time for the past or even the immediate present. There are always dreams and plans for tomorrow. There will always be tomorrow. The grass they so lightly tread is still fresh with the morning dew.

Only the onlooker realises the bitter truth of those words: "The young have aspirations that never come to pass, the old have reminiscences of what never happened."

The runs are still coming . . . but the wickets are falling quicker. Soon will come the Procession of the Boats . . . the crews in their distinctive costumes . . . white duck trousers. They glide silently up the river. In the distance we hear the strains of the *Boating Song:* Harrovians and Wykehamists may disagree with the last line – "But we'll still swing together. And swear by the best of schools," but none can be immune to the atmosphere by Fellows Eyot when multi-coloured fireworks fill the night air with sound and colour. The darkness is cut by flashing lights. The Fourth of June has ended. It has been exactly the same as previous years. And it has been just as heavenly.

Current accusations of Test cricketers throwing matches have left a nasty taste. With relief I turn to an annual fixture that still has a freshness untainted by greed and the money man.

Wisden conducted a poll to establish the outstanding cricketers of the century. The following were listed in order of merit: 1. Don Bradman: 2. Gary Sobers: 3. Jack Hobbs: 4. Shane Warne: 5. Viv Richards: 6. Dennis Lillee & Frank Worrell: 8. Walter Hammond: 9. Denis Compton: 10. Richard Hadlee & Imran Khan: 12. Sunil Gavaskar: 13. Sydney Barnes & Len Hutton: 15. Bill O'Reilly: 16. Ian Botham: 17. Harold Larwood & Ray Lindwall: 19. Sachin Tendulkar: 20. Richie Benaud with George Headley & Kapil Dev: 23. Graeme Pollock with Wilfred Rhodes & Victor Trumper: 26. Godfrey Evans with Malcolm Marshall & Wasim Akram: 29. Alec Bedser with Clarrie Grimmett, Fred Trueman & Frank Woolley: 33. Curtly Ambrose, Colin Bland, Allan Border, Ian Chappell. B.J.T. Bosanquet, Baghwat Chandrasekher, Learie Constantine, Allan Donald, A.P. 'Tich' Freeman, Lance Gibbs, Michael Holding, Clive Lloyd, Stan McCabe, Bruce Mitchell, K.S. Ranjitsinhji. Maurice Tate, Pelham Warner.

Interesting, but a somewhat predictable catalogue, rather like media tipsters for the Derby who with umbrella coverage are reasonably assured of naming the winner! Wisden's list lumps together 49 players bracketed against 33 selections!

I am more interested in compiling a shorter list of men who

made the mark, plus others not so well known but nevertheless important in the legends of cricket.

1. C.B. Fry: 2. Jack Hobbs: 3. Herbert Sutcliffe: 4. W.G. Grace: 5. Harold Larwood: 6. Keith Miller: 7. Don Bradman: 8. Ian Botham 9. Denis Compton: 10. Mike Atherton: 11. Fred Trueman: 12. Groundsmen.

My choice for the all-time cricketer: Don Bradman.

1. C.B. Fry . . . so versatile, impossible to slot into one category. Cricketing record speaks for itself. 30,000 runs with an average of 50 per innings; world record holder in long jump; gained an England cap for football; as an academic at Oxford gained first-class honours in Classical Moderations; refused the Kingdom of Albania. Enthusiastic about anything he tackled, particularly the boys' training ship. When last we met, in quirky mood, he donned an academic gown and demonstrated how a cricket bat should be held.

2. Jack Hobbs personified the grace of fluent batsmanship. Scored 61,237 runs with an average of 50; that included 197 centuries. In 61 Tests amassed 5,410 runs with average of 56. Highest score 316 not out in 1926. I was invited to field a side against a Jack Hobbs XI; he scored 37; we won; the Charity benefited. His memory is recalled in the Jack Hobbs Pavilion.

3. Herbert Sutcliffe established the legendary opening partnership with Jack Hobbs. It was a contrast in styles, but the mixture worked.

4. W.G. Grace could be controversial, cantankerous and stubborn; tactical opportunist and captain of rare achievement. Regarded by many as the greatest English cricketer. The claim is irrelevant. Any batsman who scores centuries for 38 years is in a class of his own. He recorded a thousand runs in a month against top-class bowling from Spofforth who made Larwood, Trueman and Lindwall look medium-paced. Statistics make the point. 126 centuries in first-class cricket; 54,896 runs averaging 39.55 an innings; 2,876 wickets at 17.92 runs apiece; highest scores 344, 318 not out, 301, and carried his bat 17 times through a completed innings. In Tests against Australia, averaged 32.39 including two centuries. He came on the scene a year after over-arm bowling was officially accepted. His mother's scrap-books show top-hatted

George Parr, Caffyn, Willsher, Clarke, Box and Julius Caesar. After his death, Sir Stanley Jackson phrased the inscription on the Memorial Gate at Lord's:

> To the Memory of
> William Gilbert Grace
> The Great Cricketer.

5. Harold Larwood . . . linked with the bodyline tour of 1932-33, and Douglas Jardine, the England captain, who orchestrated the leg-theory tactics that neutralised Don Bradman who disliked the fast stuff.

6. Keith Miller . . . one of Australia's finest all-rounders; devastating fast bowler with an explosive action.

7. Don Bradman . . . finest all-round cricketer, the ultimate run-making machine Bill Davies, one-time Deputy Governor of the Bank of England and treasurer of Cambridge University Cricket Club, recalled how, when the Australians played the University at Fenners, he bowled the Don for a duck. The feat went into the records, but at the time was most unpopular with the spectators.

8. Mike Atherton, who defied West Indies bowlers for over 12 1/2 hours with 83 and 108 to win the final Test against their opponents for the first time in 31 years.

9. Denis Compton . . . made cricket seem a lighthearted experience. Captained England in both cricket and football and won and F.A. Cup medal with Arsenal. Unorthodox but brilliant batsman.

10. Ian Botham, cricketing legend, larger than life.

11. Fred Trueman . . . fast bowler of pace and fury; immensely powerful, blunt character; a spade became a bloody shovel; played in 67 Tests with a world record of 307 wickets. I recall an occasion when we entertained Norman Yardly and members of the Yorkshire team. Fred sat next to Jean and never stopped talking. Afterwards she said it was juicy stuff, but unfortunately the points were missed through his strong Yorkshire accent.

12. Groundsmen are a race apart with skills that influence match results. I think of "Bosser" Martin, who reigned for 51 years at the Oval, a familiar character with untidy moustache and tilted hat. I recall how he turned the Oval pitch into a feather bed that broke the heart of every bowler, particularly the "shirtfront" wicket for the 1938 Fifth Test Match against the Australians. Len Hutton scored 364. The innings was declared at 903 for seven wickets, the highest total for an innings in England. "Bosser's" comment was true: "It all depends on winning the toss" - a sentiment that Boat Race crews would confirm.

ATHLETICS

TOP-LEVEL ATHLETES LIVE IN a split-second world and the challenge to break the limits of human endurance. Their movements are like poetry in action. Public appreciation was shared with the Oscar-winning film *Chariots of Fire*. The narrative was real life fictionalised. On many occasions I listened to its re-enactment by its inspiration, Harold Abrahams, whose ambition was the 100m in the 1924 Olympics. We used to travel on the evening train from Liverpool Street to Cambridge; Harold left at Bishop's Stortford. Over a drink in the buffet bar he relived his victory over the American favourite; his admiration for Eric Liddell, a brilliant athlete who not only won seven caps as wing-three-quarter for Scotland, but succeeded in the 1924 Olympics 400 metres. He could have won the 100 metres, but the heats were held on the Sunday. Religious scruples forced him to withdraw. The following year Liddell went to China as a missionary, but died in a Japanese internment camp. The entire story is portrayed in the film.

The character of Lord Lindsey played by Nigel Havers was based on David Burghley, the hurdler who in the 1928 Olympics won the 400 metres hurdles to break the previous American domination of this event. In 1932 he won another gold with the record time of 52.01secs.

24 years later David became the 6th Earl, Marquess of Exeter, and became a significant figure in the Olympics hierarchy, becoming chairman of the 1948 London Games organising committee. In that capacity I discussed with him the possible dangers of athletes taking performance-enhancing substances. He strongly condemned such practices and would have given short shift to the current president's indirect approval of the use of drugs

in the Sydney Games. On a lighter note he admitted quiet satisfaction that his role as President of the AAA was reflected on his Rolls Royce number place AAAI.

Four more athletes . . . Roger Bannister, the first man to break the 4-minutes barrier for the mile. Iffley Road track at Oxford was the venue. He was paced over the first half-mile by Chris Brasher at 1.58:0; then taken by Chris Chattaway through the third lap in 3:00.5; then left to battle himself, crossing the line in 3min. 59.4secs. History had been made.

Sebastian Coe's record is incredible, with eleven world records: he actually held the 800m, 1000m, 1500, and mile records in the same year. Herb Elliott, the Australian middle-distance runner who in 44 races crushed the opposition at 1500 metres and the mile. His finest victory came in the 1960 Rome Olympics 1500m final, beating his own world record in 3min. 35.6secs.

Sydney Wooderson became a legend and yet never looked the part. He broke the world mile record in 1937; did the same in the 800m the following year; but scaled the heights in the 1946 European Championships by taking the 5000 metres by 30 yards. Off the track Wooderson became a tiny bespectacled citizen, unassuming, almost anonymous.

My choice for the athlete of the century is Paavo Nurmi, the Finnish athlete who won nine gold medals and three silver medals at the Olympics, altogether claiming 31 world records between 1920 and 1932. He stands alone in athletic achievement. His farewell token appearance was in the 1952 Helsinki Games. He carried the Olympic torch on its final lap from Greece. Alongside Nurmi I add Fanny Blankers-Koen, who won four gold medals at the 1948 Games. Watching her that week brought the realisation that this 30-year-old housewife and mother of two had finally emancipated the women's athletic scene. It had come of age. Had the war years not interrupted hers would have been an even more outstanding career: she nevertheless won the 100 metres, 200 metres, 80 metres hurdles and anchored the sprint relay. She had not entered for the high and long jumps in which she already held the world records.

We honour the Flying Dutchwoman and the Flying Finn.

TURF RECOLLECTIONS

THE BEST PLACE TO APPRECIATE the unique equine succession of the thoroughbred racehorse is in a Newmarket building where past and present receive equal due. In 1777 a writer declared that "it modestly turns its back upon the street, as if to shun the public view in silent retirement." The words still apply. The Jockey Club, as befits the ultimate authority of the racing world, is conservative in habits, exclusive in membership, and dignified in repose. Within its walls are preserved reminders of the past. Here is The Whip alleged to have been given by Charles II, the wristband woven from hairs taken from the tail of *Eclipse*. William IV presented a companion relic: an *Eclipse* hoof mounted on a gold salver. It is appropriate that the Jockey Club should be the guardian of these trifles of racing history, commemorating as they do the career of the most famous horse the English turf has known. For me it was a rare moment when I held the hoof in my hand.

These relics take us back to two centuries to the Duke of Cumberland's breeding establishment at Cumberland Lodge in Windsor Great Park. The country people at that time were apprehensive. It was the moment of the great eclipse of 1764. During it a mare foaled. Not unnaturally the spindly youngster was named *Eclipse*. Until the age of five the horse was not run in public. A salesman in Leadenhall Market bought him as a yearling for seventy-five guineas. He won his first race in May 1769 – the beginning of a racing career in which he was never beaten or even extended. At stud *Eclipse* became the sire of 335 winners, who won over £160,000 in stakes alone between the years 1774 and 1796. Fees from the horse's services as a stallion were £25,000. In direct descent, a yearling filly fetched 10,000 guineas; a racehorse in training fetched £37,375; two sires produced stock that won over half-a-million sterling. No other English horse has had such a record, not even the Maktoun factory-process.

The past is always near the Jockey Club. Fred Archer's whip steered 2,748 mounts past the winning-post. It delivered the two vicious welts 50 yards from the past that spurred *Melton* to snatch the Derby from *Paradox*. Paintings on the walls show jockeys riding with long leathers up to the modern pulled-up stirrups. One canvas by John Wotton is particularly interesting. The subject is a dour, puritanical gentleman named Tregonwell Frampton, "Keeper of the Running Horses to their Sacred Majesties" during the reign of William and Mary, and trainer to Queen Anne, George I and George II. He was the first professional trainer and an intense woman-hater.

Ownership of thoroughbred bloodstock used to carry the hall mark of wealth and aristocracy, with names like the Stanley family, Rosebebery, Victor Sassoon, Waldorf Astor, James de Rothschild, and Cavendish-Bentinck. Each one in the true line of English owner-breeders, unlike the Maktoum family who have bought instant success. In 1977 they had one horse. Since then they have established a monopoly of horses in training, brood mares, several studs and shares in virtually every leading stallion. Cost is of little importance to this family from a small oil State in the Persian Gulf. Their method of block investment does not appeal. I prefer vintage memories unsullied by crude oil.

I recall the Maharajah of Baroda, who knew success and frustration; internal political upheaval in India forced him to trim racing ambitions. In 1951 the Indian Government deposed him as ruler of Baroda, a decision that killed any possibility of rivalling the Aga Khan's position in the turf. Time had run out. Memories of a more relaxed Gaekwar are linked with King's Parade in Cambridge, in particular the KP restaurant run by Grace Marsh, daughter of the Beckhampton trainer, Sam Darling. It was a unique establishment. People who walked down the narrow passageway would have featured in a celebrity *Who's Who*.

Its success was due to this lady, who in racing lore became a legend. "Mops", as she was affectionately known, presided in regal style. Her appearance never altered. Dressed with an Edwardian touch, she sat in a small, elegantly furnished room on the left as you entered. Only the chosen few were invited to have a glass of sherry in the sanctum. Her reminiscences had total recall, particularly of the days when her husband, Richard, trained *Persimmon* to win the Derby and the St. Leger for the Prince of Wales. Those familiar with the record of this spirited horse should visit the National Horseracing Museum in Newmarket, where his stuffed head is on loan from the Queen's racing collection. "Mops" used to describe how *Persimmon* almost missed the Derby altogether. His high-mettled temperament rebelled at the thought of the horsetrain-box. Attempts failed with the first two special trains at Dullingham station. The last train was about to leave without the fretful horse. Marsh took drastic action. Twelve men literally carried *Persimmon* on board. Once installed, he settled down with no further trouble.

Further memories were how Richard achieved the Triple Crown with *Diamond Jubilee,* who came to Egerton House, their family home, in 1898 as an unbroken yearling with a devilish temper that made training a nightmare. Victory in the Grand National with *Ambush II* made the Prince of Wales the only owner to have won the Derby and the famous steeplechase in the same year. In 1989 Marsh won another Derby and the distinction of recording a win for a reigning sovereign in the Classics. In "Mops'" world memories never faded. She still felt Richard's influence, a belief assuredly helped by her faith in spiritualism. Her son, Marcus, added to the family successes. Inheriting his father's flair, he won the 1934 Derby and St. Leger with *Windsor Lad* for the Majarajah of Rajpla, and the same races in 1952 for the Aga Khan. Two years earlier he won the Derby with *Palestine.*

The KP Visitor's Book was an autograph hunter's dream. Each signature invoked an anecdote, particularly those of Clark Gable and Humphrey Bogart. Grace also had an eye for future talent. Several Cabinet Ministers could look back on undergraduate days. I recall Norman St. John Stevas, now ennobled, unbelievably foppish with impeccable manners, later to become Master of my own College, Emmanuel, still having the same garish taste in clothes and purple socks in deference to the Pope. I remember Gaekwar of Baroda's satisfaction at creating a Newmarket Sales record by paying 28,000 Guineas for a yearling. Conversation that evening was interrupted when an undergraduate from Baroda about to leave, saw the Gaekwar, and prostrated himself on the ground, a diversion that did not upset the head-waiter, who stepped over the recumbent body to announce that dinner was ready. The closing of the KP was a loss.

A word about jockeys. Looking through the records I am reminded of the truism that good horses make good jockeys. That is only partly true. Successful jockeys need certain qualities seldom found in one man. I believe that Gordon Richards was the nearest to this standard. In 1931 he passed the total with 259 winners. Evaluating his jockeyship is not easy. Like Fred Archer, his record is in a category of its own. Injuries alone prevented him from winning the title of Champion Jockey 21 years in succession. He rode with a long reign, had perfect balance, and, like Lester Piggott, a highly developed will to win. In every sense Gordon Richards personified the Champion Jockey. He dominated the Turf.

Summing-up, Newmarket is to horseracing what St. Andrews means to golf. For me one aspect never changes. It is as fresh as it was in the time of the mysterious Devil's Dyke. Walk over the Lime Kilns on a early misty morning before the world is awake. The brooding silence that marks the interlude between night and day is everywhere. An air of vibrant expectancy shimmers over dew-laden grass; silence disturbed by the first drowsy notes of a thrush. Then, like the spirit of the Heath, a string of the most graceful creatures in the world emerge from the mists with smooth sweeping strides . . . festoons of breath from distended nostrils linger in the morning air . . . the thud of hooves grows faint . . . and the vision fades into a grey, meditative silence. That is Newmarket.

RINGSIDE STRATEGY

I HAVE LITTLE PATIENCE with those who cannot find dramatic excitement in the boxing-ring, whilst deploring the abuses that so often make it a "racket". A classic example was the fight at Madison Square Garden between Evander Holyfield and Lennox Lewis for the undisputed heavyweight championship of the world. After a gruelling fight in which Lennox was clearly the winner the judges declared a draw. The travesty of boxing judgement called for a Federal Enquiry, but such legal niceties are soon forgotten when a mega-million refight guaranteed both pugilists and promoter Don King personal fortunes. There is little hope for clean contests when blatant "fixing" is acceptable.

There is nothing new about the practice. I recall the fight in 1927 christened "The Battle of the Long Count" between challenger Jack Dempsey and Gene Tunney. It was a clash of styles. Dempsey, living up to his reputation as the "Manassa Mauler", was the American legend, one-time hobo; he had fought in tough saloons for meal-tickets. Now he was matched against Gene Tunney, former US marine, with a middle-class Greenwich family background. Dempsey's onslaught crushed Tunney's stylish methods. He slumped to the canvas in the seventh round. Dempsey stood over the sprawling Tunney instead of going to a neutral corner. The referee, Dave Barry, refused to start the count. The delay enabled Tunney to regain his feet, eventually winning on points.

Somehow Tunney never appealed to the American public. His style was too methodical and clinical. Effective, for he only lost once in 83 contests, retired in 1928 as undefeated champion, married a millionairess, one of the children becoming an American Senator. Years later I had dinner in London with Jack Dempsey and his actress wife, Estelle Taylor. Recalling incidents in his career, he accepted blame for the "Long Count". "Dave Barry had no alternative," but the title-fight he recalled in detail was against Georges Carpentier in 1921, "stage-managed" by Tex Rickard, the fore-runner of the Don King mould.

Carpentier was the ring's first pin-up, his good looks attracting thousands of female fans. An added appeal was the *Croix de Guerre* for bravery in the war. Dempsey admired his courage, both in and out of the ring. He never hesitated to concede weight. Superior skill was compensation as Bombardier Billy Wells and Joe Beckett found to their cost. His fight at Boyle's Thirty Acres, Jersey City, in 1921, that drew the first-ever million-dollar gates, left Dempsey with reservations. He thought the fans were short-changed through Carpentier being under-trained, though he still remembered the power behind the Frenchman's right hand. Superior weight turned the scales. Carpentier was left unconscious after four rounds.

That evening in London is still fresh in my mind. Dempsey was an American folk-hero, a media head-liner before the 1929 Wall Street crash. Time had mellowed the ferocious spirit. He was more anxious to talk about film-making in Hollywood in which his wife was involved. Georges Carpentier out of the ring was equally talkative, holding court at his favourite table in the popular restaurant he had opened in Paris. Like Dempsey, he felt fistic topics were episodes of a forgotten world, but he still felt resentful that a foul blow caused him to retire in the fourteenth round of his fifteen-round title-fight against Gene Tunney in 1924. His manager,

Francois Descamps, had argued that the verdict should have gone against the American. Wishful thinking. On both visits to Paris, conversation turned on the golfing prospects of his daughter, who was championship quality. On the last occasion her skill on the fairways was confirmed by her friend Vicomtesse de St. Sauveur, the only French girl to win the British Ladies Championship. Somewhere along the line, enthusiasm must have softened for we never saw the Carpentier offspring invading our links.

Whilst on the subject of flawed boxing decisions, I think of two bouts involving Henry Cooper. The first was against Cassius Clay in 1963. The unbelievable happened that night. At the end of the fourth round the American was floored by a wicked left hook. It looked doubtful whether Clay would recover in time. The bell sounded. Then inexplicably the American's glove was found to be split. His trainer, Angelo Dundee, welcomed the vital seconds' respite whilst another glove was fitted. Clay recovered. In the fifth round the fight was stopped because of Cooper's facial cuts. The second bout was in 1971 against Joe Bugner for the British Commonwealth and European titles. Cooper, then 36, survived the early flurry of powerful blows from his younger opponent and was cruising to victory, then, to everyone's amazement, Harry Gibbs raised Bugner's arm. Shortly afterwards Cooper retired, but even today swears he was robbed. Bugner was equally adamant that the decision was right. At that time Joe was a keen supporter of BRM, but even in the pits we agreed to differ in fistic topics, but not on a matrimonial matter. I pointed out that his estranged wife could beat him on points every time. He did not disagree. Another instance of a controversial decision was the fight for the WBO world middleweight title at Earl's Court in 1991 between Chris Eubank and Michael Watson. Up to then the Brighton boxer had never been beaten, but that night he was so outboxed that the result was never in doubt. The split points decision in Eubank's favour was given a hostile reception of disbelief with Eubank strutting round the ring in petulant style. Such are the vagaries of the ring. Only a knockout is safe. Of all the unbelievable pugilistic characters, Eubank heads the extrovert category. He postures, poses, and does anything to attract attention. It is part of a personal publicity campaign. He sat at my table for a Sportsman of the Year lunch at the Park Lane Hotel in London. He turned up wearing a Saville Row hacking jacket, jodhpurs and riding crop but was somewhat non-committal when I enquired where he had parked his horse.

There were so many extrovert fistic figures, it is impossible to list them all. I think of Carlos Monzon, the Argentian, who preened like a peacock. I watched him retain his world middleweight title in Monaco during the Monte Carlo Grand Prix week. His record was impressive. Unbeaten in 82 fights, he retired as undefeated champion in 1977.

Colourful, volatile, with uncontrollable temper, he was infatuated with motor-racing. Walter-Mitty-like, he saw himself as a racing driver, but was irritated when I said that at the wheel of a racing car around the Monaco circuit, he was an inevitable patient at the Princess Grace Hospital. He argued that you never know until you try. He ought to know. At the outset he was a pimp, then found there was money in vicious hooks. His track record confirmed the hunch. His private life was stormy. Exasperated by philandering, his wife shot him in the back. He threw his film-star mistress to her death from a hotel balcony after a row; convicted of murder, then, on parole, was killed in a car crash.

Freddie Mills was another with a ruthless streak. World heavyweight champion after winning the light-heavyweight title, he took on opponents conceding weight advantage, sometimes as much as two stone. Immense courage and capacity to absorb punishment took its toll. The end was inevitable. He retired in 1965 after 97 fights. Under suspicious circumstances, he was found dead with gunshot wounds outside his London nightclub. Asked to nominate the Sportsman of the Year, I chose Mills. At the Savoy lunch he sat with other winners, like Henry Moore, Graham Greene and Michael Wilding,

Looking for the boxing champion of the century, I narrow the choice to four champions. Mohammed Ali who was world heavyweight champion three times, losing only five fights in 61 contests. Like most boxers, he refused to retire. Pointless fights left him punch-drunk, so that today his faltering, shambling movements are heart-breaking to see. He was a rare champion, who could be remembered by such poetic quotes as "Float like a butterfly, sting like a bee", not forgetting his quote "I am the greatest." At the peak, the claim was true.

Mike Tyson must be considered. His record as world champion is awesome, but his criminal record has devalued any claim to recognition. He is a disgraced figure of New York's black ghetto community.

Lennox Lewis stands out as our first undisputed world champion having won all three titles of the same weight. The confusing triple titles reflects the untidy chaotic situation due, as in other sports, to commercial greed by match-fixers. Maybe one day there will be one genuine title-holder, but as long as promoter Don King is around it is wishful thinking.

My choice of the greatest boxer of the century is Joe Louis. Heavyweight champion of the world in 1937, he retired undefeated after twenty-five successful defences of the title. One win in particular stands out. The demolition in 2min.17sec. of Max Schmeling and the Göebbels Nazi-inspired claim that the fight was an Aryan versus black confrontation.

TENNIS

LAWN TENNIS HAS MANY PLAYERS as likely candidates. Bill Tilden, Ken Rosewall, Rod Laver, The Dominant Four Musketeers, Jean Borotra with beret, Rene Lacoste, Jacques Brugnon and Henri Cochet who from 1927 to 1932 won the Davis Cup for France – extrovert and brilliant. Even so, my choice goes to Fred Perry, the last Englishman to win Wimbledon. His views were always incisive, did not suffer fools lightly, but was amazed that his peers should have erected a statue to him that stands just inside the Fred Perry Gate at Wimbledon.

There have been so many star women players. The effervescent Mo Connolly, Suzanne Lenglen of legend, Margaret du Pont, Helen Wills-Moody, Steffi Graf, Monica Selles, Virginia Wade, who won the Singles title for England, these are but a few of the "greats". My shared choice would be Martina Navratilova. Her record is remarkable. 167 Singles titles, including nine in Wimbledon. Born in Prague, she became an American citizen in 1981. As an attacking serve-volleyer, Martina was in a class of her own. Alongside must be bracketed the 2000-Wimbledon triumph of

Venus and Serena Williams, girls of the ghetto who were taught to believe in themselves and have become the most talented exponents of the modern power-packed game. Some critics say Serena is more gifted; Venus, credited with serving the women's record speed of 127 mph, has been descried as moving across the court with the grace of a camel. Be that as it may, the fact remains that these sisters, emotionally in tune, are making tennis history.

RUGBY

RUGBY FOOTBALL HAS SEVERAL CLAIMANTS, men like Jonah Lomu, whose stature and fitness played havoc with opponents in the Nineties; Colin Meade, Rob Andrews, J.P.R. Williams, Dickie Jeeps, brilliant, but falling short of the excellence shown by Gareth Edwards, whom I regard as the best scrum-half of all time. He played 53 internationals for Wales, plus ten Tests with the British Lions. Few forget the years of Welsh dominance with Gareth Edwards, Barry John and Phil Bennett, a legendary trio.

MOTOR RACING

REGARDING PERSONAL INVOLVEMENT in motor-racing, Jean and I as Chairman and Joint Managing Director led the BRM racing car to victory in Formula One World Championship races. Among our drivers were Juan Manuel Fangio, Peter Collins, Mike Hawthorn, Graham Hill, Jackie Stewart and Niki Lauda. I include a starting-grid of our BRM drivers, plus a list of some of our wins. We have warm memories of five victories in the Monaco Grand Prix; taking the United States title was always satisfying, likewise Italy, Germany and Austria. Fangio I rate as the greatest racing-driver; the combined skills of Jackie Stewart, Jim Clark and Ayrton Senna have the edge on the current group. Michael Schumacher has flair. With an income per season of £60,000 million, sponsors and the Ecclestone squad expect a return on investment. This aspect is over the top, and obscene. I don't blame Schumacher for accepting the money, but the system has gone mad. I prefer to recall drivers like Graham Hill, who was the sport's finest ambassador without any hint of arrogance. I had immense admiration for men like Colin

Chapman, Enzo Ferrari and John Cooper, engineering pioneers.

Sadly the mega-business of Ecclestone and his colleagues has killed the old camaraderie among entrants and drivers. Even more regrettable is the decline in the sense of caring. Everything has become self-centred and selfish, everybody has a price. What happens to the other fellow, outside of a limited, self-governing elite, is of little consequence. The fact that a new young driver, Jason Button, has burst on the scene, was hailed as unique. Up-and-coming youngsters of the past who made good would today be sidelined unless they brought substantial sponsor cash. This trait runs counter to the traditions of motor-racing established by men who found in the sport a way of life. In the long run it is the sum total of the character of the men who participate, and has nothing to do with bankrolls . . .

I am entitled to the luxury of recalling an historic BRM victory that made racing history: the 1971 Italian Grand Prix and Monza. Peter Gethin had only one Grand Prix victory, but it made history. The 3.57-mile circuit set its usual challenge with high-speed curves and long flat-out straights, an examination that sorted out boys from men. That year we brought five BRMs. Jo Siffert, Peter Gethin and Howden Ganley were in the PI60s with mark 2 engines, Helmus Marko in a PI53.

In practice Siffert had lapped 1min:23.95sec. Chris Amon took pole position, clocking 1min:22.40secs, with Jackie Ickx second. Ganley was on the second row thanks to a tow from Stewart and Peterson.

The start was sensational. Regazzoni was just ahead of Siffert as the pack hurtled into the Curve Grande where the circuit had been narrowed. As the race-pattern settled the lead continually changed until lap 41 when Siffert and Ickx dropped back. Amon had fallen back to sixth place after a nasty moment. Tearing off a visor-cover, he had also lost his goggles.

Those opposed to overtaking manoeuvres, like Max Mosley today, might be reminded of that afternoon when the lead changed hands eight times. The field had settled into two groups. Gethin found himself in no-man's-land, isolated, without any hope of getting a tow. The only answer was to drive like hell. It worked. By lap 35 he was sixth, 5.6secs behind the leading bunch. By lap 40 the margin was cut to 4.0 secs with ten laps remaining. The gap fell to 3.3secs. By then Gethin was with Peterson, Cevert Hailwood and Ganley. Slip-streaming took him into the lead on laps 52 and 53. Confident that the BRM had sufficient power, Gethin dropped back on the penultimate lap. Everything depended on tactics at the Parabolica.

Cevert's ploy was to let Peterson through at the entrance, take a wider line and exit first to take the lead. Peterson aimed to lead through the Parabolica, banking on his acceleration having the edge on the Tyrrell. Gethin's challenge was discounted. So much for theory. Gethin, brakes locking, took the BRM on the inside line. Both cars were forced out wide in parallel slides. The BRM rev-limit was 10,600 rpm. As Gethin told me afterwards, he had nothing to lose. In high second-gear, the engine went over 11,500 rpm. The engine did not blow up. Gethin won by 0.01 seconds. Only 0.61-seconds covered the first four cars. It was BRM's second World Championship victory in succession. Gethin's record-breaking winning average of 151.31mph became and still is the fastest in Formula One World Championship races.

In retrospect Jean and I have the satisfaction of knowing that every Grand Prix success enjoyed by BRM, including the Formula One World championship title and the Constructor's World Championship, came during our stewardship and directive. On a more personal note I appreciated the words written by Niki Lauda, three times World Champion: . . . "Louis Stanley gave me enormous encouragement at the start of my racing career. We first met on Christmas Eve at Vienna airport to discuss the terms of my contract with BRM. We broke off so I could discuss the deal with my parents and lawyers while Louis went to St Stephen's Cathdral to hear the Vienna Boys' Choir sing the traditional Christmas Eve Carol service. I signed the contract before Louis' plane left for London. With team-mates Jean-Pierre Baptiste and Clay Regozzoni, I gained invaluable experience at BRM before moving on to Ferrari.

"Louis Stanley is a remarkable man by any standards. This was made abundantly clear when I crashed in the first lap of the German Grand Prix at the Nurburgring. My car was engulfed in flames, my injuries so severe that the medics thought I would die. I was saved due to the specialised treatment I received at the hands of Europe's finest burns specialist flown in by Louis. It was just another example of his spontaneous, selfless reaction to a crisis."

One tribute I value more than all came from Jackie Stewart:

"Louis Stanley wears many hats in motor racing, and has coats of many colours. He is a man of strong convictions. He undertakes many tasks, some of which seem impossible. He executes these with no concern for his personal popularity, because, in some instances, he is driving directly against conventions and sometimes the Establishment as we in motor racing know it. The duties he undertakes would fill the lifetime of lesser men. In all his dealings and efforts his beliefs are sincere. His interest in racing is intensive and to many drivers his presence is assuring and comforting when things are not well. In cases of accidents he has been a pillar of strength to the people most clearly affected by this side of motor racing."

Looking back over our motor-racing years, I do not think so much of the Grands Prix that we won or lost, but the skill and courage displayed. What I hold in mind and affection are those men, many close friends who lived their lives wholly in the sport and died through it. In imagination they have become immortal characters in a sporting epic. They will stay like that through the years ahead. They are no longer with us, but for those who knew them, such recollections are tinged with sadness. There is one consolation. Memories never age.

ALL TIME CHAMPIONS

SPORTING PERSONALITIES OF THE CENTURY are too many to chronicle. Instead I single out the élite across the board as a cross-section of memories, past and present. I ignore commercial interests that have made a mockery of values. Football and motor-racing are the worst. Burgeoning wages for players and drivers far exceed what the average support earns in a lifetime. In football about a hundred players net more than £1-million a season, more than ten times more than Tony Blair. Skills of men like David Beckham, Michael Schumacher, Alan Shearer, David Coultard and Michael Owen make headlines, but they are no better than their predecessors like Alex James, Jim Clark, George Best, Mike Hawthorn. The only difference is the older generation earned a pittance. Selecting the outstanding footballer of all time is difficult. My choice is Sir Stanley Matthews. When he died, the world of football paid tribute to the man whose wizardry on the pitch mesmerized opponents.

Table of the Élite

Motor-racing ~ Fangio
Golf ~ Ben Hogan, Joyce Wethered
Turf ~ Sir Gordon Richards
Boxing ~ Joe Louis
Football ~ Sir Stanley Matthews
Rugby ~ Gareth Edwards
Lawn Tennis ~ Fred Perry, Martina Navratilova
Athletics ~ Paolo Nurmi, Fanny Blanjers-Koen
Cricket ~ Sir Donald Bradman
Rowing ~ Steve Redgrave, with the remarkable feat of winning his 5th gold medal at the Sydney Olympics - a record for an endurance event at the Games.

CHAPTER NINE

SAINTS AND HERETICS

~

"GOD MOVES IN a mysterious way....." There is no doubt that the Church of England is in a distressing state and showing signs of decline. Membership has sunk to a low level. In 1957 the electoral-roll membership was nearly three million. In 1994 the total had dropped to 1.4 million. The fall has continued. The number of stipended clergy in the established Church is at its lowest since 1851, declining to 9,180: as a proportion of the population, the lowest number since the Reformation. There are several contributory factors. We now live in a multi-faith society with different standards. Our reassessment has been flawed. Some church leaders, apprehensive of being thought intolerant or narrow-minded, have adopted wishy-washy trendiness. Their message has lacked a Christian clarity. Maverick bishops have become preoccupied with secular politics, the ethics of investment and the morality of business practices, but failed to give comfort or guidance to the laity.

Instead of pronouncing what is a sin in the eyes of the world, the answer has been left to individual consciences. The Church has become silent about sin in an attempt not to alienate sinners. Inevitably this meant a clash between those for whom traditional answers are not negotiable and those for whom they are merely a starting-point for new thinking. Many clerics have abandoned the moral code of which the Church is the guardian.

Not only has the Church failed to provide moral leadership, but many clergy are denying the Bible's teaching. An instance of this occurred when the Reverend Anthony Freeman was sacked by the Bishop of Chichester for claiming he did not believe in God. His reaction was to produce a declaration signed by twenty-two Anglican priests expressing regret for the dismissal. Freeman later claimed in a BBC interview that his views were shared by a significant number of priests. Obviously the Church has to work within the framework, but that does not mean accommodating everything. Unfortunately this has spread. Certain bishops have drifted with the tide of fashion and embraced the trendy sociology distrusted by traditionally-minded congregations, excursions that have undermined the patient work done by parish priests year-in and year-out. Pews may be half-empty, but those who attend feel strongly about this type of approach to theology, its modification of ethical beliefs activated by the wish not to condemn the contemporary mores of society.

The malaise is deep-seated. There is reluctance to acknowledge that the Church of England has always had great breadth of view from High Church to Low Church, from Catholic to Evangelical, held together by accepting the same system of Bishops and Priests and believing the same three Creeds. There have been crises but in spite of the Reformation all three essentials remained intact. Despite divorced Kings, Spanish marriages, Protestant zealots and Catholic martyrs, the Faith survived. The Gospels are clear, but confusing issues over the past few decades have brought unease over controversial issues.

Elevation to high ecclesiastical office tends to encourage an intellectual snobbery that questions the tenets of the Faith, clever-clever attitudes that undermine fundamental teachings of the Church. Debates in academic circles about such radical views, often heretical in substance, are acceptable, but using the media to gain publicity has done immense harm. Bishop John Robinson was guilty of causing such distress. Here was an agreeable cleric who became self-centred after being labelled the most controversial theologian of the century. Although denying the charge, Robinson loved to shock people. It did something for his ego. Occasionally we lunched in a Coton cottage presided over by Mrs Barker of

Grantchester renown. Awkward topics were avoided, no mention of *Honest to God,* the book in which Robinson rubbished the concept of God as an old man in the sky, arguing that Jesus Christ was a normal human being not a perfect being. In *The Human Face of God,* Robinson warmed to the theme by declaring that Christ's conception was the result of a relationship outside marriage, later condoned by Joseph. He speculated that as nothing is known about Jesus' sex-life, he could have been homosexual.

Robinson wanted to rid himself of sexual inhibitions. He agreed to be called as a witness for the publication of D.H. Lawrence's *Lady Chatterley's Lover,* declaring the book was against promiscuity, and recommended it as suitable reading for Christians. In 1972, when Dean of Trinity College, Cambridge, he appealed for the age of consent to be lowered to 14. I recall an inflammatory speech made in the Cambridge market-place in which he condemned the Government over-reacting aggressively during the Falkland crisis. John Robinson found it hard not to upset conformists. He justified his actions by arguing that to be honest with himself did not mean encouraging credulity. He was irritated by suggestions that the good he did as a pastor was diminished by a tactless urge to be intellectually superior. He felt outraged, but the criticism was valid.

Another Cambridge intellectual cleric with near-heretical views was Don Cupitt, Dean of Emmanuel College. Like Robinson, he was preoccupied with justifying a reputation as a provocative writer on theology. His aim was to make Christianity meaningful to modern sceptical thinkers by refuting the truth of dogmas and doctrines, leaving a metaphysical-less Christianity not even similar to the Christianity of any of the major churches in Britain.

As an individual Cupitt was not easy to know. He had a slow, melancholy smile and gave patient thoughtful replies that conveyed the impression of a brooding mind, then, chameleon-like, would adopt a persuasive style, a mood convincing to listeners, even though they found it difficult to grasp the trend of the arguments. Hardly surprising, such facile approval did not last. Cupitt's radicalism was greeted either by silence or direct refutation. He was entitled to redefine words as he liked, but, in so doing, forgot that the meaning of Christianity is not an exclusive property. He contended that the Jesus of History and the Christ of Faith are incompatible. One or the other had to go, along with miracles, answers to prayers and the supernatural in the popular sense.

Such iconoclastic thinking invited strong reactions. Scholars felt that his theological horizon was suspect in a number of vital areas. Surprise was expressed that an academic who knew so much could indulge in such sweeping generalisations. Considering the unorthodoxy of his views, his appointment as Dean of Emmanuel raised several eyebrows. It was ill-advised.

It promoted the question by what authority such priests question the authenticity of the Gospels and the teaching of the Church. This applied to David Jenkins, former maverick Bishop of Durham, who dismissed the Resurrection as a conjuring trick with bones and categorically refuted the Virgin Birth. Christians were confused by such authoritative opinions. The chalice offered was not the wine of communion, but the poison of doubt. In Jenkin's case it was the preening of an intellectual peacock. He is not alone.

I link him with Richard Holloway. As Bishop of Edinburgh and Primus of the Episcopal Church in Scotland, his observations to the media were equally foolish. In a misguided attempt to show Christian understanding rather than condemnation of human frailty, he blamed infidelity on chromosome genes that cause men to "go out and propagate as widely as possible". He reduced the Ten Commandments to nine, with adultery the odd one out. The Episcopal Church has some 55,000 members compared with 700,000 of the Presbyterian Church of Scotland. There was unanimous criticism. Holloway did not retract. In an attempt to attract further publicity, he argued in favour of legalising drugs and prostitution, opposed the Government's decision to hold a Gulf War Thanksgiving in Glasgow Cathedral. He used the media as a substitute for the pulpit. Occasionally he had an original idea like the BBC series "When I Get To Heaven", even persuading Joanna Lumley to be optimistic. He also supported the demand for ordination of women. To the relief of many, this maverick bishop has now retired and hung up his mitre. The most unguarded tongue in the episcopate belongs to history.

In spite of carpet-bagging off-beat ideas, his name was put forward as a candidate to succeed Robert Runcie as Archbishop of Canterbury, later as a possible successor of John Hapgood of York.

LEFT: Allan Macfie was the first amateur champion in 1885, and a member of the Royal and Ancient Golf Club for 61 years.

BELOW LEFT: Harry Vardon created a record by winning the Open Championship six times, in 1896, 1898, 1899, 1903, 1911 and 1914.

BELOW: Jack Nicklaus—power golf at its best.

LEFT: Ben Hogan, one of the greatest golfers of all time, sightseeing with the author at Christ Church, Oxford.

ABOVE: Cricketing legend C.B. Fry, so versatile he is impossible to contain in one category.

ABOVE RIGHT: Denis Compton (right) captained England in both cricket and football, and won an F.A. Cup medal with Arsenal.

RIGHT: Ian Botham amassing his historic 149 in the third Test at Headingley against the Australians in 1981.

Photograph by Patrick Eager

RIGHT: Leading the pack, the Dutch athlete Fanny Blankers-Koen, who won four Gold medals at the 1948 Games.

MIDDLE RIGHT: The Olympic torch bearer enters the stadium in 1948.

BELOW RIGHT: Jean Stanley with Jean-Claude Killy, the French skiing champion who won three gold medals at the 1968 Olympic Games.

FAR RIGHT: The author in The Jockey Club holding the hoof of the legendary *Eclipse* mounted on a gold salver, with the Stubbs painting in the background.

LEFT: Gwen "Mops" Marsh who ran the KP restaurant in King's Parade Cambridge.

BELOW: Richard Marsh and William Jarvis at the Edgerton Stables in 1924. Richard the husband of "Mops" trained *Persimmon* to win the Derby and the St. Leger for the Prince of Wales.

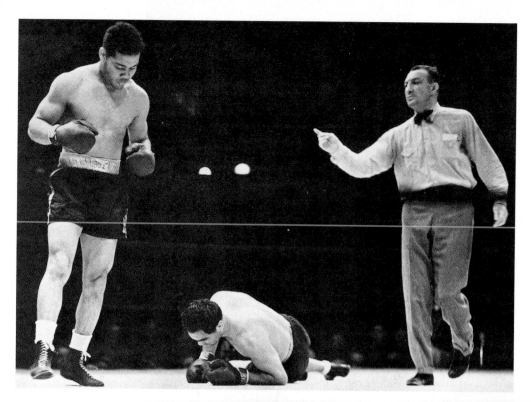

ABOVE: Joe Louis, the author's choice of the greatest boxer of the century, defeating Max Schmeling in two minutes, 17 seconds.

RIGHT: Georges Carpentier was the ring's first pin-up, his good looks attracting thousands of female fans.

ABOVE: Primo Carnera (left), Italian heavyweight champion of the world from June 29 1933 to June 14 1934, with Larry Gains and Louis Stanley.

LEFT: Bernie Ecclestone with Louis Stanley. In the background is David Benson, for years motor racing correspondent for the *Daily Express*.

ABOVE: **The BRM line-up. With Tim Parnell, Alex Stokes, Aubrey Woods, Jackie Oliver, Pedro Rodriguez, and in the foreground Louis and Jean Stanley.**

LEFT: Graham Hill, Jean and Louis Stanley and Josef Strauss.

BELOW: Victory at Oulton Park for Pedro Rodriguez with Alex Stokes, gearbox genius, in the background.

BRM in action. From the top Harry Schell, Graham Hill and Mike Hawthorn.

LEFT: Bishop Trevor Huddlestone, a familiar figure denouncing apartheid through a megaphone outside South Africa House in Trafalgar Square.

RIGHT: Lord Soper. To listen and watch how he handled vast crowds at Speaker's Corner in Hyde Park was an experience.

BELOW: The evangelist Billy Graham. An opinion poll made him the fourth most admired man in America.

BELOW RIGHT: William Temple, Archbishop of Canterbury.

ABOVE: The author with Yehudi Menuhin. Menuhin's search for fresh musical interpretation brought him into contact with jazz violinist Stephane Grappelli.

LEFT: Vaugham Williams went through life with a subtle twinkle in his eye. His music was part of England, a breath of the open air of his beloved Malvern Hills.

RIGHT: Benjamin Britten, son of a Lowestoft dentist, started composing aged five.

Such ideas were rejected by Anglo-Catholics who distrusted the off-the-cuff remarks of this loner who was a scholarship product from a working-class background.

Historians of the Church of England recognise that the worst misfortune to befall its leadership was the premature death of William Temple, aggravated even further by such successors as Geoffrey Fisher and Donald Coggan. The latter, a dour product of Cambridge University, was described in Crockford's Clerical Directory as a man "who rides out with his mind made up, a latter-day Don Quixote". The schoolmaster approach by Fisher made him a prickly Primate. Laying down his office, he displayed typical complacency. "I leave the Church of England in good heart"!

A rare opportunity was missed by ignoring the claims of George Bell, Bishop of Chichester. His background was impeccable. Having worked closely with powers of leadership in the churches of Europe he had seniority as a diocesan bishop. The credentials for the Primacy of All England were right. The only snag was Bell himself. Serving with him on several committees, I found him an unusual mixture. He lacked charisma, eloquence in speech was absent, could be incredibly dull, made no claim to be scholarly or academic, yet possessed a natural dignity. The German theologian, Dietrich Bonhoeffer, regarded Bell as one of the most influential Christians of his time. Bonhoeffer was hanged at Flossenburg just before the war ended on Hitler's personal orders. It was to Bell that his last message was sent as he was led away to execution.

A contributory factor to non-selection was Bell's pleading for humanity in war and controversial speeches about obliteration bombing. In his opinion indiscriminate use of atomic bombs made a mockery of the distinction between a just and unjust war. When Dr. Temple died, Bell's name was submitted to Winston Churchill by Lord Halifax as a possible successor, but at that particular time, anyone taking such a stand was unacceptable. The Crown advisor was vindictive when Bell had acted as conscience dictated. The Church was denied a potentially outstanding Primate.

On occasions Prime Ministers have not been in sympathy with Primates. Robert Runcie came in that category. Dogged by indecisive fudging, on several occasions he was to blame. Thorny issues were side-stepped, an attitude at variance with his early training. After school at Merchant Taylor's, Crosby, he read "Greats" at Oxford, but undergraduate days were interrupted by war. He served four years as an officer in the Scots Guards, led a tank unit and was awarded the Military Cross. He then returned to Oxford to finish his degree, was ordained in 1951, spent nine years as don at Trinity Hall, was Principal of Cuddesdon Theological College in the Sixties, then Bishop of St. Albans and finally became Archbishop of Canterbury in 1980.

Indecision did not feature in the C.V., yet courage often failed when important decisions had to be taken. He dithered over the ordination of women priests, declined to tackle the problem of homosexuality among priests, became indifferent to domestic issues, preferring instead the international scene. Accepting that the Anglican Communion had only a modest role in the World Church, he admitted the Anglicans were only a fraction of the world's Christians and was luke-warm about emphasising the Established status of the Church. Unfortunately his years as Primate coincided with the Thatcher period. There was no empathy. The Brixton and Toxteth riots led to a Commission's Report on the Church's role in the inner cities, which when published was condemned by the Cabinet as a Marxist document. Runcie further antagonised Thatcher by his sermon at the Thanksgiving Service after the Falklands War. Hardly surprising his name was never mentioned in her autobiography.

Runcie's tendency to dither on matters of religious import led to a tragedy. It began when the editors of Crockford's Clerical Directory published their annual anonymous preface in which the writer could indulge in critical judgements without any comeback from their victims. This time the scribe launched an attack, not bitter or vitriolic, but prompted by sheer exasperation about policies not pursued by Runcie. The Primate was accused of a seven year reign of failure, neglect and indecision, depicted as lacking firm principles, without conviction or courage, preferring to drift with the mood of the moment. The writer stated that Runcie had systematically failed to preach the traditional faith as found in the Creeds and the Prayer Book. He was soft on trendy issues, possibly handicapped through not being a trained theologian, but such a weakness was no excuse for deferring all questions until someone else made a decision. Runcie nailed his colours to a fence. There were allegations that a high proportion of senior church appointments had been allocated by Runcie to his own circle, described as élitist liberals, who viewed both Anglo-Catholics and Evangelicals with dislike for being unstylish. Runcie's clear preferences were for men of liberal dispositions with a moderately Catholic style falling short of having firm principles.

Controversial stuff, but nobody anticipated the tragic sequel. The style of the preface suggested somebody well-schooled in the politics of the Church's upper échelon, someone with a theological background and pronounced conservative disposition. Dr. Gareth Bennett, a cloistered Oxford academic, medieval historian and chaplain of New College, fitted all three criteria. Bennett hoped the shield of anonymity would be a protection. He did not anticipate a tirade from John Hapgood, Archbishop of York, who condemned the piece as "scurrilous, sour and vindictive". This denouncement sparked-off a witch-hunt. Bennett denied authorship and left Oxford for a dinner at Emmanuel College, Cambridge. Normally Bennett was reserved, but that night he was in good spirits and enjoyed a meal of parma ham and figs, sole, pheasant, and pear pudding accompanied by a fine claret. The dinner ended about 11.00 pm. He retired to bed in the guest room behind the Wren Chapel. The next day the *Daily Mail* linked his name with the anonymous preface and printed his photograph. Deeply shocked, Bennett walked for some time in the Emmanuel cloisters before returning to his small Oxford home in Marston where he lived alone. Anxiety proved too much. He committed suicide and was found in the passenger seat of his car, a hosepipe running from the exhaust. By his side was a copy of the *Daily Mail* offering to pay £10,000 to a charity if the anonymous author would write an article based on the Crockford preface. Hapgood's denunciation had been the final straw. As the Romans sourly observed 1800 years earlier, "See how these Christians love one another." The matter was badly handled. After all, the preface had been seen before publication by Runcie and Hapgood. The contents were discussed over the telephone. Runcie opted to remain silent. Hapgood was asked to make a statement. There was no reason why Runcie could not have done so himself.

Changing the subject, there have been occasions when bishops have failed to address themselves and their dioceses to the financial need of wealth creation and rarely explain how to generate the wealth in order that it may be shared. They have given the impression that money grows on trees, pennies from heaven. George Carey has been one of the worst offenders. Purblind to the gambling aspect of the Church's finances, he pontificated about the evils of avarice and speculation, preaching sanctimoniously about ethics and the wickedness of "big money". He ignored the fact that the Church Commissioners, who are responsible for investments, had secretly lost £800 million in a greedy attempt to make money - *make* not *earn* - on the Stock Exchange in a manner that made wide-boys look like choir boys.

An obvious question was how such a could disaster happen. There are 94 Church Commissioners, including all the bishops, Prime Minister and the Chancellor of the Exchequer. Between them they should have realised that all was not well. Unfortunately too much trust was placed on the two architects of the catastrophe, Sir Douglas Lovelock, then the First Church Estates Commissioner, and James Shelby, former Assets Committee Secretary. The enormity of their lack of judgment and ineptitude is not fully understood by the public. These two men did more than any single act to destroy the parish system of the Established Church. They wasted millions on a proposed new town development at Ashford, Kent, later valued at less than £3 million. They were also criticised for setting up 37 companies in Britain and America, partly to circumvent the rules on charities. Their transactions were investigated by the Commons Social Security Committee. Their findings were damning. The Commissioners - Lovelock and Shelby - were castigated for gambling on highly speculative projects. Their actions were "ethically suspect and did not sit easily with the ethics of the Church." Suggestions were made that fraud, even theft, could not be ruled out, but the Report concluded that the Commissioners were such easy prey for developers that fraud was "probably superfluous". The very secrecy of their dealings contributed to the débâcle. Another financial liability was added. The decision to ordain women priests had created a rift in the clergy. The Synod recognised the problem. It was agreed to pay compensation and housing aid to clergy who had resigned from the Church in protest. The cost, topping £3 million, was added to the £800 million scandal.

The Lovelock-Shelby fiasco resulted in churches closing, priests losing part of their pensions as cash-strapped parishes had to dig deeper into their resources. Apportioning them, another figure can be added, Michael Hutchings, former head of the Commercial Department. I know little of this gentleman or his qualifications professionally in the property field. He lived in a rented Church Commission property in Bayswater, was adviser to restaurants on their wine lists as well as being a property consultant. In retrospect the naivety of these financial experts was astonishing. Equally surprising was the fact that Lovelock and Stacey refused to apologise for their culpability in spite of the harm inflicted on the Church. The Archbishop of Canterbury merited censure. He admitted that the first intimation came after reading an article in the *Financial Times*!

No one doubts the sincerity of George Carey, but the modern church desperately needs dynamic leadership. The 103rd occupant of the throne of Canterbury failed. He tried to be all things to all men and women.

After commenting on some of the contributing causes that have left the Established Church in such a confused state, it is refreshing to name some of the men of God who pursued their vocational path with firm conviction and dedication, a cross-section of theological belief.

I think of Michael Ramsey, the 100th Primate of All-England, a true son of God rather than a contrived leader, whose instincts turned to prayer, meditation and Retreats. A devout Anglo-Catholic, he strove nevertheless to gain approval for union between Anglicans and Methodists. In the House of Lords he advocated liberalism, accepted modern-style Services, recognised that homosexuality had become a vocal part of society, and distrusted some of the restrictions on immigration.

When a topic lacked interest, he did not hide his feelings and lapsed into silence: he had mannerisms that could irritate, including an annoying habit of finishing your sentence before that moment had arrived. He indulged in facial contortions when emphasising a point. Eyebrows would twitch, mouth wobbled, and cheeks puffed out, giving a misleading impression, particularly during television interviews. The Archbishop was a formidable apologist and an expert on manoeuvring an argument. On financial matters he could be unpredictable, but not as incompetent as the Church Commissioners. I recall an instance during an advisory monthly committee meeting in Lambeth Palace. We were running late trying to solve an awkward financial problem. The session was adjourned as Ramsey had to be at a City luncheon, but, before leaving, he reassured us that all would be well, the short-fall headache cured. Unfortunately he forgot to mention how.

The Archbishop was often complimented on his remarkable stamina for someone of such advanced years. He did nothing to discourage the myth. He liked a patriarchal appearance. The topic came up one afternoon when his aunt invited me to tea in an almshouse where she lived on Castle Hill, Cambridge. The London train as usual was late. Duly apologetic, the Primate told how he had to sprint down the platform at Liverpool Street to catch the train. The guard expressed concern in case the effort had been too strenuous, on a par with the belief that he was his aunt's aged father, whereas she was his senior by more than twenty years.

I was intrigued by a large coloured signed photograph of Pope John XXIII that occupied pride of place on the Lambeth study mantelpiece. He told me that, in his opinion, Pope John was loved and respected by more non-Catholics than any other occupant of the Throne of Peter. Deeply human, with a rare sense of humour, I believe the Primate envied the Italian's simple charismatic appeal and spirit of poverty, a role that did not come naturally to Ramsey. He had rare powers of recall, particularly of his historic visit to Rome, the first official meeting between the Heads of the Roman and Anglican churches for over 400 years since Henry VIII broke with Rome. It took place in the Sistine Chapel in front of Michelangelo's colossal fresco of *The Last Judgment.* The Common Declaration marked a stage in the development of fraternal relations, based upon Christian charity and of sincere efforts to remove the causes of conflict and re-establish unity, but Pope John did not minimise the great difficulties that barred the way to reunion.

Pope Paul was another remarkable man. As Cardinal Montini,

Archbishop of Milan, he was one of the last men on earth to speak to Pope John when he brought the Pope's sister and three brothers to the bedside where the much loved Pontiff lay dying. Two days later Pope John XXIII died. The conclave that followed was unlike any other in history. It was the largest ever. Eighty Cardinals met in the Sistine Chapel, only a third Italian and half of them the creations of Pope John. Speculation as to the possible successor had short-listed such Cardinals as the liberal Lercano, the popular Agagianian; the Canon lawyer, Cardinal Roberti; the youthful Suenens; Marella, of the gift of tongues; Urbani, Pope John's successor at Venice; and Montini, who had spent almost his whole life, except for seven years as Archbishop of Milan, within the Vatican's corridors of power and was known as the Dauphin.

The Cardinals retired in conclave. Dark smoke rose from the improvised chimney of the Sistine Chapel indicating that the ballot papers had been burned. With surprising speed, puffs of little white clouds confirmed the choice had been made. In the case of Pope John it had taken three full days and twenty-four ballots. This time only twenty-three hours were needed. Giovanni Battista Montini was elected the 262nd successor to the Throne of St. Peter, taking the name of Paul, unused for three centuries.

As an Anglican I am fascinated by the trappings of the Roman Catholic hierarchy that presides over the Vatican City, the greatest power-house in the world. With such thoughts in mind, I visited a prosperous 19th century house, overlooking Wimbledon Common, the official residence of Archbishop Ignino Cardinale, the Apostolic Delegate. The title sounded impressive, but, as the Cardinal said with a resigned smile, it was misleading. It meant that the British Government did not recognise his existence and the title carried no diplomatic standing. He was just the link-man between the Pope, whom the Government did not recognise, and the Roman Catholic Church in Britain that had no legal status. The historic breach with Rome by Henry VIII, constitutionalised by Elizabeth I and rubbed home by Parliament in 1688, had seen to that. All is now changed. In 1982 Britain and the Holy See established full relations. The Apostolic Delegate is the Apostolic Pronuncio in Britain, recognised as a diplomat, with the privileges involved, including the inviolability of the Wimbledon house, though still without any recognition of the Vatican as such. The lack of such recognition did not seem to worry the Archbishop unduly. Born in Italy, but brought up in America, he had acquired a trans-Atlantic ease of manner that was refreshingly relaxed. Through his influence, a private audience with the Pope was arranged, but he reminded me that Vatican protocol was strict. I would have to observe the ruling and allow the Holy Father to guide the conversation. Direct questions would be frowned upon.

The road from Rome to the Pope's summer residence at Castel Gandolfo went past a ruined aqueduct, across the plain and into the Alban Hills, up a steep, narrow street into a piazza and the entrance to the huge Renaissance Papal Palace built by Maderna, the architect of the facade of St. Peter's. I attended a Service in a small chapel for a group of pilgrims from Yugoslavia. For a non-Catholic it was strange to hear continuous outbursts of cheering in church, yet somehow the Pope, by the obvious sincerity of his manner, the delicate impact of his hands outstretched to bless, avoided any jarring note. One had the impression of the head of a large family, speaking to everyone *en masse*, yet addressing us individually at the same time, *a tour de force* worthy of a diplomat or head of state. Meeting the Pope was an arresting experience. In appearance he was dignified, if a little severe, but in conversation the mood became affable and outgoing. His English was somewhat hesitant. He recalled a previous meeting when he was Archbishop of Milan. On that occasion our BRM racing car had just won the Grand Prix of Italy. He admitted he had a slight affinity in that he was the only Cardinal to have driven round the Monza circuit in a high-powered sports car, at the invitation of Enzo Ferrari. But now it was different. Here was a man whose sacred office stretched back to the time of Imperial Rome, the Father-in-God of some 550 million Catholics and some 420,000 priests. El Greco would have committed to canvas the likeness of an intellectual aristocrat of the Church with long slender fingers and dark penetrating Italian eyes. The audience ended on a light note. He asked how as an Anglican I had reacted to the Service in the Chapel. I replied it had about it a sense of warm humanity; in fact, the spontaneous cheering made it seem like a football match, an ecclesiastical Inter-Milan. He smiled and said that was as he liked it, the emotions of a family circle.

Pope Paul's attitude showed that the age of religious neutrality had ended. Religion was not a clerical specialisation. He broke the self-imposed Vatican ruling that restricted previous Popes from travelling to the Holy Land, becoming the first Pope to do so since St Peter, followed by the first visit by the Head of the Roman Catholic Church to the United States of America. I was in New York at the time and listened to his address to the United Nations. It was a magnificent sermon, creating a limited alliance between the spiritual authority of the Roman Catholic Church and the temporal authority of the United Nations. Afterwards delegates reacted by saying he was undoubtedly right, they should mend their squabbling ways; then went on squabbling. In St. Patrick's Cathedral he was given a tumultuous welcome on his arrival with Cardinal Spellman. Then at night, Jean and I went to the floodlit Yankee Stadium where 90,000 worshippers watched the Pope celebrate Mass for Peace before returning to Kennedy Airport and the flight home to the Vatican.

Physically Pope Paul was not strong. One diplomat accredited to the Holy See commented that he seemed intent on martyrdom . . . and so it proved.

In October 1978 Cardinal Karol Woztyla became the first non-Italian Pontiff for 455 years. At the time of writing John Paul II is the longest-reigning Pope this century, overtaking Pope Pius XII. His influence has been far-reaching and was personally responsible for the fall of Communism in Eastern Europe, as Mikhail Gorbachev acknowledged. On his missions the Pontiff has undertaken 84 gruelling overseas journeys, often in searing heat. Increasingly frail and showing distressing signs of Parkinson's Disease, the Pope refuses to admit physical decline and is determined to consolidate the Church and Christian values. The possibility of a breakdown has been anticipated. Dr. Corrado Manni and a team of surgeons led by Professor Francesco Crucitti are on constant standby at the Gemelli Hospital in Rome, part of the University of the Sacred Heart, where a papal suite is kept permanently ready, whilst his Lear Jet has special equipment for intensive care, life-support and monitoring systems. There is no tradition of papal resignations. The last Pope to step down voluntarily was Pope Celestine V in 1294.

I turn now to one of the most controversial diocesan bishops of the century. Mervyn Stockwood was a charismatic rebel whose experience as parish priest in the slums of Bristol made him a Christian Socialist. He took part in demonstrations against Fascism, joined Stafford Cripps on political platforms and became known as the Red Parson. As Bishop of Southwark his far-reaching, at times controversial, experiments were vigorous attempts to get social justice and a Church revival. Seldom out of the news, he created opportunities for the voice of committed Christians to be heard.

It is difficult to make an appraisal of such a fractured nature. Mervyn was a man of moods, egocentric, and could be an accomplished hand in the acerbity business. He had no time for irrelevant doctrines or ecclesiastical mumbo-jumbo. When an evangelical minister rebuked him for praying for the dead, he retorted, "My dear fellow, if I didn't pray for the dead, I couldn't pray for 80% of the Church of England."

On occasions Mervyn visited the Old Mill House. One such visit coincided with problems over a troublesome cleric. The incumbent, double-first at Peterhouse, was over-qualified for a hamlet parish. Unable to get on with his parishioners, he had insisted on introducing a form of churchmanship that was unpopular. It led to a revolt. The Church Council resigned, both churchwardens left, the choir melted away, the organist retired and finally the entire congregation of ten people went elsewhere. Every Sunday the vicar turned up, opened the church, lit the candles, read a modified Order of Service to empty pews, extinguished the candles and locked the church door. Work for the week was completed. The stipend went into the bank. Mervyn's attempts to resolve the dispute failed. I listened to a litany of exasperation that ended with the heartfelt words, "Well, as long as there's death, there's hope."

He once analysed his early dislike of Sundays. At school, after reading the Collect for the Day to the master on duty, the pupils were taken to the local church which was Low, with interminable Matins and the Litany every fortnight. Mercifully an outbreak of measles put the school into quarantine with substitute House prayers. Later a High Form was introduced with vestments, processions, candles, incense and, most important, the Service was half-an-hour shorter. Mervyn was so attracted by the ritualistic detail that he asked to be confirmed: such was his road to

Damascus. He was not always at ease with formal worship, predicting correctly a substantial drop in clerical intake. He used to say that one of the reasons so few people attended church was sheer boredom with what happened inside the building.

Mervyn was such an anecdotal person that it is difficult to separate fact from fiction, but the authentic ones were enough to make him a legend. In spite of the vicissitudes of his episcopate, he enriched the ecclesiastical world. His virtues were far greater than his very human shortcomings. Sadly retirement did not bring tranquillity. He moved into a modest terrace house overlooking Bath Abbey and the Mendip Hills, but the change of life-style brought a sense of loneliness. Everything was so different. Even domestic incidents became important. Midge was a cat that he spoilt with affection, but felt it was cruel to take her away from the spaciousness of Bishops House into a strange cramped space. She was left behind. Unfortunately the new bishop's cat objected, so, like Humphrey at No.10, Midge was despatched to Bath where Mervyn plied her with delectable meals and affection.

Mervyn died on 13th January 1995. In his will he requested a Requiem Mass in the Anglo-Catholic church of his childhood. It would have met with his approval. A former Archbishop of Canterbury and eight other bishops robed in the sanctuary. The preacher at the private cremation was the Dean of Westminster. The ashes were scattered at Chanctonbury Ring. Robert Runcie was the preacher at the Memorial Service in Southwark Cathedral.

So passed a remarkable cleric. I recall his favourite quotation: "Death is nothing at all. I have only slipped away into the next room" - such was his simple faith. Surely his beloved Midge was patiently waiting.

Selecting those clerics outstanding in the 20th century is not easy. The range is wide and diverse. It includes eccentrics, evangelists, controversialists, pastors, monks, reformers, scholars and martyrs . . . a motley assembly under the heading of Men of God. A priest who could be identified with the last category was Joost de Blank whom I knew when, as Bishop of Stepney, he lived in a Georgian house by Highbury Common.

He was no meek-and-mild church bazaar cleric, but a tough prelate who looked bull-shouldered in a purple cassock. His interests included foreign films, American musicals, modern paintings, literary items from American thrillers to Shakespeare. He once edited an *avant-garde* review, was something of a gourmet, and an addict to fast driving. There was never a shortage of topics. In a way they were safety-valves to ease the frustrations of seeking answers to the social problems of the dockland parishes of his diocese. He was also an opponent of the death penalty. I recall his comments about a visit to Ruth Ellis in the death cell. He did not go on his own accord but by the invitation of the prison chaplain. It was ten days before she was hanged. He found her calm and composed. She would not appeal and gave the bishop her reasons. Grief stricken at what she had done, she told him that such was her love for David Blakely she could not explain her act. It was an inexplicable tragedy. She was ready to take the consequences. Joost de Blank said he had visited several condemned men and had confirmed five. Each man had been reconciled to the thought of sudden death, but he felt the system should be abolished.

Joost de Blank's appointment as Archbishop of Cape Town was an imaginative stroke. Some felt that his Dutch stock would be less offensive to the anglophobic Government. It was a daunting challenge that failed. His spirit could not cope with the vicious intensity of South African opposition. I saw him once more before he died disillusioned. In Nelson Mandela he would have found an understanding ally. If only he could have witnessed the victory over the All Blacks in the 1995 World Cup. It was a day when race and creed were joined in celebration.

The reverse was the case of Trevor Huddlestone, a priest of immense courage remembered as an outstanding figure of the 19th century. Ordained in 1937, he joined the Anglican Order of the Community of the Resurrection at Mirfield. In 1943 the Order sent him to their Mission in Sophiatown in the native quarter of Johannesburg, where he later became Provincial of the Community in South Africa including responsibility for the school which trained the most prominent lawyers, politicians and agitators of that period. It was there that Huddlestone became involved in the campaign to improve employment conditions and better living standards for the Africans. He denounced the pass-laws and spoke at political meetings. His anger took shape in a book published in 1956 *Nought for your Comfort,* a copy being smuggled out of South Africa. Fierce reaction by the South African Government led to threats of imprisonment. The Community Superior, Father Raymond Raynes, recalled Huddlestone.

Restrained by the Order's vows of chastity, obedience and poverty, Huddlestone reluctantly returned to this country. For the next five years he worked from Mirfield and became a familiar figure denouncing apartheid through a megaphone outside South Africa House in Trafalgar Square. Aided by Canon John Collins, the *International Defence and Aid Fund* was established. The money made it possible to finance a brilliant team of lawyers to defend Nelson Mandela in 1962 when he faced the death penalty for plotting a military campaign. Instead the verdict was life imprisonment. In 1968 he was appointed Suffragan Bishop of Stepney by Robert Stodford, but found it difficult to be gainfully occupied in complacent attitudes. There were rumours that he might be chosen for the vacant see of Canterbury, but persistent ill-health and diabetes caused the Prime Minister to be cautious. The Archbishop of York, Donald Coggan was appointed, a misguided nomination. In 1978 Huddlestone became Bishop of Mauritius and was later elected the first Archbishop of the Church of the Province of the Indian Ocean. It was a further challenge, to create an indigenous reflection of Anglicanism in a remote part of the world. Retiring in 1983, Huddlestone lived in the rectory of St. James's, Piccadilly, long associated with controversial issues, and continued campaigning as President of the Anti-Apartheid Movement.

In retrospect Trevor Huddlestone's achievements were remarkable. Archbishop Tutu said it was due to his persistence that apartheid became a world issue. He once told me that he greatly valued the African National Congress's highest award. Further tribute came at the end of 1997 when he received a knighthood in the first New Year's Honours List controlled by Tony Blair.

Trevor Huddlestone died in 1998 at the Community of the Resurrection in Mirfield. He had become very frail, but the spiritual core was unchanged. The self-discipline of a monk was evident. The family background had firm religious traditions. He once recalled how an ancestor, John Huddlestone, as a priest received Charles II into the Roman Catholic Church on his deathbed. Today those who wish to remember him will find his bust in South Africa House, a tribute to the end of apartheid.

The next choice must include warts and all. Dean Hewlett Johnson was an ecclesiastical self-publicist with a taste for relaxed luxury. Appointed by the first Labour Prime Minister to the deanery of the industrial diocese of Manchester, Ramsey MacDonald next moved him to the Mother Church of the Anglican community. Keen ritualist, Canterbury provided the right backcloth. By any standards Hewlett Johnson was an odd mixture. When politics were discussed, he immediately became dogmatic. Discussions were misleading. Over dinner he never stopped talking about his beliefs. He was convinced that God intended him to be the interpreter of the inherent goodness of Communism, rather like Yeltsin in gaiters. Stalin was rated a great leader whose politics made it possible for Russians to have an improved life-style. He saw what he wanted to see and no more. He enjoyed overseas travel, but did not visit Russia until 1937. Well primed with experience of Fascism in Germany and Italy, sympathetic to the Republican Government in Spain, the Russian trip fully converted him to Communism and he was rewarded with the Stalin Peace Prize. The Red Dean's views became a source of embarrassment to the Church, so much so that in 1947 the Archbishop of Canterbury disclaimed any responsibility for the Dean's speeches. Not that it made any difference. He was a vain man. At the enthronement of Geoffrey Fisher as Primate of All England, Johnson was a striking figure in blue vestments, domed balding head, white hair and sun-tanned features. A magnificent pectoral cross was worn with pride. In the blaze of television lights, Dr. Fisher, in white vestments, was made to look insignificant, which perhaps was not too difficult. One last vanity. The Dean once told me that in the Soviet encyclopedia he had 75 lines against the nine lines devoted to Christ. The inference was left to speak for itself. To counter such crass thinking, there was another side. At heart the Dean was a compassionate pastor when it came to personal problems.

Martin Sullivan was a complete contrast. His appointment as Dean of St. Paul's in 1967 came as a surprise and upset traditionalists. He was a New Zealander and the first cleric in this post for many years with no claim to scholarship. He was a fluent speaker, agile wit, popular in the City, especially with children, but could not handle the Press. Liberal in doctrinal matters, very Protestant in churchmanship. Sullivan was averse to ceremonial gatherings, which made life difficult in St. Paul's. He welcomed experimental worship in the Cathedral but refused to tamper with the Prayer Book. His great successes were with youth. We met several times to discuss plans for a Youth Festival in the Cathedral that was labelled "Pop in St. Paul's". Purists were upset, but surprised when the attendance reached capacity proportions. Another occasion that attracted large teenage support was a Service of Holy Communion attended by the cast of *Hair,* the American rock musical.

As a preacher Sullivan commanded attention, but admitted that unorthodox success had widened the gap between the Cathedral and the Dioceses. He was not popular with the clergy but made his mark with the younger generation. A final recollection was the Service of Thanksgiving and Blessing which he conducted on the steps of the Cathedral before the Mobile Hospital of the International Grand Prix Medical Service left for the Grand Prix circuits of Europe.

VIGNETTES OF MEMORY . . . I recall an overnight stay at Bishopthorpe in Aberdeen on the eve of the outbreak of the Second World War. Bishop Deane over breakfast was confident it would be of short duration. Although 60 years ago, the events of that 24 hours are still vivid. Neville Chamberlain's emotional broadcast; George VI's firm message of resolve; France joining us six hours later; German U-boats sinking the passenger ship, *Athenia,* in the North Atlantic; all that was happening as life went on peacefully in the Bishop's household. It all seemed unreal . . . Coffee with Dr. Matthews in the Deanery. Outside, Ludgate Hill was the scene of blitz devastations dominated by St. Paul's. On the Dean's mantelpiece was a framed photograph of the Cathedral encircled by flames. The Dean said that in moments of near despair, and there were many, that picture personified for him the hope for the future.

Morning prayers in the private chapel at Bishopscourt, Rochester. Bishop Chevasse, who lost a leg in the First World War and was decorated with the Military Cross, conducted the simple

Service standing. I sat next to Mrs Chevasse, behind was their officer-son, Guy, home on leave. Deep in prayer, I felt a tap on the arm . . . Guy whispered, what did I fancy for the Chester Cup. Sadly there was no divine revelation.

The Church has had its quota of eccentrics. Ernest Barnes was no exception. Appointed Bishop of Birmingham in 1924, he stayed there for nearly 30 years. At Trinity, Cambridge, he was bracketed 2nd Wrangler in 1896 and took a First in Part II of the Mathematical Tripos. Convinced pacifist in the First World War, but on other matters belligerent and controversial. He argued for the evolutionary theory accepted by Natural Science to replace the traditional scriptural version. He objected to the doctrine of the Real Presence in the Eucharist and upset his High Church diocese. His persistence in giving "gorilla sermons" led to denunciation as a heretic with demands that he be brought to trial. Instead Archbishop Davidson merely slapped his wrist for the views on sacramentalism.

Used to hitting the headlines, Barnes accused the Cement Makers' Federation of holding back the supply of cement urgently needed for air-raid shelters so that profits might increase. The Cement Workers sued the Bishop for slander and were awarded damages. Still persistent, Dr. Barnes repeated the allegation in the House of Lords. Seven years later his book *The Rise of Christianity* was fiercely attacked, particularly the chapter precluding the recognition of miracles. Archbishop Fisher took a firm line and condemned the book in Convocation. No one could say that Barnes was an easy man to please. Away from the limelight, it was a different story. He had immense charm and thoroughly enjoyed the social graces, particularly the company of ladies.

Durham has had its quota of unusual prelates. David Jenkins outraged both clergy and laity by flaunting intellectual limitations, but Hensley Henson was more of an irritant who provoked without adding to the chaotic state of doctrinal and moral theology in the Established Church. He was an entertaining speaker though hardly a persuasive advocate. More often than not members flocked into the Upper House of Convocation when he rose, listened to him with delighted cheers and laughs, then voted solidly on the other side. This never ruffled him, in fact he expected it. He decried false modesty, quoting as an example his autobiography *Memories of an Unimportant Life* in three substantial volumes. Never afraid of controversy, he advocated closer relations with the Free Churches. At one stage, Charles Gore, Bishop of Birmingham, forbade him to preach in a Congregational church in the city. Henson defied the order and went on denouncing Anglo-Catholicism. When Parliament rejected the Revised Prayer Book, he retaliated by advocating Disestablishment. Henson was stronger intellectually than any English prelate of his time. As to personality, he was undoubtedly combative, but charitable and lovable as well.

Cyril Alington did not fit the Durham mould. A former Headmaster of Eton, the Dean brought an air of quiet scholarship to the cloisters. He had a deep love for all matters of cricketing and needed little encouragement to recall the feats of a relative, Edward Lyttelton, also a former Eton Headmaster. I knew Lyttelton after he retired to the rural obscurity of East Anglia, but he was always reticent about his cricketing prowess. Not so Alington. He was a Lyttelton encyclopedia. He described how a few months before he died, Edward used to say his evening prayers standing before the fire and leaning on a walking-stick that had special significance. In 1882 when English batting was led by W.G. Grace and the Australian attack was powered by Spofforth, one of the immortals of the game, Lyttelton used to describe graphically what it was like facing the hurricane bowler. For the first few overs it felt like "standing on the brink of the tomb" before settling down. When Middlesex beat the Australians at Lords by 98 runs, it was largely due to Lyttelton's innings of 113. Afterwards Spofforth presented him with an inscribed walking-stick as a memento. It was this stick that he used for prayerful meditation. When Alington came into the room, he found Edward batting away merrily with it, then returning to his devotions after a minute or two. Even in full white canonicals, this grey-haired cleric admitted that he never went into a church without visualising the spin of the ball up the nave. His favourite memory was the match at Lords under his captaincy, Australia against Cambridge University, the tourists losing by an innings and 72 runs.

Cyril Alington also had his moment of national fame. Every morning he tackled *The Times* crossword. One clue was particularly troublesome until he realised it was his own name. He told me afterwards that a life's ambition had been realised.

Clerical cricketing feats are usually parochial affairs. Not so with David Sheppard. He set standards that make today's Test batsmen look like novices. Statistics speak for themselves. In 1950 Sheppard made 1,000 runs for Cambridge University, including opening partnerships with John Dewes of 343 against the West Indies and 349 against Oxford, both University records which I watched from the old Fenner's pavilion. Selected for the final Test against the West Indies at the Oval, toured Australia and New Zealand that winter. Examinations delayed his start in 1951 but finished the season with 2104 runs, more than 1000 in matches for Sussex. Cambridge captain in 1952, Sheppard made a century in the University Match and scored more runs than any other undergraduate in one University season. He played in the last two Tests against India, scoring his maiden Test century and topped the first-class averages with 2262 runs. To beat Worcestershire against the clock, he made 239 not out, his highest score in first-class cricket. Although reading for Holy Orders, an illness to Len Hutton in 1954 brought an invitation to captain England in the Third and Fourth Tests and he made his first century against Australia, the first priest to play in Test cricket. His career came to a close against New Zealand at Auckland in 1963. If only the England selectors had such talent available today.

Sheppard's career in the church was equally outstanding. As a student at Ridley Hall, he would talk in the evenings, sometimes with his tutor, John Earp, about his future in the Ministry. Ambitions were realised. Zeal found an outlet in the Mayflower Family Centre as Warden, both before and after his second visit to Australia. He then went to Woolwich as a suffragan Bishop and was still only in his early 40s when he became Bishop of Liverpool. There he established a remarkable working relationship with Archbishop Derek Worlock, the friendship between two overlapping episcopal regimes, forging a unique partnership.

Derek Worlock brought great experience to his task. A year after his ordination, he was chosen as private secretary to Cardinal Griffin. A potentially gifted administrator, he became an authority on the internal machinery of English Roman Catholic institutions and was an obvious candidate for Westminster on the death of Cardinal Heenan. Surprisingly the appointment went to the Abbot of Ampleforth at the same time that Worlock was transferred to Liverpool. Previously Worlock, as private secretary to three incumbents of Westminster, had a reputation of being a hatchet man who carried out stringent decisions in the name of his superiors. Being side-lined must have been a blow but it did not affect his loyalty and support. He was present when the Benedictine monks were led into Westminster Abbey for vespers when the freshly consecrated Basil Hume was installed at the Cathedral.

Worlock concentrated on his work in Liverpool. At the time of the Toxteth riots he joined David Sheppard in interceding with the police and the black community. Together they tackled the problem of this northern working-class city, opposed factory closures, advocating the values of a free port, faced with a disastrous local government headache and seeking to improve the economy. They comforted relatives in the football tragedies of Heysel and Hillsborough. The Sheppard/Worlock ecumenical co-operation resulted in extraordinary acts of Christian ministry, carrying out Pope John XXIIIs exhortation "to do separately only those things we cannot do together".

To this list of men of God, I add the name of a fervent convert. Malcolm Muggeridge was an odd mixture. We were friends for many years and I had seen him striking varying poses, but the closing years of his life were more rewarding. He had one fault, an inability to stop talking. Conversation over a meal was impossible. Just one long passionate monologue. At least the food could be appreciated.

Malcolm was obsessed by the thought of death. He likened himself to a man on a sea voyage nearing his destination. On embarking he worried about having a cabin with a porthole, whether he would be asked to sit at the captain's table, who were the important passengers. It became pointless when he realised that he would soon be disembarking. He believed earthly things could not bring lasting satisfaction, so the prospect of death held no terrors. He considered that those saints who pronounced themselves in love with death displayed the best of sense. He recalled how Pastor Bonhoeffer told his Nazi guards, as they took him away for execution, that for them it was an end, but for him a beginning.

In one sense Malcolm did not want to die. He found the world he was soon to leave, more than ever beautiful, especially in its remote parts with the sea, mountains, streams and trees. The image of eternity seemed more closely stamped there than among streets and houses. He would get quite lyrical in his belief that life was a blessed gift, that the spirit which animated it was one of love, not hate or indifference, of light not darkness, of creativity not destruction. He was certain that whatever lay beyond would be similarly benevolent.

I only hope he was not disappointed.

Canon John Collins: essentially a man of action, a scholar, who could not resist taking up controversial issues of the day. The range included racialism, disarmament, co-existence, capital punishment and any quirky campaign that appealed. Free-thinking clerics do command attention. Sometimes counter-productive, like Bishop Montifiori's pointless aside that Christ was probably homosexual. I think of Owen Chadwick, rich with academic honours, including the Order of Merit. As Primate of All England, he would have restored the office to its former importance, not a wishy-washy liberal nonentity. I think of Chadwick in lighter vein as a strict referee of Cambridge University rugby matches at Grange Road. Not much escaped his eye.

I recall Father Hope Patten, whose dream of revitalising the Pilgrimage to Walsingham became reality; his life-sized figure rests on a tomb in the Shrine. Eccentric Conrad Noel, vicar of Thaxted, who used to hoist the red flag of Communism on the church tower. In his magnificent church of cathedral dimensions is a bronze Epstein bust in his memory, whilst a hammer and sickle is engraved on a chest. Noel was a prickly character who found empathy with the *Planet Suite* composer, Gustav Holst, who lived in the High Street and often played the church organ.

Leslie Wethered's years at the City Temple in London were remarkable. He exercised a magnetic appeal to packed congregations and reached thousands more through religious books that went into endless reprints. Not scholarly but readable, they proclaimed a simple faith, uncomplicated but challenging, maybe appealing to the credulous but nevertheless of real comfort. I remember a cleric, St. John Grocer, telling me how he shared an interdenominational service with Wethered. The atmosphere that evening was electric. On leaving, hundreds were waiting in the street. No one took notice of him, but when Wethered appeared there was a surge forward. He responded like royalty with a gracious wave before entering a car. It was the same wherever he preached. His message was the simplicity of the Disciples brought up-to-date.

Lord Soper was another with magnetism that attracted Christians and non-believers. To listen and watch how he handled vast crowds at Speaker's Corner in Hyde Park was an experience. Some listeners were hostile, even belligerent, but never once did I see Soper put off his stride. Fluent oratory and logical arguments silenced agnostic elements. Soper had a rare gift, patience and conviction to convince doubters.

Turning to more conventional clerics, when Archbishop Temple died there were many who hoped that Cyril Garbett would succeed. It was not to be. Garbett remained at York to continue his role as spokesman of the national Christian conscience. Some 50 years have passed since I spent a day with him at Bishopsthorpe, an impressive centuries-old manor house. After the bustle of Stonegate, the atmosphere of lawns fringed by the slow-moving Ouse was peaceful. In his own background, Dr. Garbett was just as serene. In many ways incalculable, he never spoke badly but often put a limit to the standard he intended to reach, giving the impression of a man keeping himself in hand. He talked of his global travels, of meeting Molotov in the Kremlin and finding him phlegmatic and intractable. His visit to Moscow had followed hard on the announcement of the installation of the Metropolitan Sergius as Patriarch of the Orthodox Church. He commented on the Russian methods of collective farming. He was one of the few Englishmen with first-hand knowledge of that system; of the suffering of the persecuted Church in China; the situation in Poland and Germany; the rising divorce rate and its consequences on society; the disturbing drop in the number of ordinands; plus an explanation why such a high percentage of potential candidates were rejected by selection committees; the case for pluralities; the rise in juvenile crime and the increase in immorality. His main preoccupation concerned the problem of parish administration and the growing crisis of the retreat from Christianity. Not much has changed over the past half-century. Sadly we never learn.

I turn to John Hapgood who was 12 years as Archbishop of York before retiring two years before the mandatory age of 70. The backgrounds of Garbett and Hapgood could not be more different. Hapgood was the first English Archbishop to be trained in the Natural Sciences. At Cambridge he had Firsts in both parts of the Tripos, took a Ph.D in research on the effects of pain, followed by three years as a demonstrator in pharmacology and was elected Fellow of King's in 1952. Twenty-one years later Edward Heath offered him the bishopric of Durham. Ten years later he moved to York. A distinguished life span, but anything but peaceful. Mistakes were made. It was unfortunate that shortly after arriving at York he had to cope with the inflammatory outburst by David Jenkins before he was consecrated Bishop of Durham. With hindsight, Hapgood should have exercised his authority and cut down the rebel to size, deflating an outsize ego.

Then during the Miners' Strike of 1984 Hapgood convened a meeting at Bishopthorpe to which were invited Derek Worlock, Roman Catholic Archbishop of Liverpool, Arthur Scargill and the N.U.M. General Secretary. The motives were well intended but with the strike at fever pitch, the Scargill presence hardly endeared Mrs Thatcher to the Archbishop. It proved an ill-timed gesture. In 1986 Hapgood supported The *Sun's* attack on Gay propaganda being distributed in schools. In so doing, he alienated the Gay and Lesbian community by describing their sexual inclinations as a misfortune. The Crockford Preface tragedy, dealt with elsewhere, was badly handled. He was made the scapegoat through Runcie's reluctance to make his own defence.

Hapgood was also the dominating liberal figure who backed the ordination of women and effected the compromise-deal that kept the loyalty of some of the alienated traditionalists when the first woman was made a priest in 1994. Many mistakes were made, particularly in 1971 when the Church in Hong Kong and the American Episcopal Church were allowed to ordain women. It split the world-wide Anglican Communion and created an intolerable position. Hapgood has had second thoughts. He considered that the move to allow women to become priests was too hasty, and blamed pressure groups and activists who had seized leadership of the

Church from the bishops. It was true. Pressure groups favouring the ordination of women were very nasty when the extremists took over.

Hapgood's departure from York left a void in the Anglican hierarchy. He was a man of profound learning and extensive Christian experience with an intellectual background far superior to any of his colleagues, yet he was not promoted to Canterbury. The Prime Minister's power to appoint is limited to two names submitted by the Crown Appointments Commission. It is probable that Hapgood was one of the two names, yet Mrs Thatcher preferred the virtually unknown George Carey. Maybe there were semi-political reasons. Hapgood had incurred the displeasure of the Anglo-Catholics, whilst the Evangelicals, whose turn it was to be represented at Lambeth were lukewarm in their support. Mrs Thatcher considered Hapgood a 'wet' both politically and spiritually. So the Church was encumbered with George Carey, who came with an undistinguished track record that still remains the same.

Monseigneur Gilbey belonged to an English way of life that has ceased. Son of a thriving wine merchant of the gin family, he inherited from his father many of the traditions and customs linked with the cycle of country life, to which was added the devout Catholic influence of his Spanish mother. In deference to her wishes, the boy was educated by the Jesuits of Beaumont.

Enjoying the advantages of private means, Gilbey's years as an undergraduate at Trinity College, Cambridge, were so enjoyable that a pass degree reflected a cavalier approach to academic studies. His friends were surprised when Gilbey disclosed an ambition to become a priest. He went to the Breda College and was eventually ordained in the private chapel of his home, Mark Hall in Essex. So began a fulfilling priesthood in which a deeply spiritual sense of vocation was combined with a capacity to appreciate temporal pleasures.

He was probably the most meticulously dressed cleric in England. Sartorially it was frock-coat, broad-brimmed hat, cassock, later trimmed with the purple of a Domestic Prelate to the Pope, and the patrician dignity of Protonotary Apostolic. At the outset Gilbey served as secretary to the Bishop of Brentwood, and then accepted the post of Roman Catholic chaplaincy at Cambridge University. During his 33 years there he instructed some 170 converts, often without direct proselytisation. Focal point was Fisher House, the chaplaincy head-quarters where he kept an excellent table and cellar, hospitality often extending to the *Lion, Bath* and *Pitt Club*. During the Second World War the club moved to a temporary home with rooms over the post office in Trinity Street and was renamed the *Interim Club*.

Gilbey was a frequent visitor. In the afternoons he would sit at one end of the long table. An elderly man, heavily built, with an old-fashioned high stiff collar, starched cuffs and rimless glasses attached to a cord, presided at the other end. The routine was predictable. The club servant was not allowed to pour the tea. Unfortunately the teapot handle was too hot to hold for more than a few seconds. Gilbey's offer to help was declined. The stubborn masochist was the King Edward VII Professor of English Literature, Sir Arthur Quiller-Couch, better known as "Q". Both men might have stepped out of the pages of Trollope, who in turn would have appreciated the view from the club window of the Great Gateway of Trinity College.

In 1965 it was decreed that women would be allowed in Fisher House. Gilbey was unhappy. He felt that limited space would be inadequate for the basic requirements of female undergraduates. He resigned. The blissful years had ended. He found himself homeless but was soon offered a permanent base in the *Travellers Club* and began what was virtually a new ministry. He turned the boot-room at the top of the back staircase into a tiny oratory. Cardinal Heenan gave him a licence to reserve the Blessed Sacrament in this chapel and permission to say the Tridentine Mass on all occasions. This privilege indicated the status granted to Gilbey by the Vatican. Others, like Archbishop Lefebvre, were not so fortunate. He was excommunicated for doing so without permission.

The Travellers Club period marked a change in life-style. At Cambridge this debonair priest was a familiar landmark, sometimes with the Trinity Foot Beagles or graciously doffing the wide-brimmed hat on arriving every Saturday morning at David's bookstall in the market-place. Now, as an ageing cleric the routine was different. One duty was constant. Every morning he would leave the Club, board a No.14 bus to the Brompton Oratory where he said a 7.30 Mass in St. Winifred's Chapel according to the Tridentine Rite, which was a comfort to many Catholics who disliked the post-Vatican II liturgy. In 1940 the kindness of a friend made life easier. He was given the comfort of a limousine and chauffeur. Five years later Gilbey went on a coast to coast American tour to promote a new edition of his book *We Believe*. He enjoyed the experience, particularly an interview with Mother Angelica. Although frail and in his nineties, Gilbey's company was always stimulating. I recall his indignation at the rumour spread by his great-nephew, James Gilbey, the fellow who became involved emotionally with Princess Diana, to the effect that she was receiving instruction from the Monsigneur. He dismissed the suggestion as utter rubbish.

Alfred Gilbey's death broke the link with a distant past that can only be recalled in the pages of an Evelyn Waugh novel.

In sharp contrast, I think of the Forties when a great deal was heard of the Oxford Group, a religious movement founded by Frank Buchman after experiencing a spiritual conversion at the Keswick Convention of 1908. Having seen the light, Buchman returned to America and did not surface again in England until 1920. Originally called Buchmanism, his movement became the Oxford Group, a disingenuous use of Oxford that annoyed many people, whilst critics pointed out that its so-called conversions were emotionally short-lived. Nevertheless it had an appeal, initially among professional and upper-classes, later involving trade unionists and industrial workers. It certainly had an enthusiastic response from Cambridge students in 1946. I was invited by Buchman to a "house-party" for a session of sharing and counselling. About a dozen undergraduates came to a house in Coates Crescent, Edinburgh. After tea and scones, we sat silent in a circle. Eventually a man stood up and poured out his inner thoughts. In rotation each one did likewise. A girl next to me, quiet, almost mouselike, rose and confessed to a remarkable string of lurid, erotic thoughts, then demurely sat down having experienced a pious orgasm. It was my turn. I confessed it would be difficult to match the previous speaker. I begged to pass and retired. So ended my flirtation with the Oxford Group.

I recall an evangelistic movement that gained global recognition. The reaction to Billy Graham was sensational. In 1954 he attracted nearly 1,500,000 people to his Rallies. Twelve years after the sensational debut, a repeat campaign drew 18,000 people every night to Earls Court. The eighties saw a concentrated mission to the Universities of Oxford and Cambridge, again a remarkable response, and so on. Every time the impact was memorable. Clerical reaction was somewhat lukewarm. Critics argued that after the friendliness and theatrical effects of these meetings, potential converts would find the austerity of chapels and half-empty churches an anti-climax. This muted response possibly had a touch of sour grapes. There was no disputing that Graham claimed the ear of the people. Personality undoubtedly played a part. The tall, good-looking, square-jawed, wavy-haired evangelist from North Carolina knew its value. His voice was strong, with an accent neither flat nor mid-West. His rhetoric was skilful. He was an extrovert. An opinion poll made him the fourth most admired man in America, though for a time his allegiance to Richard Nixon caused uneasiness.

Billy Graham is a wholesaler. Using the media of Established Churches, he claimed to reach more than 80,000,000 consumers and became ecclesiastical Big Business. President of a communications empire, the Billy Graham Evangelistic Association owns a city block in Minneapolis, has an annual budget of some 12 million dollars, deals with 80 million items of mail every year, including 4 million copies of the monthly magazine *Decision* for the United States and Canada with a Spanish translation for Latin America, and editions for Great Britain, Germany, France, Japan and Australia. It claimed to have the largest circulation of any religious magazine. Other articles included the *World Wide Pictures* of Burbank, California, the world's largest producers and distributors of religious films. The radio programme *House of Decision* went out to over 1,000 stations with an audience of 20 million. Television specials of edited tapes of personal crusades were shown on 250 stations without commercials. In Minneapolis, a team of clergymen answered letters from people with problems or were in distress.

The very range was staggering, motivated by a man who greets you with wide-eyed simplicity. This disarming approach could be misleading. On an early visit to England, Graham joined me for dinner in London with his personal assistant, Gerry Beavin, and a supporter from Texas. I was curious to know why he was staying at the *Ritz*. It seemed out of character. If there was a Second Coming, I imagined that Christ might have stayed at a Salvation Army hostel rather than a luxury hotel. Graham agreed with all that, but added the choice was influenced by the fact that work came easier in such surroundings. I enquired why he favoured a somewhat expensive car only to be reassured that as it was used by the Queen, there could not be much wrong with the choice. My point seemed to have been missed. After dinner we left for Euston to catch the night train to Glasgow. We arrived early so Beavin asked us to stay in the car while he checked the platform. He returned accompanied by a group of women. Graham adjusted the angle of his hat, straightened his tie, stepped out and spoke to a woman who was not in the group. He took her copy of the *Evening Standard,* autographed it and returned the newspaper to the bemused female who had no idea who he was or what it was all about. That particular picture found its way into the next day's newspaper with the caption of a prayerful woman wishing the evangelist well at the start of the Scottish campaign.

Even without her support there was no doubt about its eventual impact. Some publicity gimmicks are bound to fail. Another incident occurred at Gleneagles Hotel. Returning from a round of golf, I noticed Graham by a ground floor window gesticulating and making facial contortions. I mentioned to the concierge that perhaps Graham was unwell. It was a false alarm. He was only practising mannerisms and facial expressions in the mirror. Nothing was left to chance. Everything was professionally stage-managed, skilful blending of mood music, mingling of colour effects, controlled volume of sound and choral backing with strategically placed supporters who led the way to the conversion-walk to the platform, slightly hesitant so as to encourage others. The overall effect was convincing.

Orthodox clerics with a conservative outlook may eye these evangelistic jamborees with suspicion, but the fact remains they worked. The flavour cannot be to every taste but they demonstrated how the communication-media can be used. Maybe Billy Graham's personal success was due to the fact he is a good man without the "grey areas" of some of our bishops, not least the Archbishop of York. Graham is the Mark McCormack of evangelism and just as effective.

Lastly the man who was the greatest clerical personality of the 20th century, whose activities deeply influenced the social and ecclesiastical life of the country. The background of William Temple was coloured through being the son of an Archbishop of Canterbury; as an Oxford undergraduate he became involved in the Worker's Educational Movement; Headmaster of Repton; Bishop of Manchester; Archbishop of York, and an all-too-brief period as Archbishop of Canterbury. He understood the problems of the social, economic and religious life of his time and renewed an assuring belief in the power of religious faith, unlike the Established Church of today that lacks moral leadership.

There are so many memories of William Temple. One in particular concerns the B.B.C. It began after a discussion group that I shared with Bishop Stephen Neill, Bertrand Russell, Harold Laski and Field-Marshal Lord Ironside. The balance favoured agnosticism. Russell and Laski were formidable debaters on ethical questions, but Neill more than matched their arguments. Not so clear-cut was an edition of the Brains Trust on which Joad and Huxley were resident members. They dominated with a professional bedside manner. The producer, wanting someone to speak for organised religion, invited C.S. Lewis, author of *The Screwtape Letters* to defend that corner. Unfortunately Lewis became nervous, almost tongue-tied, and was swept aside by Joad and Huxley. Ethics and religion had been beaten by agnosticism and atheism.

The Primate was upset. James Welch, Director of Religious Broadcasting and known in Broadcasting House as the *Proud Priest of God,* was summoned to Lambeth Palace. A new programme was devised called *The Anvil.* The team included men like Canon Cockin, later to become a bishop; Nathaniel Micklem, President of Mansfield Hall, Oxford; Father Agnellus Andrew, representing the Roman Catholic viewpoint, and occasionally Dr. Temple. Chairman was Quentin Hogg, now Lord Hailsham. Questions were known a week before so there was no danger of being unprepared. One snag developed. As many of the questions could never be answered this side of the grave, replies had to be speculative; not so for Agnellus Andrew. With Roman Catholic foresight, he stated they were all wrong. This was the truth. Listeners felt he was the only man who knew what he was talking about. The programme became a robust endorsement of Roman Catholicism. After a three month stretch, Hogg left. I took his place. Final verdict, the most telling contribution came from the Primate.

One last memory. Some years ago my guest for dinner at the Dorchester Hotel was a rotund man wearing plain-rimmed glasses and a good trencherman. There was no doubting his ability to enjoy the occasion. Occasionally he unleashed a body-shaking laugh that was infectious. The head waiter tactfully whispered to me that perhaps the unrestrained mirth might be modified if only for the sake of other diners. On leaving after the meal, I introduced my guest to the restaurant manager. It was William Temple, Archbishop of Canterbury, who said he felt duly rebuked!

CHAPTER TEN

INSPIRED BY MUSIC

~

T HE LAST TIME I SAW VAUGHAN WILLIAMS was a glorious summer's morning, with sunlight flooding the rooms of their house in Hanover Terrace. Standing by the open balcony door was the majestic, leonine figure of Vaughan Williams, his hair flowing in the soft breeze. His very bigness, not only physically, but in mind, heart and thought, showed in his insatiable curiosity about any new works and the possibility of utilising instruments not currently used in the classical armoury. He was a man of enormous energy and industry, whose eighty-five years were filled with all sorts of musical activity besides composition. He occasionally complained of a fallow patch, but his output was large. Like Blake, he had the type of mind that sees heaven most readily in a wild flower.

I think of his eternal sense of youth and his enchanting sense of humour about things and people – not always quotable, for it was salted with his own particular brand of Rabelaisian wit. In spite of his shaggy grandeur, there was also a little of the sprite in him. Ursula recalled when they acquired their Hanover Terrace house, she said, "I'm afraid we can only get a twenty-year lease," to which Vaugham Williams, then in his early eighties, replied: "Never mind, my dear, we can renew it."

I remember the last Cheltenham Festival he attended, it must have been only a month or so before he died, it closed with his *London Symphony*. After an unforgettable evening and a wonderful ovation, he said afterwards that this Symphony was really his favourite, adding with a gamin look, "but don't tell anybody."

There were so many, like the lovely *Eighth Symphony* and its beautiful Cavatina with the first theme announced by the cellos; in *Santa Civitas*, possibly his first choice among the choral pieces; the lovely ideas buried in the *Poisoned Kiss*; the genius that emerged when he set Synge's beautifully shaped *Riders to the Sea*; and *Job*, his one masterly ballet, which, by virtue of its grand scope and its good-and-evil conflict, paved the way for the crowning achievement of the three central symphonies, Nos. 4, 5 and 6. These works, together with smaller scores, like *On Wenlock Edge*, the *Tallis Fantasy* and *Serenade to Music*, were music that used dissonance not as a new language, but as enrichment of the old. Much of it recalls the harmony and tenderness of the English countryside.

One aspect of Vaugham Williams's approach was not known. He cared so passionately all his life about hymns and carols, spent so much of his time in setting to music Herbert and Bunyan, the Bible and the Liturgy, even the Catholic Mass, yet he was a youthful atheist and lifelong agnostic. He used to tell a story how as a young man he was conducting one of his own works at the Three Choirs Festival! Understandably anxious, he turned to the first violin section and to his consternation saw the famous Kreisler playing at one of the back desks. He said the shock was shattering, but the explanation was simple. The next item was a concerto to be played by Kreisler, but since there was nowhere to "warm up" in the cathedral, Kreisler had taken the obvious course of joining in the first violins to do so.

He was criticised for the use of the vibraphone in his *Eighth Symphony*, but countered by saying it made a lovely noise. He took immense care in mastering the technical possibilities of the harmonica when he wrote that charming piece for Larry Adler.

Vaugham Williams found it impossible to still an instinctive curiosity about new instruments. He went through life with a subtle twinkle in his eye. There was no pastiche, no affectation. His music was part of England, a breath of the open air of his beloved Malvern Hills.

ARTURO TOSCANINI

STRAVINSKY ONCE SAID that great conductors, like great actors, were too often unable to play anything but themselves and that every member of an orchestra knew that a conductor could be less well equipped for his work than the least of his players. I know the type. The conductor who seeks the "effect" to show-off; who makes a gesture for the benefit of the audience's back-view of him; who bows alone. I could name half a dozen who play-act this charade at the end of every performance. Instead I pick out six conductors who effaced themselves in the service of music. First was Arturo Toscanini who insisted on perfection. Handicapped by shortsightedness, he learnt his scores by heart – first his parts as a "cellist", then as a conductor. It became a legendary musical memory. No score at a performance. In this way works were recreated. Every piece of music became more penetrating, almost translucent.

Toscanini's first demand was unlimited rehearsal time. An instance occurred in 1927, the centenary of Beethoven's death, when Italy waited for the performance of Beethoven's *Mass in D* with the orchestra and choir of La Scala. After thirty rehearsals, he laid down his baton with the words . . . "Ladies and gentlemen – next year." Insistence on precision occurred whilst conducting the Bayreuth orchestra in *Tristan*. He stated that an *appoggiatura* should not have been there. The players disagreed and brought the score to prove their point. Toscanini still insisted, and referred to Wagner's manuscript in the archives. The little note had been cancelled by the composer's hand with a faint stroke in faded ink. Purists of the Wagnerian persuasion had to admit that *appoggiatura* should not have been played over the years. At times frustration led to caustic comment. During a rehearsal he asked the orchestra "Can't you read? The score demands *con amore*, and what are you doing? You are playing it like married men!" Politically he became a symbol of anti-Fascism, but stayed at La Scala under Mussolini. Opposition caused his passport to be withdrawn, and the break with Italy. When Hitler came to power and Jewish music and musicians were banned in Germany, Toscanini no longer went to Bayreuth; occupation by the Nazis of

Austria, meant withdrawal from the Salzburg festivals. Instead he went to Tel-Aviv to help Bronislaw Huberman organise a Jewish orchestra.

On the musical landscape, Toscanini recaptured the purity and precision of the composers he interpreted, the very essence of their work.

GLYNDEBOURNE AND THE CHRISTIE FAMILY

NO LONDON SEASON IS COMPLETE without the musical occasion on the South Downs of Sussex and the Elizabethan Manor House of Glyndebourne. Part of the original house with its panelling remains and has belonged to the same family for seven hundred years, but it was not until 1934 that it was known outside the county. John Christie changed all that by announcing a Festival of Mozart operas. There was already a strong musical tradition, with a magnificent music-room, large organ and a musical library unequalled in any English private house. An opera house was added, with perfect acoustics. Fritz Busch was appointed conductor and Carl Ebert as producer. The cast came from established European singers. Everything was on a low key. During rehearsals the cast had the freedom of the grounds. Special trains left Victoria for the first performance of *Figaro* that would have been praised in Mozart's home-city of Salzburg, but behind the scenes there were problems.

The next day I lunched with John Christie. Having read the reviews, he was in a mood to talk. The season was only to last two weeks, but on the strength of public reaction he planned to extend it to five weeks with four operas, but there were difficulties. Opposition had come from several sources. Roy Henderson dismissed them as "a bunch of amateurs with a couple of pianos"; on the second night only seven people had boarded the special train when it left Victoria. He was surprised by the vituperative opposition from Lord Keynes and the lukewarm support from the Duke of Norfolk. I recall Christie's fondness for dogs, of Osbert Lancaster's amusing line-drawing showing him clutching a pugnacious-looking pug. It was indeed a dog full of character and tit-bits. As he spoke I moved my leg under the table and felt a sharp pain. Christie assured me it was only a friendly nip, reassurance that did not stop the retaliatory kick. "We have always been fond of dogs, in fact I named a son after one of my favourites." That offspring has been in the news lately. Internal friction has caused Sir David Davies, one of the four directors of the Glyndebourne Opera House, to be turned out to grass by Gus Christie, its new chief executive and son of the owner. Glyndebourne spokeswoman justified the dismissal because Gus wanted someone nearer his own age. It is interesting to recall that his father, Sir George Christie, was named after one of John Christie's favourite dogs!

SERGEI RACHMANINOV

I LOOK BACK WITH PLEASURE to a lunch at the Adelphi Hotel in Liverpool with the Russian composer, conductor and pianist, also with us was Leigh Ibbs, friend and senior partner of Ibbs and Tillet. He talked of his past; how after the 1917 Revolution he emigrated to America; of his friendship with Tchaikovsky; how when he was conducting the first performance of *Aleko* in Kiev, he received a telegram from St. Petersburg saying that Tchaikovsky had died suddenly from cholera after suffering for only three days. He said how deeply he felt the loss, not only of a fatherly friend, but a patron and adviser.

In reminiscent mood, he recalled success and failures. *Prelude in C sharp minor* became world famous, but his *Piano Concerto No. 1* was not a success, whilst the *First Symphony* played in Russia was a fiasco. The set-backs left him depressed, only cured by hypnosis and auto-suggestion treatment. Recovery brought fresh inspiration. Result . . . *Concerto No. 2 in C minor* which he dedicated to his doctor and first performed in London in 1901 with the composer at the piano. Its lyrical passion and rhythmic spirit won praise from public and critics. Reputation as composer and pianist consolidated, he became conductor at the Imperial Theatre in Moscow. Took a sabbatical to compose and produce *Piano Concerto No.3 in D. minor*. Moved to Dresden where he composed two large orchestral compositions, the symphonic poem *The Isle of Death*, inspired by Arnold Bocklin's oil painting, and his *Symphony No. 2* which he felt was his finest orchestral work. Then his last major work, *Rhapsody on a Theme of Paganini* for piano and orchestra.

Self-imposed exile in the United States left him lonely and isolated, depression made worse when in 1931 his music was banned in Soviet Russia because it represented "the decadent attitude of the lower middle classes" and was "especially dangerous on the musical front in the class war."

It was fascinating listening to a legend of the world of music. Whatever the decade emotions do not date . . . to quote his own words ". . . when I compose I am a slave. Beginning at nine in the morning I allow myself no respite until after eleven at night. A poem, a picture, something concrete helps me immensely. There must be something real before my mind to convey a definite impression, or the idea refuses to appear."

One incident of that lengthy lunch. I asked what inspired him to compose his most popular Prelude. There was no answer, just a sharp tap on the ankle from Ibbs. Afterwards Leigh explained that by mutual consent talk of this particular composition was avoided. The reason was partly financial. Inexperienced or absent-minded, Rachmaninov signed away all rights to royalties. Although a best-seller and best-known, he had to be content with a modest once-for-all payment. That wouldn't happen today.

Impressions that flit across the mind include flash-backs of *Frederick Ashton*, the sensitive British choreographer with the gift of nostalgia, who developed ballet into an art form. I think of Moira Shearer, who in 1946 danced three of the great roles of classical ballet – Aurora in *The Sleeping Beauty*, Swanilda in *Coppélia* and Odette/Odile in *Lac des Cygnes*, also dancing in the first performance of Ashton's *Symphony Variations*. To dance even one leading role in classical ballet is a considerable achievement, but all four in one season underlined her development as a ballerina. Moira's career did not clash with Fonteyn. Her interpretation was lyrical, pathos rather than tragedy; seldom has ballet been blessed with two such leading dancers, perfect foils to one another.

Moira developed from pert schoolgirl into a ballerina of real stature with an aura of beauty and Titian hair. Over lunch with her in London, she asked when I went to Monte Carlo for the Monaco Grand Prix, the most glamorous event in the racing calendar, if I would show her daughter where the railway station had been. The reason was that this station featured in *The Red Shoes* in which

Moira starred. Maybe it was over-extravagant, but, released at the peak of post-war austerity, it provided light relief, becoming one of Britain's best-loved films. The balcony was ideal: it recalled vignettes of Monsieur Froggier playing his violin between puffing an obnoxious pipe in the resplendent Louis XV restaurant . . . the natural amphitheatre of Monte Carlo with sides rising to Alpine heights in a series of tiers . . . the Casino where audiences listened to operas specially composed by Saint-Saens and Massenet . . . Diaghilev used it as a base for the Ballets Russes de Monte Carlo . . . not forgetting the interior with naked women smoking cigars painted on the ceiling.

About the same time, Robert Helpmann appeared on the scene. No dancer of his day, with the exception of Massine and later Nureyev, so influenced the ballet of our time. He was the most innovative choreographer since Balanchine, bringing drama to ballet with the pulsating touch of Fokine. No ballet was ever dull when Helpmann was on the stage, such was the subtlety of mime, wild extravagance of burlesque, gift of drollery and virtuosity in make-up. He used to say that when Ninette de Valois first saw him she said "I can do something with that face." He had an uncanny sense of characterisation and grasp of drama. He never had a bad performance, but it is not in negatives that I remember him.

To me the finest performance was his second ballet *Hamlet* that he set in the seconds after the Shakespearean play had ended, taking as the theme that line "For in that sleep of death what dreams may come" – a Freudian footnote to that moment when Hamlet's corpse was borne off by Fortinbras' four Captains . . . the milling mind of Hamlet in the split-second before death . . . his past life passing before dulling eyes . . . the image of his mother meeting with that of Ophelia, then merging. The ghost stalking the stage. The funeral cortege passes. Ophelia, enveloped in the blue folds of the river, replaces the Queen. The King is killed . . . all in the time it took four captains to tread four paces bearing his body to the ramparts. The ballet rounded off with the perturbed spirit's rest. Tchaikovsky's dramatic music reinforced the pageant and highlit the dark dream in Hamlet's mind, tempo integrated by Leslie Hurry's teeming decors. The theme had its roots in our literature. His ballets were English influences and were as national in flavour as Shakespeare's Falstaff.

Helpmann came to London from Australia in 1932 and took lessons from Ninette de Valois and worked with Constant Lambert. In his first ballet, *The Haunted Ballroom* by de Valois, to music by Geoffrey Toye, he had the male role.

I always found Helpmann unpredictable, with sparkling wit, highly developed ego, and pernickety about food. Taste buds had to be wooed. He regretted not being taller, superstitious, added an *n* to his name to avoid having nineteen letters in the name; conscious that, as a son of Aries, he was affiliated to the pioneer sign; admired the memory of Anna Pavlova; had fond recollections of playing Oberon to Vivien Leigh's Titania in Tyrone Guthrie's production of *A Midsummer's Nights Dream*; enthused about Moira Shearer's colouring in *The Red Shoes*, for which he did the choreography. Had some odd habits that caused Ninette de Valois's eyebrows to be raised, but "Madame did nothing!" He swore never to retire with so much still to do. One ambition was never realised. He returned from a Middle East tour and described how visiting Jerusalem and the traditional sites inspired the choreographic dream of a ballet recording the life and crucifixion of Christ. Some years later he said that perhaps it was just as well that nothing had come of the idea. Casting might have caused problems. He would probably have been chosen as Judas Iscariot . . . and some critics could be vicious!

Among many shades, I end with the entrancing Lydia Lopokova, whose appealing face was the mask of comedy. She abandoned the world of ballet to be the wife of Lord Keynes, becoming a provocative Cambridge hostess with vehement opinions. Today in the Arts Theatre that Keynes founded their memories are kept alive with a painting of these two legendary figures.

IGOR STRAVINSKY

I REMEMBER NOT LONG BEFORE HE DIED in 1971, talking with Stravinsky in his suite at the Savoy Hotel. He was rather miserable, kept flourishing an outsize handkerchief, dabbing his face and forehead. In a resigned tone, his wife said, it was no use, he had decided the symptoms were influenza. No temperature, just perverse, conversation fragmentary. Eventually sitting in a spacious limousine, his face was still hidden by the handkerchief. As predicted by his wife, once in the Royal Albert Hall, the phobia was forgotten.

Later that evening, having made a remarkable recovery with quite an appetite, he was ready to talk about his work. There is no doubt that he dominated the history of 20th century ballet from his first commissioned ballet score *The Firebird* in 1910. His perverse rhythms and lush writing inspired choreographers as opposite as Fokine and Balanchine to produce some of their greatest works. Studying under Rimsky-Korsakov, he created music for the Diaghilev ballets, but that evening I was anxious to hear his views on *The Rite of Spring*. He said it was about attracting the attention of God and had tried to compose something very old by inventing music entirely new with the orchestra making noises never heard before. He said that Nijinsky's choreography was out of touch; Rambert found it inspiring. Stravinsky felt that Massine's interpretation was clearer. Opinions varied so much he was resigned to the fact that no choreographer could match the score's epic greatness. It is interesting to speculate how Stravinsky would have developed had he not left Russia as early as he did.

YEHUDI MENUHIN

THE LAST TIME WE met was in 1998 at the University Concert Hall in Cambridge when he conducted the double string orchestra. At the reception given by Richard Sotnick, who, with his wife Ruth, has done so much for young musicians, I talked with Menuhin about future plans.

Fit and mentally alert, his conducting gave no hint he was an octogenarian. Fixing a date proved difficult. The provisional day would be confirmed if I rang his diary secretary, I was given a Vienna number. In due course we met in his impressive Belgravia home. Over the years we had many discussions in different countries. This time the topics were more personal. Being a child prodigy, when aged eleven he made his debut as a virtuoso at the Carnegie Hall with the New York Philharmonic Orchestra, the prelude to a world famous career. Outstanding in his memory was when the Elgar *Violin Concerto* was conducted by the composer. His solo repertoire extended from Vivaldi to Enesco. Like Toscanini, Menuhin had a phenomenal memory and attributed it to a three-fold cause . . . memory of the mind, the eye and the fingers. The instrument helped, in his case the favourite *Prince Khevenhueller* made by Antonio Stradivari, was used to good effect at the 60th birthday concert in the Royal Festival Hall when the composer Bela Bartok dedicated a violin sonata to him.

Menuhin's search for fresh musical interpretation brought him into contact with unlikely sources. He recalled meeting Stephane Grappelli on Michael Parkinson's chat show. It was a fusion of minds. Grappelli's rhythms of jazz, classical and popular, led to duets with Menuhin, as well as having played with legends of jazz like Duke Ellington, Fats Wallers, Glen Miller and Oscar Peterson. Menuhin also paid tribute to the free-ranging skills of Nigel Kennedy.

Yehudi Menuhin's sudden death came as a shock, at a moment of personal anxiety. His wife, Diana, devoted partner for over 50 years, had suffered a stroke four days earlier. It was the end of an era. Without her, Yehudi's life would have been empty. Although constantly busy, often abroad, she would be waiting. Maybe it was just as well that he died peacefully of heart failure in his sleep.

DUKE ELLINGTON

TO CELEBRATE WINNING the Formula One World Championship in 1962, we held a victory dinner in the Penthouse and Pavilion of *The Dorchester* as a tribute to Graham Hill, who had driven out BRM for seven years. One guest of particular interest to Graham was Duke Ellington. Neither composer nor musician nor a leader in the usual sense, he was a combination of all three, had the finest jazz ensemble in the world at that time and was acclaimed the most accomplished composer of Negro folk music. Fascinated by the skills required to drive a racing car at incredible speed yet under cool control, he asked what had been the highlight of the lethal, almost gladiatorial sport. Graham replied by recalling the trauma when he won the German Grand Prix under horrific weather conditions and an incredible win against Jim Clark in the

International Trophy at Silverstone. He asked the same question of Ellington.

He spoke of the satisfaction gained by achievement. Topping the list was receiving America's highest civil award, the Presidential Medal of Freedom from President Nixon, and the memory of a hit recorded under the title *"Take the A Train."* Then added in more thoughtful vein, that maybe his real ambition had not been realised. He spoke of his plans to compose an extended work expressing the history of his race . . . in rhythm, tracing the story of the American Negro from Africa through slavery, emancipation, and the urban settlements, adding, I tried to go forward a thousand years . . . to express the future . . . when the Negro could take his place, a free being, among the peoples of the world. He made his dream come true by performing the suite *Black, Brown and Beige* at Carnegie Hall in New York. It ran for about an hour, but the piece was received by the critics with something less than rapture. He said the unfriendly reception deflected him into never recording it in anything resembling its original form, cannibalizing various sections for other projects. It was an ambition frustrated.

I find the alchemy of the big band in jazz mysterious. I found Ellington's band played jazz more modern than John Coltrane's, more steeped in tradition than Louis Armstrong's. For Ellington and his men, the awful harmonic dilemma at that time of the contemporary soloist simply did not exist. The fruit of forty years of bandleading and composing was there fore all to see.

VIGNETTES OF MUSICAL LEGENDS . . . of Sir Henry Wood, who raised his baton at the opening of the first annual concerts in London's new Queen's Hall, later known as the Promenade Concerts. He promoted national interest in music and encouraged many young composers. I recall several meetings with him and Robert Meyer in the Langham Hotel and the conductor's home at 49 Hallam Street in Portland Place, discussing plans for the 1938 Henry Wood Jubilee Fund. Everything in those days was so simplistic, yet still yielded results. He is remembered today by music lovers as composer of *Fantasia on British Sea Songs*, which ends every Promenade season on an enthusiastic, rumbustious note in spite of protests of jingoistic sentiments and the ridiculous attempt by conductor Mark

Elder to remove *Rule Britannia* because of Argentine's feelings in the Falkland War. Tradition prevailed, we still have the festival of music ending with funny hats, Union Jacks and people roaring jingoistic verses whilst the bust of Henry Wood, garlanded, looks down benevolently on Royal Albert Hall ritual.

One conductor who would approve was Sir Malcolm Sargent. He was perhaps our most charismatic wielder of the baton. He felt he was Wood's natural successor in the Promenade Concert series, superstitiously recalling that his birth in 1895 coincided with Wood's first of these concerts. His antics and mannerisms were constant. Stabbing stick technique, agile footwork, immense energy, ability to get the best out of singers; always succeeded in inspiring a feeling of nervous tension in Walton's First Symphony.

As a private individual he exuded an exhilarating sense of companionship; like Peter Pan he never seemed to age. In his flat next to the Albert Hall, he was surrounded by signed photographs of the Royal Family. Confessed he never took exercise. Waving arms six hours a day was quite enough. Little interest in food; ordered meals but lost interest when it arrived. Never lived down the nickname *Flash Harry* that came after a Brains Trust with Joad and Huxley. The announcer said they were going over to Manchester for a concert by Malcolm Sargent. It came across that he had gone there straight away – in a flash. Later Sir Thomas Beecham learnt he was conducting in the Far East and commented it was just a "Flash in Japan"!

Malcolm took it all in good part. Admitted he liked well-fitting clothes, not flashy just well tailored, and, of course, with a carnation.

He was an active member on the Council of the Zoo and President of the R.S.P.C.A. This affinity was shown with his budgerigar, Hughie III. Whilst I was there he was free to fly from picture to picture, occasionally settling on my shoulder hoping for a tit-bit. This procedure happened regularly in the Ritz Hotel lounge, always the same table in a corner by the pillar. Well-trained, the bird sat on his shoulder expecting a sip from a sherry glass. Malcolm was proud of training it to say when the telephone rang – "Of course, I remember you."

I will never forget his appearance at the last night at the Proms.

In the final stages of terminal cancer, he was too frail to conduct. He just stood on the platform. Promenaders gave a tumultuous welcome of love and admiration to the man who had so richly contributed to the world of music. His example and courage during the last weeks of his life were an inspiration.

It is difficult to complete the choice, which has to be personal, not definite, more the arbitrary first growth from one's vineyard covering the century. People who have enlivened and enlightened our times. In this realm I am particularly conscious of those omitted . . . Jacqueline du Pré, who, for me epitomised emotional expression; of Mstislav Rostropovich, one of the last direct links to Dmitri Shostakovich; of Lionel Bart, who wrote some of the world's best loved songs; in the mysterious world of Tin Pan Alley he had his finger on the common pulse from the days of playing the washboard behind Tommy Steele in Soho coffee bars, yet died penniless in a small flat above an Acton shop after being fabulously wealthy; of many happy memories of Ernest Ansermet, the veteran Swiss conductor. I am certain that few conductors today have a tenth of the charisma of their forerunners. In this category I place Sir Thomas Beecham, volatile and colourful. He used to say his earliest ambition was to be a concert pianist but was foiled by a wrist injury. The loss was compensated by intuitive influence as a conductor, establishing the Royal Philharmonic Orchestra and becoming closely associated with the music of his great friend, Frederick Delius. In private he had several liaisons, particularly Lady Cunard. Some of the Beecham observations were incisive. He maintained that in the course of his lifetime a great sameness had come over singers. "In my youth," he said, "there were a dozen baritones, all very good and all as different as chalk from cheese. Maurel, Ancona, Scotti, Renaud, Bisham, Battistini: three consecutive notes from any of them, and you were never in the slightest doubt as to the singer. Whereas now, however rich the vocal tone, I always have to consult my programme." Would we could have an update on their successors. More trenchant was his general verdict . . . there are two golden rules for an orchestra: start together and finish together. The public doesn't give a damn what goes on in between! So there you have it!

One final thought about an artist I find difficult to categorize.

Here was a man who would wear a full-length chinchilla coat, wear so many outrageous rings it was hazardous to shake hands, flirt with over-sexed matrons, playing with shattering extravagant flourishes on an ornate grand piano complete with candelabra. My initial acquaintanceship came in the Hollywood studios of Warner Bros. Escorted to a set in which Liberace was featuring in a film with Maureen O'Sullivan, I watched several takes. In intervals I listened to him extolling the virtues of his devoted mother and brother George. Later went to their caravan, which I was assured had been used by Judy Garland, and was introduced to a formidable lady capable of taking on Mike Tyson. It was an illuminating experience. Before leaving the studios, a security guard gave me a small package with Mr. Liberace's compliments. It was a pair of gold cuff-links in the shape of a grand piano complete with candelabra . . . some day I may have the courage to wear them!

I think of the days when Aldeburgh was a little seaside town of 3,000 at the end of a single line railway track, when it took three hours and two changes from London. I was sitting in a comfortable lounge of a large red house having tea with Benjamin Britten and Peter Pears, his friend for many years. We talked of how the Aldeburgh Festival came into being. It happened when Britten, Pears and Crozier were driving to Lucerne in 1947. Fed up with continual chasing round to endless places, Pears aired a rhetorical question, Why not have a Festival at home? Britten dismissed the idea as financially impossible – but that was how it began in spite of pessimism. Britten poured out another cup of China tea. The very simplicity appealed to the public. They never advertised and refused ticket agents, yet every year hundreds were turned away. Railway posters were printed but were only displayed as far as Saxmundham station. Venue was the village Jubilee Hall, an archetypal Victorian building only holding 320, but the intimate atmosphere and informality seemed right. Should a musician be late, the entire audience was taken round the corner to the Festival Club – converted garage – until the performer turned up.

Success brought change. In 1967 a large auditorium was built at the Maltings; Snape was erected, destroyed by fire in 1969 and restored the following year. The creative output was remarkable: some ten operas, seven of them major vocal works for the concert hall; four large-scale orchestral works; three canticles; two string quartets, as well as works for small choirs, like the *Hymn to St. Cecilia*; small groups of all kinds, music for all occasions. The sheer scale of Britten's accomplishment was staggering.

Britten, son of a Lowestoft dentist, started composing aged five. He described his daily routine. Rose early, started work immediately after breakfast; after lunch continued until teatime, then a long walk, work again in the evening. He was fond of tennis. On the lawn was a pole with tennis ball attached to a rope given to him by Lady Harewood.

Britten used to live in a house in Aldeburgh itself on the sea front, but it became untenable with tourists gaping through the windows and following them everywhere, the last straw being when a woman set up her canvas on the doorstep. Continuous hard work with great gifts so vibrantly alive set Britten on top of the world alongside Shostakovitch. Early promise. At the age of twelve, he had already written ten piano sonatas, six string quartets, an oratorio and dozens of songs, yet I found him always modest, easy smile, heavy-lidded eyes, and salient nose. He composed fluently, setting down on manuscript paper music perfected in his mind's ear.

Out of this creative flood, I isolate two works; the opera *Peter Grimes*, based on verses by George Crabbe, and created for his life companion, Peter Pears, the English tenor who collaborated with Britten in a rich catalogue of song cycles and operatic roles, but most memorable was *War Requiem*, that combines poems of Wilfred Owen with the text of the Requiem Mass, that had its first performance at the consecration of the new Coventry Cathedral. I heard it for the first time in London at Westminster Abbey. The experience was overwhelming.

Benjamin Britten died in 1976 at the Red House in Aldeburgh.

LOUIS ARMSTRONG

DRINKS WITH LOUIS ARMSTRONG had a special significance. He had many imitators, but none could match the piercing flare of his trumpet. He made jazz an international language, but fame never robbed the man from the honky-tonk band background of New Orleans of his unspoilt honesty. He never forgot the early difficulties in a State Home for Delinquent Children, or the money earned as milk-roundsman, newspaper seller, rag-and-bone man, and coalman. The rate for hauling coal was 15 cents per load working from seven in the morning to five in the evening. He would recall making a four-string guitar out of a cigar box and copper wire. His only chance to blow the cornet was at funerals.

He was always the same, bubbling over with high spirits. His voice was in a category of its own. It sounded like a hoarse shout for beer, yet had a melodious and rhythmic touch. The effect was right. His first and only million-dollar disc was a vocal – *Hello Dolly* – that stayed in the U.S. charts for 22 weeks. He said that one of his most enjoyable experiences was the role in the film *High Society* in which he sang with Bing Crosby *Now You Has Jazz* specially written by Cole Porter. In a way Louis seemed to be searching for his identity. This aspect came during a flight from New York to London. We talked about a Mobile Hospital I had designed, equipped and sent to Ghana where it was received by the President as the prototype unit inaugurating the Ghanaian National Health Service. Louis' reaction was unexpected. He said he felt instinctively drawn to Africa as if his roots were in the Third World, a feeling shared by his fourth wife, Lucille, rarely apart from him over a 23 years span. "It's a feeling of kinship. We don't know where exactly we came from because our identity was taken away. Ghana was our first taste of Africa. We made many friends." Louis added a practical note. When he retired, he would build a summer house in Ghana. He liked the local fare . . . soul food . . . stews, beans, tripe, a poor man's diet.

Sadly that ambition was not to be realised. On that flight, passengers settled down to get some sleep, but Louis was restless. Periodically he took a mirror out of his pocket, directed the beam of light on his face, then twisted his features into varying contortions. After breakfast I spoke to Dr. Alexander Schiff, who accompanied Armstrong abroad as his personal physician. He shrugged and said the crumply lips showed the punishment by his trumpet playing. Musicians often asked what was the secret. The answer was simple. All you had to do was harden jaw muscles and develop air pressure to the point where you could strike and hold high C longer than any other swing trumpeter. It sounded easy, but Louis Armstrong was the only one to make such a grade.

POSTSCRIPT

~

THE BEGINNING OF THE MILLENNIUM found us speculating what fortunes it had in store for us. A laudable instinct makes us wish each other a Happy New Year. It is an interesting custom, in many ways contradictory. Cynics with a Socratic turn of mind agree that it is impossible to determine the precise moment when a thing ceases to be new and becomes old. Even the heartiest of New Year celebrants must find it difficult to pin-point how 12.5 a.m. on 1st January was essentially different from 11.55 of the day before. Nor was it. The astronomer can inform us to the tick when year merges year and century into century. We have become so enamoured of these compartments of our own making, we erect them into individualities. We endow each century with characteristics that make it stand out clearly from the rest. Predestination on imponderables is never satisfactory. It is almost better to adopt a fatalistic attitude of taking things as they come. Even so, nothing will suppress the desire to measure something that does not exist.

Time. As Aristophanes told us, man measures the hour by the number of times his shadow is greater than the length of his own feet. But what are the hours? It is only since the fourteenth century that man has divided the day and night into a total of 24 hours and in some parts of the world they divided periods of night and day into a number of "temporal" hours, usually twelve. In Japan temporal hours were the measure until 1870.

Anthony Powell's approach to the passage of time is more laconic . . . "Growing old is like being punished for a crime you didn't commit." Bernard Darwin's reaction was not so cynical. In a volume entitled *What Life has Taught Me* he reflected, "To spend a good part of your life doing the thing you happen to like best, in pleasant places and in pleasant company, seems to me not unenviable. I'm afraid I would do it all over again."

If only one could!

To return to my former theme. Past, present and future are intangible, but from the dawn of mankind the space of a man's duty has been measured by the rising and the setting of the sun. Time-measures have been many and varied, one of the oldest and most familiar being the sun dial, that speaks to us across the centuries with thought-provoking sayings. I close with my favourite:

Life is a passing shadow.
The shadow of a bird,
in his flight.

INDEX

~